Acknowledgements

This book wouldn't have been published if not for the encouragement of at least twenty readers of the manuscript.

I hesitate to name everyone who told me these tales because I know I will leave someone out. Several of them are dead. So I will just say: "Many thanks to those of you who did. If you read this, I'm sure you will know who you are."

I do want to give special thanks to several of you who helped me in the typing, proofreading, and editing of this book. These include my wife, Sissy, Donald Gray, Betty Gray Laniel, Betty Fischer Gray, Brenda Halbrook Tyler, and Ashley Prince Tyler.

A special thanks to Linda Schumacher and Jana Hudson Rhinehart who encouraged me the most to publish it.

I hope you enjoy reading this book of tales of the Iron Ore Mountain, Pea Ridge, and surrounding areas as much as I enjoyed writing it. It tells of my mother and father and some of their relatives in their struggle for survival during the great depression.

Randall Gray

For additional copies or comments
call   479-967-0858 or email
randall2@gmail.com or amazon.com
address 5438 Morgan Rd. Russellville, ar
72802

High on a Mountain

Randall Gray

Arkansas Tales

The triumphs and tragedies of raising a family in the depression years of the 1930's.

This book is printed in the USA.

First Print

Part One

High on a Mountain

Chapter 1

TO A NEW HOME

The air was clear and crisp on that bright and sunny February day in nineteen twenty-eight as Lois Maxwell Gray and her new husband, Boyd, traveled up the Iron Ore Mountain road in Pope County, Arkansas. They sat on the wagon seat as Rhody and Jude, the faithful and surefooted little brown mules pulled them on their way. The road was rocky, steep, and winding in places, but Lois didn't mind. She was on her way to her new home--a home of her very own, which she had never seen and beside her sat the man she loved.

The two of them made a nice-looking couple, with both being dark-headed and sun-tanned from being in the open air so much. Lois was a pretty and pleasant-looking young woman of twenty-two, and Boyd was a handsome, curly-headed man of twenty-six. He had a positive and ambitious attitude in everything he did, and that was one of the things that had attracted Lois.

He wasn't a large man, standing about five feet, eight inches in his stocking feet and weighing one hundred fifty pounds, but he was all muscle, as most mountain boys and men were back then. They had to work hard in the fields and the woods. Even when not working, they were climbing up and down the hollows and the hills, either hunting or going to different places in the valleys below.

Lois stole a look down into the valley from which they had just come. The scenery was stunningly beautiful. The village of Oak Grove, with Isabel Creek bisecting it, lay almost a mile from the mountain. The Baptist church and the scattered outbuildings looked like toys from up here. A few people walking along the roads and around the houses and other buildings and the people riding horses or in wagons looked like ants scurrying along.

The Maxwell house that Mom left, to live with Boyd on the Iron Ore Mountain. The road from Atkins on north passed right in front of the house.

She could see the narrow road as it twisted and turned while making its way toward Atkins to the south and Caglesville, Hector, and Appleton to the north and northeast.

Across the valley on the west, a narrow road ran toward the little village of Moreland and Buck Mountain, which was framed by the clear blue sky and dotted with pine trees, giving it a welcome green color on that winter day. To the south lay the Crow Mountain, farther than the Buck, and having a luster of dark blue. She could see Pea Ridge between the Iron Ore and Crow Mountains. There was her old home, one of the few white houses visible in the distance. How beautiful it looked!

A touch of sadness gripped her heart. She was leaving that house forever. How she loved her old home and the family she was leaving behind. She had known many happy times in that house---with the singing, the talking, the laughter, and sometimes the tears.

Many times as children, Lois and her brothers and sisters would be playing outside, when one of them would suddenly shout, "Here comes a Mountain Boomer!" Everyone would stop their play as a covered wagon tossed and rolled toward them, coming from the north in the direction of the Ozark Mountains.

The wagon would usually be pulled by two mules, but sometimes by horses, as it made its way toward Atkins in the Arkansas River Valley. A woman, man, or child would be sitting by the driver. Sometimes someone would be walking along beside or behind the wagon.

Once when Homer, Lois's oldest brother, yelled at the wagon, the man walking beside it started running at him like he was going to assault him. The man had a black beard about six inches long, which made him look mean to Homer. When Homer started running around the house, the man stopped and burst out laughing.

How far and mysterious those Ozark Mountains had seemed to Lois back then. From her home on Pea Ridge, she had been able to see only mountains and more mountains to the north. Beyond the Iron Ore loomed the White Oak Mountain, several miles from it and much higher. To her, the Ozarks could just as well have been called the Mystery Mountains, because that's what they were to her---a mystery.

Lois and Boyd

Now she was married to a Mountain Boomer, and she would soon be one, but Boyd had promised that he would take her home to visit her folks each weekend. They would go to church at Shiloh on Sundays, just like always. Then, after a year on the mountain, they would move to Pea Ridge---close by her family.

Her father and mother owned an extra house they could live in and they had forty acres they could farm. Sharecroppers now lived there and worked the land.

They already had a good start, since Boyd owned one hundred thirty acres of land on the Iron Ore and was almost free of debt. He also had the new wagon they were riding in and the pair of mules that was pulling it.

Her father owed her $120, which she had saved while teaching school and had loaned to him. They were in much better financial shape than a lot of people their age---at least around there.

"What do you think of the Iron Ore Mountain?" said Boyd, interrupting her daydreaming. Before she could answer, he continued, "Look down there to the south past Pea Ridge. You can see Atkins, and a few miles farther, the Arkansas River. Just across it is the Petit Jean Mountain. Then there's Mount Nebo to the southwest."

Petit Jean Mountain stood pretty and majestic, being flat on top and lying several miles east to west along the river. It ended abruptly at each end with what appeared to be bluffs. At its base flowed the Arkansas on its way to the Mississippi River. It turned south reaching the east end of the mountain for a half-mile or so, then swung east again. This gave it the appearance of a lake from up there, and it was beautiful. The light haze gave it a silvery look. It and the other mountains, valleys, and the river were so beautiful that as Lois looked at them, her breath was almost taken away. It filled her with awe.

Boyd said, "I feel closer to God when I'm up here. I have sat outside many a night and watched the lights of Atkins and of houses in the surrounding countryside glimmering in the darkness ten miles away."

She had heard the 'Legend of Petit Jean Mountain'---how the French maiden, Jean, had stowed away on a ship bound for the new world so she could be with her sweetheart who was on board. After she was discovered, it was too late to turn back, so she was allowed to continue on with him. Accompanying him to Arkansas, she had become sick and died and was sadly buried at the top of the Petit Jean Bluffs overlooking the Arkansas River. Since she was small, they called her Petit, which means "little" in French. France claimed Arkansas then, even though the Indians had lived here for thousands of years.

Iron Ore Mountain Home

"It's beautiful!" Lois exclaimed. "I didn't dream that you could see so far from up here. It looks as if most of Arkansas is made up of mountains."

"That's because you can't see the valleys between the mountains," Boyd replied. "They call it the Iron Ore Mountain because it has so much iron in a great many of its rocks.

A long time ago a man had an iron ore mine on the side of the mountain and hauled the ore to a blast furnace in Russellville. It wasn't profitable, so he didn't work the mine long, but to this day, it is called the Iron Ore Mountain.

The sweating and puffing Rhody and Jude had finally pulled the last steep stretch of the mountain. Boyd had stopped them often to rest them on the climb up the mountain. "Why don't you stop and rest them again?" Lois asked him. "They sure are puffing and blowing."

"They will get their breaths back now without resting," Boyd assured her. "After the long climb up the mountain, pulling the wagon on level ground is almost like resting them." He was right. After a few minutes, the mules' breathing was back to normal.

Soon after reaching the mountaintop, they came to a weather-beaten house out in the middle of nowhere. It was unpainted, as all the houses on the Iron Ore Mountain were, and its oak-shingled rooftop was weathered the same color. The chimney was built of red brick, causing it to stand out from the rest of the house. The bricks were neatly mortared together with cement.

All the other chimneys on the Iron Ore were mortared with clay. A silent cloud of smoke was rising from the chimney, announcing the owners were home. As the smoke ascended into the heavens, it slowly dissipated into the air around it. Then it was gone as if it had never been there, to be replaced by more smoke rising from the chimney.

"This is where Uncle Bud and Aunt Mary Davies live," Boyd said. "They are from Illinois. They came down here a long time ago in a covered wagon with a wagon train.

Uncle Bud is almost blind, so when he has to do close work like cutting wood or hoeing cotton, he has to bend way over so he can see. Doing that so long has made him hump-backed.

They are pretty old, and their only children, two girls, are married and gone. So the Davies must be pretty lonesome people. Their nearest neighbor is over a half-mile away."

"Poor things," Lois said. "Maybe we can visit them some. And we can help them when they really need someone."

Boyd said, "I already do. They call on me and others up here from time to time. Different ones of us help them cut wood, and we help with their cattle and things like that."

The road was sandy and not so rocky for a mile or so as they passed the Davies' fields, standing bare and empty in the winter gloom, but it became rough and bumpy again before they reached their destination. Bedrock showed in the road where the soil had washed away due to the many wagons that had come over it, and the many rains.

Suddenly Boyd stopped Rhody and Jude. "Get down and I will show you the Rockhouse that I have told you about.

The Rock House

Lois had heard of the Rockhouse from him many times. It was a cave with a mouth forty feet across and it went back into the bank twenty-five feet. The roof, which was three or four feet thick, had little soil on it, and it had a hole eight feet long and two feet wide. This hole was the opening through which smoke escaped from the many campfires built by the Indians and early pioneers. A small branch of water flowed by, and a nearby spring which never went dry allowed anyone to get water.

Men from the valley below used the Rockhouse for a hideout during the Civil War. They were not outlaws but for one reason or another didn't want to fight. Some of them were "Yankee sympathizers" but didn't want to fight against their southern friends. Others didn't care one way or another who won the war and some had simply been cowards.

But Lois wasn't interested in the Rockhouse just now. She was tired, aching and wanted to get to her new home. Her father owned a car, so she wasn't used to riding in a wagon.

"Come on, let's go. We can see it later," she said. So they continued on their way. The house was less than a half-mile farther and she was anxious to see her home of the next few months.

But first they had to stop at Boyd's father's house, which was between the Rockhouse and Boyd's house. Mr. Gray was married to Lois's Aunt Mollie, so Boyd's stepmother was Lois's Aunt. They didn't visit for long. It was only a courtesy call. They said their hellos and goodbyes so they could get home.

Lois was pleased when the house finally came into view. She saw that it was a nice place for a newly married couple---especially since it was paid for. Although it wasn't painted, it was well-built and had a large living room, a large bedroom and a good combination kitchen and dining room. The oak shingle rooftop and the weather-beaten boards on the sides of the house were of the same gray color. The front porch went all the way across the front of the house. A honeysuckle vine enclosed one end reaching all the way from the ground to the rooftop. The back porch occupied as much space as each of the three rooms of the house. If it had been enclosed like the rooms, the house would have been a perfect square, plus the front porch.

The back porch didn't have a floor. Perhaps the original owner, Will Singleton, had intended to floor it someday, but had never gotten around to it. Boyd told Lois that when Mr. Singleton lived there, he always kept a big dog tied up under the open porch.

There were wooden pine floors, which were weathered the same color as the outside of the house. There were small cracks where the boards fit together. They didn't go all the way through the floor, only about one-eighth of an inch deep. Lois thought they would be good dirt catchers, and it would be a hard job to keep the floors clean. Maybe soon they could get rugs for the floor. She was sure that when the house was first built, the boards had fit together snugly, but as time passed and the boards dried out, they had shrunk, so the cracks had developed.

In the kitchen was a cook stove which burned wood. It was a good stove, but she was disappointed. It didn't have a reservoir for heating water or a storage space overhead. It did have a good oven. In the back of her mind, she filed another item she wanted as soon as possible---a better cook stove.

Boyd had a coal-oil lamp for inside light and a lantern for outside light. Neither were very bright but they were the best available in most of Arkansas rural areas. Lois had been exposed to electricity when she had attended Normal (Teacher Preparatory School) at Arkansas Polytechnic College in Russellville and when she had lived with a relative in Atkins while going to school there. "Maybe someday," she thought to herself, "Just maybe."

Another thing she would have preferred to be different was the fireplace. Its rocks were cemented together with clay. Sometimes a chunk of clay would fall out, and until it was replaced, a tiny crack was left, which let wind blow through and send smoke into the house. It became so cold at night after the fire burned down that water froze in buckets and pans and the damp washcloths and dishcloths froze before they could dry out.

When the wind blew from the north, it would come down the chimney and fill the house with smoke. And if anyone stood close to the fireplace, he got too hot on the side near the fire, and would still be cold on the other side. He had to keep turning around and around to get warm. But Lois was used to that, because her mother and father's house was the same way.

Grandpa and Grandma Maxwell

Chapter 2

GETTING ADJUSTED TO MOUNTAIN LIFE

The next few days were spent getting adjusted to married life and cleaning the house. Boyd had lived by himself and hadn't kept house very well.

Then he took her to visit his folks. They went to see his father and stepmother first. Lois had only seen Mr. Gray for a few minutes on their way home. Mr. Gray and Lois's Aunt Mollie had become acquainted through Lois and Velma, Boyd's younger brother, Bob's, wife. Aunt Mollie was Velma's aunt, too. Mr. Gray and she had only been married for a few months. Aunt Mollie's first two husbands were dead. The first one, Tom Duvall, had died young, and her second one, Ned Coffman from Hector, had been dead for several years.

Lois felt right at home at Mr. Gray's that Sunday. She had known Aunt Mollie all her life. She was almost like her own mother. But Mr. Gray was hard for her to get to know. He was a very serious man, perhaps because his life had been hard. It hadn't been easy raising his six children after his first wife, Betty, had died fourteen years ago. His family was grown now, except for sixteen-year old Leonard and fourteen-year old Sewood.

Mr. Gray hadn't always lived in the mountains, having come to Arkansas from Alabama with his mother and father and their other children forty years before, when he was sixteen. They had made their home in Tennessee for a few years after times got so rough in Alabama following the Civil War. His Great Grandma and Grandpa had been wealthy farmers with several slaves before the war but they had lost most of what they had. His Great Grandpa had once loaned $2000.00 in gold coins to Thomas Jefferson's grandson and the war resulted in him losing that. That was a lot of money in those days.

In Tennessee they had raised tobacco for their money crop. But the price had gone down so much they decided to start raising cotton again. Cotton took more land, which they didn't have, so they had decided to come to Arkansas, where they had heard from relatives already living here that land was available, and that jobs picking cotton were plentiful.

They had rented two railroad cars and with their kinfolks, the Haneys and the Parkers, and some friends, the Gardners, had come to Pope County. The Haneys had stopped at Atkins, and the Grays, Parkers and Gardners had continued on to Russellville. The Gardners had become business men, which they were in Tennessee, while the Grays and the Parkers rented land and farmed. Mr. Gray's father had farmed some of the land that was to become Arkansas Tech. Then he had landed on Buck Mountain and then at Oak Grove. Each move he had made seemed to be worse than the one before. The land he had at Oak Grove was poor and it was very thin. Only a little way down was solid bedrock.

After they lived in Arkansas for a year and grew cotton, the price went down and the price of tobacco went back up but there was no market for tobacco here.

Mr. Gray had become interested in the Iron Ore Mountain after hearing reports of the good crops Will Singleton had grown up there. He sold his house and land at Oak Grove and bought forty acres from Mr. Singleton.

But he and his family endured hard times. Half of the land he bought was rocky and rough. The shack he built was only makeshift and they had to carry water from a spring a hundred yards from the house, because the well he had spent so many hours digging was dry. Then his wife contracted tuberculosis soon and died a few years later.

Ben, Boyd's older brother, and his wife, Nora, who lived a half-mile to the north of Boyd and Lois, were also at Mr. Gray's that Sunday. Ben and Nora already had five children, though Ben was only a year and a half older than Boyd. He had started his family at an earlier age.

Nora was a nice young woman and Lois and she became good friends right from the start. She had her hands full with her seven-year old twins, Corene and Irene, and the three younger children. Raymond was five years old, Ruth three, and Avanelle one year old. But, even with her busy life, she seemed as happy as could be. Her earlier years had been spent on Buck Mountain, so, unlike Lois, she was used to mountain life.

Sewood had gotten himself a new bicycle from money he had made picking cotton, and he was very proud of himself for having finally learned how to ride. Leonard, who was crippled from having polio while a baby, teased him.

"I could outrun you on that bicycle."

"You could not!" Sewood responded.

"Could, too!"

"No, you couldn't!"

"Yes, I could!"

"Do you want to try it?" Sewood challenged.

"Yes, and I can beat you, too!" Leonard declared.

So the two brothers lined up, ready to go, while the rest of the families went outside to watch. There wasn't much entertainment on the Iron Ore Mountain and they weren't going to miss this race. They didn't think Leonard would win, but he seemed pretty sure of himself.

When the race began, Leonard leaped ahead, running like the wind. He was very fast, in spite of his handicap. Sewood was afraid he might get beaten, but he continued to pump the bicycle pedals as fast as he could. He was finally overtaking Leonard, but when he did, he didn't go around him---he ran over him. Down went Leonard, and off the bicycle tumbled Sewood in a heap on top of him.

My, was Leonard angry! He was also hurt. The skin was stripped off one of his big toes, and it was spurting blood. His bare foot had become entangled in the spokes of the front wheel and he had come out second best.

"You didn't have to run over me!" he groaned, as he limped up the hill toward the house.

Sewood, walking beside him while pushing his bike, was sorry he had hurt him. He hadn't planned to run into him. The idea had just come to him on an impulse.

Here came Mr. Gray, Boyd and Ben. Oh, was Mr. Gray angry! "Why did you have to go and do that? Don't you have a lick of sense?" he shouted.

Boyd thought he was going to give Sewood a thrashing, but he didn't. He helped Leonard to the house as Mr. Gray raked Sewood over the coals so badly that it may have been worse than a whipping. He felt sorry for Sewood.

It took a while for Lois to get used to the silence of their house when Boyd would be gone. Back home someone was always talking and laughing. People were often stopping by to sell apples, peaches and other things, or just to get a drink of water. The road by their house was the main one from Atkins to the northeastern part of Pope County. It went through Oak Grove, where it turned northwest and hooked up with the road from Russellville and Moreland and then went through Caglesville on the way to Hector and beyond. Sometimes those from the mountains would stop by to spend the night when the weather was bad, or when they were late in the day as they made their journey home from Atkins.

Lois recalled when a peddler had come by their house late one evening and traded her dad a new pair of check lines (leather strips used for controlling horses and mules) for his old ones, which looked to be about worn out. He had given almost as much to boot as a new pair would cost. The peddler had spent the night with them, and he had brought into the house new brads and a bradder. After he finished working over the old check lines, they looked almost as good as the new ones he had sold her father.

Mr. Maxwell was astonished. He thought he had been gypped. He wasn't one to throw away money carelessly. "Why didn't you just offer to repair my old check lines and charge me for that?"

The peddler laughed, "I have to make money some way, and you got what you wanted." Mr. Maxwell couldn't argue with that. He wouldn't have known about the repair job if the peddler hadn't spent the night with them.

Not long after their marriage, Lois's brother, Homer, and his wife and daughter, Joella, came for a visit and stayed all day. Boyd killed a young rooster and dressed it for Lois to cook. Soon it and the dumplings to go with it were simmering in the pot on top of the cook stove.

As it neared lunch time, she checked the chicken and dumplings. The dumplings were delicious, but the chicken was only half-done. She almost panicked. She had so wanted to show everyone she was a good cook, but now they would know she still had things to learn.

"The chicken isn't done," she informed them. "We'll just have to eat the dumplings and vegetables now, and have the chicken tonight."

They teased her about not knowing how to cook chicken, but they did enjoy her dumplings. The chicken would be ready to eat later.

After eating, they hitched up the mules and showed Homer and Goldie the mountain, first taking them to the Rockhouse, then to the Chimney Rock. The Chimney Rock was an outcropping of beautiful rock formations near the northeastern side of the mountain. Pioneers had given names to different formations.

One was called the Needle's Eye, which was a horizontal hole on the crest of the Chimney Rock. Another was the Devil's Chair, a rock shaped somewhat like a rock that anyone could sit in. Names were carved all over the Chimney Rock. People had used nails to scrape away the soft sandstone to make the letters.

Under the Chimney Rock were places you could walk beneath bluff overhangs and still be far above the base of the bluff. One such place was called the Goat's Den. Tame goats that had become feral (wild) had the run of the surrounding woods and rock formations. The Goat's Den had gotten its name from the many goat droppings still visible on the floor.

Calvin Kinslow on top of the Needle's Eye.
Note the eye below Calvin's left. Nov. 1958

The Tater Hole was a small cave that went back into the hillside for fifty feet or so. No one had ever been to the end of it, because it got too small for anyone to crawl back there. Pioneers had stored potatoes in it, thus the name. Later on, during World War II, Lois was to tell her children, "If the Germans ever come over here, we'll go into the Tater Hole and hide."

The Panther's Den earned its name from the time a hunter killed a panther in it. It was a large crack in the bluff, and no one had ever ventured to the end of it.

Last of all, and probably the most spectacular, was the Yellow Rock, on the eastern most point of the mountain. It was a large bluff, and it went out to a point so you could see in three different directions. You could see many miles toward the north, east, and south. In the wintertime, after a big snow, when the snow started melting, huge icicles would form on the underside of the Yellow Rock. They would be as big as a man's body and several feet long.

They didn't have to point out to Homer and Goldie the other beautiful scenery off the mountain. They had noticed it on their way up.

Chapter 3

FARMING

Lois soon learned that Boyd was quite a worker in the fields, and he expected her to help him. This was nothing new to her, because all the farm women she knew helped their men in the fields---if they weren't too sickly or too frail.

Boyd was clearing a piece of ground when they married. After Lois came, he cut the trees and brush down and trimmed the large saplings, while Lois piled and burned them.

One day while she was working, she smelled burning cloth. Examining her dress, she found nothing on fire, but she could still smell smoke close by. She removed her sunbonnet. It was on fire! Throwing it to the ground, she stomped it out. That had been a close call! A little more and her hair would have caught on fire.

After the land was cleared, the rocks had to be hauled off, then more carried off the old fields. Even though many had been removed in the years past, each winter's freezing and thawing seemed to bring up more, and each time the land was plowed, additional rocks were brought to the surface.

Then there were persimmon and sassafras sprouts to be cut, piled, and burned. Lois got many welts on her face and arms from a persimmon sprout as it lashed out at her when she hit the grubbing hoe against it. How she grew to loathe those things!

Next, the fences had to be mended, and a new fence built around the 'new ground' just cleared, to keep the cows and mules out of the fields.

There was also the never-ending job of keeping wood for the fireplace and cook stove. It took an enormous amount to keep them both supplied.

As soon as the ground became dry enough, Boyd hitched Rhody and Jude to the turning plow and started turning the sod. It took eight hours of constant work to break an acre of land. He wanted to plant fifteen acres each of cotton and corn. The corn was for Rhody and Jude, the milk cow, the hogs, and the chickens, while the cotton would be to sell.

Boyd arose from bed at 4:00 a.m. each morning and built the fires, then awakened Lois to cook breakfast. She was greeted to a new day by the familiar smell of coal-oil burning in the lamp and lantern, and by the odor of burning wood in the fireplace and cook stove.

He walked to the barn to feed the mules and milk the cow and then returned to the house to eat breakfast, while Rhody and Jude ate theirs.

By working until sundown every day, he was able to get the thirty acres broken in time to start planting the crops. As Lois often took him water to drink, the newly-turned sod smelled fresh and clean.

They started planting corn first, since it could stand cool weather better than cotton. Ben and Nora swapped work with Boyd and Lois now. In the mornings Lois drove Rhody and the harrow and leveled the ridges the men had put up with their cultivators, while Boyd followed with Jude hitched to the fertilizer distributor. Ben then planted the corn behind him.

At noon Nora would take Lois's place, and Lois would go to the house. She was thankful, because the five hours of walking in the soft ground exhausted her. Her mouth and throat stayed so dry from the dust stirred up by the harrow that she craved water so badly she could hardly stand it. She got some of the warm drinking water, but it relieved her thirst for just a few minutes. Then she craved water once again.

They had thirty acres of corn to plant and then they could wait until the first of May to start on the cotton. All of them were very thankful for the time off between the plantings, especially the women, because it gave their bodies time to recuperate.

One day when Lois and Ben met as they drove their mules along the cotton rows, he said to her, "Boyd isn't going to move off this mountain."

"Yes, he is," Lois replied. "He said he would."

"Naw, he won't move off this mountain," Ben repeated, as he moved on past her.

That kind of talk aggravated her. But in the back of her mind, a little voice told her that he just might be right.

Then the rains came. It rained and rained and rained. They didn't have to work outside then, except to milk the cow, but they knew that as soon as the rain stopped, they would have one heck of a job in the corn and cotton fields. The rain was making the grass grow thick and tall, as tall as the cotton was and way up on the corn. Both crops needed plowing and hoeing in the worst way.

Late one day Aunt Mollie and her daughters, Barbara and Agnes, came to their home to stay overnight. She seemed very sad. She said, "Lois, John and I are just about the same as separated. He's always griping. He doesn't seem to want me. He keeps talking about going back to Tennessee or Alabama to live. I did so want us to have a family. The girls did, too. Leonard and Sewood are not helping matters either. They are always pestering the girls and trying to stir up arguments with them."

Lois was really sorry to hear this but there was nothing she could do to help. She knew Mr. Gray could be a very stubborn man. She only hoped the two of them could make a go of it.

After two weeks it finally quit raining, the skies cleared, and the fields dried out. Then Boyd and Lois stayed in the fields every waking hour. He plowed the corn and she thinned it. The cornstalks were waist high, so it was all she could do to pull up a stalk. It took all her strength, but she knew she couldn't quit. The corn had to be thinned, or it wouldn't make anything. When she finally finished thinning the corn, she ached all over, her back worst of all. But she had to keep going, because the cotton was waiting.

Boyd was now plowing it. The only time he could help hoe would be when it rained and was too wet to plow, or when he finished plowing it. The grass was so bad Lois could only hoe an acre in a week, so it looked more and more like they might lose some. As she hoed in the field, she had to take the small rocks and grass away from the cotton. She had to thin it so the stalks left were about five or six inches apart. Many times when she dug the grass out, the cotton stalks fell over, then she had to rake loose soil around them for support.

At 9:00 a.m. she could hear the whistle at the railroad station in Russellville. At 12:00, 1:00, and 5:00 it would sound again. She didn't need a watch to tell time. She had worked in fields so much she could glance up at the sun and tell within a few minutes what time it was. The beautiful views of the valleys below and the mountains were forgotten as she worked hard to keep the grass from taking the cotton.

After each round, one row to the end and one row back, she got a drink of the lukewarm water. It didn't quench her thirst that much, but it kept her going. She also filed her hoe and then looked up at the sun to see how long it had taken her to go the round. If she had slowed any, she had to speed up again.

As she looked at the many rows of cotton left to be hoed, she didn't think she could possibly get all of it done before the grass took it. Many times she wished she could be back in the classroom teaching children. That $30.00 per month would look mighty good now.

But teaching also had its drawbacks, just like most jobs. It had been very nerve-racking. Many of the over-age boys had given her trouble, as they had many teachers. She remembered hoping and praying that certain mean boys would not be in school that day, but they were the ones who never missed a day.

Boyd hired Annie Miller from the farm down below the Rockhouse to help. She was a good worker, and Lois was very happy to have her, but Annie had read a good book recently, and she was determined to share it, cover to cover. Lois got so tired of hearing about that book.

Boyd finished plowing the cotton two weeks after Annie started helping, and he could now start hoeing. They were glad to see him come, because he could hoe as much as both of them. He never let up, working like he was fighting fire. He didn't think he could let up, since they had borrowed the money to put in the crop. If they didn't make money to pay the bank, they risked losing their farm.

After two more weeks they finished hoeing, then Boyd had to start plowing the cotton again and Lois and Annie had to start re-hoeing. This time it was much easier, because it didn't have to be thinned, nor did it have much grass.

Boyd and Lois picked up their mail at one of the stores in Caglesville, which was operated by the Reverend Walter Kinslow. Down the path it was only two and one-half miles from their house, but around the road it was three and one-half. Boyd's Uncle Mace and Aunt Mamie lived by the Kinslow's. The two families together were a dozen bodies or more, and the children often got into it with one another. It wouldn't have been normal if they hadn't.

Mr. Kinslow was a little man, standing about five feet, four inches tall when he had his shoes on and he weighed right at one hundred thirty pounds. He was comical without meaning to be. He had a rough voice, and he talked in a way as to sound somewhat bossy.

Uncle Mace kept a few goats and one of the billy-goats had been giving Mr. Kinslow trouble. He had been coming around Mr. Kinslow's store and Kinslow would have to run him off. He even went into the store a few times, because in the summer it was impossible to keep the door closed all the time. Mr. Kinslow was getting tired of him. He hated that goat.

One day when Boyd was picking up his mail, the goat entered the store and ambled down the aisle opposite the one Mr. Kinslow was in. Quickly shutting the front door so the goat couldn't escape, he told Boyd, "I'm going to teach that goat a lesson this time." The Reverend grabbed a broom and started after him. But the goat was always one jump ahead. The goat wanted to go out the front door as he usually did, but finding the door closed, he was forced to go down the other aisle to avoid the pursuing preacher and postmaster.

With Kinslow close behind and swatting at him with the broom, but not quite hitting him, around and around the store they went. Mr. Kinslow then stopped at the front of the store and waited for the goat to come around again. He was going to get him now with that broom!

When the goat reached the front and saw Mr. Kinslow blocking the path in the other aisle, he didn't even slow down. He crashed through the front window and took it into the store yard with him, panes and all. Oh, was Mr. Kinslow angry! "Why, that S.O.B.," he shouted.

The whole episode didn't even phase that goat. He hit the ground running and headed toward home.

In July when Boyd and Lois finally got their crops laid by, they could relax a little, but not much, because potatoes and other maturing vegetables from the garden had to be harvested and processed or stored. She canned all the vegetables and fruits she could, enough to last two years, realizing that some years might be too dry to have a garden. Since she didn't have a pressure cooker, she couldn't can everything. Apples and peaches were dried, after which were made jams and jellies. She made delicious jam from blackberries that grew wild and plentiful in the woods and fields nearby

The first of June Aunt Mollie's grown son, Hubert, from Pea Ridge, visited her. She sent him to her other son's house and had him bring his wagon up and move her.

Mr. Gray didn't want her to leave. He thought he would be glad for her to go, but when the showdown came, he was sorry. But it was too late. Her mind was made up. She took her two daughters and never looked back, showing that she could be stubborn, too.

Mr. Gray made a few trips to the rented house she had moved to and tried to get her to come back, but he didn't succeed.

Sewood and Leonard played a joke on him a month after she left, writing a letter to him and signing her name. Among other things, it asked him to bring her some potatoes. He was so happy when he read the letter, the boys were sorry they had made it up. They had to tell him that it wasn't from his wife. He took her some potatoes anyway, but he never did get her back.

Boyd and Bob often took Aunt Mollie vegetables from their gardens. They also gave her meat when they killed hogs.

Chapter 4

THE CONFEDERATE REUNION

Boyd and Lois always headed for Pea Ridge on Sunday mornings and returned home late in the afternoons. Lois looked forward to these visits, but she dreaded the trip to and from there. The roads were so rough and the mountain so steep. She knew they shouldn't be subjecting Rhody and Jude to all the extra work on Sunday after their long hours pulling the plow on weekdays, but she just couldn't stay away from her folks. What faithful servants Rhody and Jude were. They didn't get anything for all their toil either, only what they could eat.

When the crops were laid by each year, around the first of August, the protracted or revival meetings began. Then the farmers took a vacation from field work and attended church each night as well as on Sunday. But this year Boyd and Lois wouldn't go, because Rhody and Jude couldn't be expected to pull the wagon up and down the mountain every night.

Lois missed being at the meetings. Those meetings and church on Sundays were practically the only social activities most farm families had, other than visiting with friends and relatives. People from miles around would come. These were special times for the young and the old alike. The aisles of the churches would be filled with sleeping babies and small children lying on pallets. Outside, dozens of wagons would be parked, with the teams hitched to trees and other restraints.

Saddle horses would also be there. Older boys and young men would be looking through the windows at the girls.

After each nightly service, the boys and young men who weren't too shy would line up and ask certain girls if they could walk them home. Sometimes they accepted. Sometimes they didn't.

Boyd recalled when he was fourteen years old that he had asked a girl if he could walk her home. He only weighed about ninety pounds, and he must have looked even younger than he was.

She had told him, "You better wait 'til you quit a nursing'."

Many a night he had walked down the mountain pathway hoping he would get to walk a girl home, and many a night he had walked back up that same path, wishing he had been able to. But that was where he had met Lois, so everything had worked out all right for him.

Lois was needing a sewing machine badly, and she kept asking Boyd to buy her one. "I can save us enough money on clothes in six months to pay for it," she explained to him.

So he asked around until he heard that Henry Freeman on Buck Mountain had one for sale. Boyd hitched Rhody and Jude to the wagon and he and Lois made the six-mile trip. This was their second trip off the mountain looking at a machine. The first one they had looked at was worn out, so Lois kept her fingers crossed, hoping this would be a good one. It was just what she was looking for, being almost new and only costing $20.00, so they bought it and loaded it into the wagon to take home.

On their return trip to the Iron Ore, the road just northeast of Moreland was badly rutted from a recent rain and from the traffic passing through while it was muddy. The wagon wheels sank deep into the ruts, and the front wagon axle caught on a stump in the middle of the road. The wagon gave a lurch and Boyd was thrown headfirst down on the wagon doubletree at old Jude's heels.

"Boyd!" Lois cried out.

"Be quiet and stay still," he whispered to her. He knew that Jude was bad to kick, and that he was lucky he hadn't already been kicked in the head. But this time Jude stood as still as a statue. Boyd eased himself up with his hands out of the reach of her heels, then breathing a sigh of relief, he stood up and got back into his seat. He was trembling after the narrow escape.

He backed the mules up and moved them out of the ruts so they could get by the stump. It was hard to get the wagon wheels out, but with his urging, the mules put their backs into their work and soon had the wagon on the road again. He cautioned himself to watch out for that stump from then on.

Once a year in August, a Confederate Reunion was held on Gravel Hill, seven miles west of their house, and three miles or so west of Moreland. It was a three-day affair, and Boyd and Lois decided to go and spend a day there. They had worked hard all spring and summer and they would soon be picking cotton. They felt they had earned the right to a little fun.

After reaching the reunion grounds that day, they watered Rhody and Jude and tied them in the shade. They ate lunch they had brought before going inside the grounds so they wouldn't be tempted to buy lunch there. 'A penny saved is a penny earned,' someone had said.

There was one of the largest crowds they had ever seen anywhere. Hundreds of wagons and cars and trucks were parked all over the place. It was hard to move around because of so many people.

"Let's get some ice cream and lemonade first," Lois suggested. This was the only place she had ever eaten ice cream. Her father had brought her here a few times.

After finishing the refreshments, they walked around. They could hear bands playing in the huge covered arbor in the center of the grounds.

Lois recalled her mother telling about coming here in the eighteen hundreds as a little girl. She was in the audience while candidates were making speeches.

A Republican was speaking, and their neighbor on Pea Ridge didn't like what he was saying. The neighbor was wearing a dress coat and a vestment, which made it look like he had on a white shirt. He stood up from his seat, took his dress coat off, ran up to that podium and gave the Republican a good whipping.

When he had pulled his coat off, it revealed a fake white shirt. It only covered the front of his chest. The undershirt he had on was as dirty as could be. The crowd roared with laughter. Most of them were Democrats, and it did them good to see a Republican get a whipping.

Several booths sold food and drinks, and there were others where you could try to win prizes and money. One of these had some very pretty blankets. The man running it saw Boyd looking at them. "You!" he yelled at him. "You look like you have a good arm. Come try your luck! Three balls for a dime! Win one for your pretty wife! A blanket will come in mighty handy on those cold winter nights!"

"I'm going to try to win one," Boyd told Lois.

"Oh come on," Lois urged. "You'll just be throwing your money away." She had been here enough that she knew that in order to win a blanket, he would have to be lucky.

Boyd put his dime down and picked up three balls. He expected to win, because he thought this would be much easier than throwing at squirrels, but he didn't. Sometimes he got one, and sometimes two, but never three. The balls he was using were too light weight, and the wooden loaded bottles he was throwing at were too heavy. He threw and threw. Their money was going fast. Lois begged him to stop, but he was a man obsessed. He wanted to win just for the sake of winning much more than he wanted the blanket.

Finally he gave up. Their money was over half gone. He had thrown away $20.00, enough to buy a cow in nineteen twenty-eight, and he had won nothing. That blanket could have been bought for $2.00 in a store.

Despite their loss, they were still determined to have a good time. After meeting some close friends and going around with them, it was better, because now they had someone to talk to.

A man dressed like a cowboy was bragging about how good a bronc rider he was. He was from Oklahoma, and he was visiting relatives in this area. He was dressed to the hilt, with a ten-gallon western hat, cowboy boots, colorful chaps, and a gaudy shirt. He even had fancy spurs on. He felt like he was the cock of the walk---everybody could see that.

As he told about all the broncs he had ridden, and about all the prizes he had won, he impressed everyone who was gathered around him---that is, all except one man. That man's name was Rube Russell, and he had the reputation of being just about the toughest and meanest man in that part of the country. And he had seen blowhards before.

"You're just a big old windbag," he told the cowboy.

The cowboy laughed. He had just been insulted, and he didn't like it. "What do you know about it?" he asked Russell.

"You couldn't even ride me!" Russell told him.

"Ha! You're about the dumbest man I ever saw."

"Come on, try to ride me. I'll let you put a surcingle on me and you just try to ride me."

The cowboy did think that Russell was crazy now. Then someone ran up with a rope that could be used for a surcingle and it looked like the two adversaries would either have to put up or shut up. Someone tied the rope around Russell, as he got down on his hands and knees.

Boyd and Lois were very interested in what was going on, because Rube was Lois's cousin. They both knew how tough and mean he was.

When the rope was securely tied around Russell, he got off his knees and assumed a position with his hands and feet on the ground. The cowboy hadn't said he was going to ride him, but now he didn't think he could do anything but. Either that, or lose face. So he mounted his human bronco.

There were no betters on this ride, like there would have been if the event had been in a movie. No one thought

Russell could possibly throw a genuine cowboy, one who had actually ridden full-grown unbroken horses.

The two went around and around. Russell seemed to go higher and higher into the air, but he couldn't dislodge his rider. It looked like he was going to lose out on this one. He had to be getting tired. The cowboy rode him like he was a horse, as he held his left arm high in the air.

There was a wagon parked close by where the two were putting on the show. It didn't have a tailgate, and Russell bucked up into the open end. He bucked his way to the front of the wagon, and then went over the front end gate. On his way down, the cowboy lost his seat on him, and high into the air he went. As he came down, Russell's feet were going up and he kicked the cowboy in the rear end. There was an open dug well a few feet from the front of the wagon, and the cowboy was thrown headfirst into it!

Everyone gasped as they watched the cowboy disappear down the well. They thought he would be killed. They heard a splash down below as he hit the water. Luckily, the water was deep enough that the cowboy didn't break his neck at the bottom of the well, and the well was big enough around that he could turn over and come back up with his head above the water. Someone quickly threw him a rope, and he was pulled out of the well without any damage being done to anything except his pride. After he climbed out of that well, he didn't tarry around there very long.

After he left, everyone had a good laugh about what had happened. They hadn't laughed at all when he was thrown into the well, because they had been afraid they were seeing him getting killed. Rube Russell got so many thumps on the back, he was very sore when he went home that night.

In the middle of the afternoon, speeches were made by dignitaries and political candidates. Veterans of the Civil War told stories of things which had happened to them on the battlefield. Finally, they bowed their heads as the roll call was made of their departed comrades who had died since their last reunion.

Lois noticed that there were only a few veterans left and they were in their late seventies and eighties. They looked nice in their Confederate uniforms but they also looked sad.

Lois and Boyd's families had been touched by the Civil War. They had grandpas and great uncles who had fought on both sides. They also had ancestors who had owned slaves. But they were all gone now.

Chapter 5

AUTUMN HARVEST

The middle of August found Boyd and Lois in the corn field most of each day, as they drove the mules down the rows and gathered the corn. Boyd took two rows on one side of the wagon, while Lois got the down row, the row the wagon straddled as it went through the cornfield. She only had half as much corn to get as Boyd, but since the rows were knocked down by the wagon, she had to bend over as she gathered it.

No one had to guide the mules. They knew where to go, and what to do. All Boyd had to do was yell, "Giddup," and the mules would take off. When he said, "Whoa." They would stop.

The wagon had high sideboards, so it would hold more corn. An hour after they began gathering, it was full and ready to take to the barn and be unloaded in the corn crib. While Boyd unloaded it with a scoop, Lois went to the house and rested. She was thankful for that. She wasn't as tough as he was. He was a little Superman. That's how Jerry, one of his sons, described him after his death fifty years later.

The corn made good, which would come in handy to feed the livestock during the next year. They almost had it all gathered by the first of September. But before they could get the last few loads, Boyd decided it was time to start picking cotton. The corn could wait. They had to get the cotton to market as soon as possible, because the earlier cotton often brought a better price than that brought in later.

Lois was happy they would be earning some money, but she knew they would be very busy for the next two or three months. They would have to go over the cotton twice. When half the bolls were ready, they would start, which would be the next day. By the time they had picked it over once, the remainder of the bolls would be open and they would start picking them. She would have to let a lot of housekeeping go until the pickin' was done and the corn was gathered.

That night Boyd cleaned out the wagon, making sure the trash from all the corn gathered was removed. They would use the same sideboards with the cotton as with the corn. Early the next morning, he hitched Rhody and Jude, drove to the part of the cotton field where they would be picking, unhitched and took them back to the pasture. They were through for the day. He then took the cotton scales and hooked them to a wire at the end of a pole he had fastened to the wagon. Each sack of cotton would be weighed after it was full.

When the wagon held 2,000 pounds, he would take it to the gin at Atkins where the seeds would be removed. (Cotton gin was short for cotton engine.) It would then be pressed into a 500-pound bale. He would sell it to a buyer from a cotton mill. There would be several buyers and Boyd would sell to the highest bidder.

Lois liked to daydream as she pulled the eight-foot-long sack along the rows. It felt good to be picking cotton again. The bolls were big and fluffy and didn't hurt her fingers the way knotty bolls did. The smell of the cotton bolls was pleasant. They had the same aroma as that of new cotton cloth.

"How much cotton do you think we'll get?" she asked Boyd.

"At least half a bale an acre," he answered. "This is as good as it was last year, and it made half a bale an acre then."

"Do you think we'll get out of debt?" She didn't like to be in debt. It cost too much money to pay the interest.

"I hope so," he replied. He wouldn't say he was certain, because he had seen the price of cotton plummet too many times to venture a guess as to how much money they would receive this year. The wagon was full by Friday night. The cotton had been trampled down many times as it was filled, because Boyd wanted to make sure he would have a big bale when he took it to market. They were in good spirits as they got ready for bed that night, even though their bodies ached from the long hours of work. They were getting on in the world. The cotton would bring a good price at Atkins the next day, and it would be welcome money, because they hadn't earned any since their marriage began.

The next morning they arose earlier than usual. Long before daylight Boyd and the mules started for Atkins. It would be a long trip there and back, for one day.

As he drove along, he hoped he wouldn't have a long wait at the cotton gin. If only he could reach there before many other farmers did, he wouldn't have to wait all day. But he didn't have much hope for that, since so many others lived nearer the gin than he did.

It wasn't yet daylight when he reached the brink of the mountain and was ready to start down. Stopping Rhody and Jude, he took the eight-foot-long chain lying on top of the cotton, climbed down from the wagon, and proceeded to chain one of the rear wheels to the wagon bed frame. This locked the wheel so it couldn't turn. Although the nearly-new wagon had a good hand brake, it wasn't strong enough to hold the wagon back when it was heavily loaded.

Boyd thought of the time when his father, grandfather, and brother, Ben had been going down the Iron Ore with a load of cotton, when the chain which locked the wheel had broken, and the wagon had rushed down upon the frightened team of mules, causing them to start running. They had gone faster and faster until the wagon had finally overturned, dumping its occupants and then its contents on top of them.

Ben had crawled out from under the cotton first, and he had burst out laughing when his father and grandpa had come digging out. It hadn't been so funny to the two older men, for they had been badly frightened, though unhurt. They were also thinking of the hard job that lay ahead of them. The wagon would have to be lifted back onto the road and all the cotton picked up and put back on it. That is, after it was repaired, if it could be.

Boyd didn't want the same thing to happen to him. He had enough work to do already without adding to it.

When he reached the bottom of the steep part of the mountain, he was on the bench overlooking Pea Ridge and Oak Grove. The bench was level, so he had to unlock the wheel until reaching the point where the road again started down. Then he relocked it. At the foot of the bench, he unlocked it once more and went on his way. It was just getting daylight when he removed the chain and put it back on the load of cotton.

As he passed through Oak Grove, the roosters were crowing at almost every house. Smoke poured from the cook stove chimneys, as people were cooking breakfast, getting ready to start picking cotton, or to go to town. Some of the men were going to their barns to feed their livestock and to milk their cows. Boyd waved to each one as he passed by, and they waved back. He had gone to school and sometimes church at Oak Grove, so he knew almost everyone who lived there.

The cotton fields were as white as snow as he rode along. Almost all the open land along the road was either cotton, corn, pasture, or gardens.

When he reached the bottom of Pea Ridge hill, he could see many men busy working on the road. He had heard they were starting on the new gravel highway between Atkins and Hector. They had been talking about it for years.

Most of the workers had teams of mules or horses hitched to small grader blades called Fresnoes, which they used to move earth. They were shaping the roadbed. After it was finished, the roadway would be called a highway because its bed would be higher than the land on either side. This would allow drainage and help keep it from getting muddy.

When he reached the cotton gin a mile north of Atkins, it was 9:00 a.m. He had pushed the mules hard. There was only one other farmer ahead of him, so he had accomplished what he set out to do. There were several other wagons and trailers full of cotton under a shed, but they would be ginned only when there were no farmers waiting with cotton. It wasn't long before he was able to move his wagon into the gin, where the cotton was unloaded by suction.

The old road that once went from Atkins to northern Pope County. The picture was taken just north of Grandpa Maxwell's home place. It was abandoned in 1929 for the new Highway 105

"I see you're early," the gin foreman said. "Must have gotten an early start from the Iron Ore this morning."

"Yep," Boyd answered. "Had to. Didn't want to wait in line all day."

"Got a good crop this year?"

"Sure have," Boyd beamed. "Fifteen acres, and a half-bale to the acre. What's it going to cost me to get it ginned?"

"The price has gone up to ten dollars. We don't like to charge so much, but our costs keep rising. It's hard to get good help with everyone picking cotton."

"How much are you paying for cotton seed?" Boyd asked.

"Twenty dollars is all we can give," the foreman apologized. "The mills still have cottonseed meal left over from last year."

"That will take care of the ginning and still give me ten dollars," Boyd replied. "Can't complain about that. Things aren't too bad. I hear they're paying a good price for cotton."

They were yesterday. But I don't know about today. You can't ever tell about the market. Remember when cotton was selling for forty-eight cents a pound for a while, but started falling in price, and finally ended up at six cents?"

Boyd remembered only too well. That had been five years ago, and it could happen again. When the cotton was at forty-eight cents, a lot of farmers held several bales of their cotton after it was ginned, waiting for it to go even higher. When it started falling, instead of selling then, they waited for the price to go back up. But it kept going down. Boyd finally sold his for twenty cents a pound, but Mr. Gray held onto his. When the price had reached six cents a pound, and there was no hope of it going back up, he sold.

It only took thirty minutes to gin his cotton, and when they finished weighing it he had a large 530 pound bale. He ate an early lunch from the food Lois had sent then he drove to the cotton yard to find a buyer for the cotton.

Since this was Saturday, Atkins was alive with activity. This was the day all the farmers and their families came to town. They drove in from far and near. Today there were at least as many people from out of town as there were living in town.

Atkins was a thriving, progressive, and modern city of fourteen hundred in 1928. It had sprung up along the railroad in the early eighteen seventies, replacing the town of Galley Rock, which was five miles south on the Arkansas River. Now the only things left of Galley Rock were the cemetery and the foundations of some of the houses and businesses there.

Atkins had a busy main street, with several brick buildings, and there were as many more across the railroad tracks. There were several churches, a brick high school, many businesses, and a large white train depot. Two wagon yards allowed people to park their wagons all day and even overnight if they lived too far away to return home that day. There were probably as many people sleeping in the wagon yards on Saturday night as there were in the hotels, because most farmers didn't want to spend their money on hotels.

The small city boasted miles of sidewalks, electricity, phone service, running water, sewers, natural gas, and even electric street lights. It also had two banks, two hotels, and several cotton gins in the vicinity.

Arkansas was in its 'heyday'. Its population had been growing steadily since the Civil War. There was much cheap and plentiful land to offer newcomers, and they had bought it. Most of them didn't settle in the towns and cities. They hadn't come here for that. They were after land, which offered them food, shelter, jobs, and hope for the future.

When the railroad had come through in the eighteen seventies, the government had deeded it land to sell in order to finance the building of it. The railroad company had brought in many people from the eastern states and from Europe to sell their land to. By nineteen twenty-eight, most of the land in Arkansas that would produce food, feed, and fiber had been taken, so the population of Arkansas was as high as it was to be for many years.

Chapter 6

THE MOVE TO PEA RIDGE

That October, when the tree leaves turned red, gold, blue, orange, purple, and brown, mingled with the green of the pines, the dazzling colors leaped out at everyone who lived on the Iron Ore Mountain. It would have been hard for any painter to capture the beautiful panorama that nature had created up there and at other places like it in the Ozarks.

Autumn in the Oxarks

New vigor came to Boyd and Lois as they worked in the cotton fields. Gone was the heat of the energy-sapping sun. The smell of autumn was in the air. Not a cloud appeared in the brilliant blue sky. A light breeze played with the tree tops, as it gently swayed them to and fro. There was a chill in the early morning air, but it was soon chased away by the now friendly sun, as it peeped over the eastern horizon. The sparkling dew soon evaporated and was soon forgotten.

The golden pumpkins and the shocked corn waiting patiently to be taken to the barn gave the feeling of serenity to all those who lived high on the mountain. All was right with the world.

In November they finally got their crops gathered and they were ready to move to Pea Ridge. Mr. and Mrs. Maxwell had moved to Atkins for the winter school term so their two children, Norma and Earl, who were still of school age, could attend. Shiloh, the Pea Ridge School only had eight grades, and Mr. Maxwell wanted his children to have more education than that. They wanted Boyd and Lois to move into their house on the ridge until they returned in the spring after school was out.

It had a separate dining room and kitchen. A large screened-in back porch could be used for a dining place during the hot summer months. There was also a small screened in porch on the other side of the house.

The young couple was happy to oblige them, because it was much nicer than the sharecropper's house they would be living in later. It had two bedrooms. The ceiling of the house was high overhead, to allow the warm air to rise above the occupants' heads. The chimney was tight because the rocks were mortared together with cement, and best of all, the house was painted a beautiful white. But the high ceilings also allowed warm air to rise in the winter time, so the house was rather cold in the winter.

Homer and Goldie lived across the field just one-fourth mile to the south, so it took only a few minutes for Boyd and Lois to get together with them for a visit.

One trip was all it took to move their essential household goods to their new home. Boyd could bring the rest when he returned to the mountain to check on the place there. He also had to haul the corn and fodder down in order to have feed for the livestock.

Sometimes he hauled wood from the mountain for the fireplace and cook stove. This wasn't really necessary, but he enjoyed going back to the 'ole' home place from time to time. Although he had left the mountain, his heart still belonged up there.

In February on one of his return trips to the mountain, he came upon Mace Singleton with a whiskey distillery. Mace told him he was moving to Bebee, a town seventy-five miles to the east, and he couldn't take the still with him.

"I'll trade it to you for the saddle you have in your barn."

"I don't know how to use a still," Boyd told him.

"I'll show you," Mace replied. "I have some beer we can use to make whiskey with."

So they set out to make some Iron Ore Mountain moonshine. Boyd brought his brother, Bob, along to help.

They were about half-way finished, when the sound of crunching leaves reached their ears. It sounded like some men walking toward them.

"It's the law!" Bob yelled. He and Mace started running as fast as their legs could carry them, and they didn't stop until they were out of sight.

Boyd sat down. He wasn't going to run if it was the law; he would just be caught.

A few minutes later, some cows came strolling up and he called Bob and Mace back. As they returned, they were grinning from ear to ear, but Boyd was laughing and feeling very proud of himself for not running away.

After the whiskey was made, they tasted it. It was so terrible that Boyd thought he had just as soon drink green persimmon juice. Mace didn't say anything, but pretended it was good. He left soon afterwards with his saddle. Boyd and Bob poured the whisky out, because it wasn't fit to drink. Boyd wondered how he had let himself be talked into trading for the still. That was a good saddle, even if it was old.

A few days later, Boyd had a visitor, Claude Blankenship, from the Buttermilk community east of the Iron Ore. "I heard Mace Singleton traded you my still," he said.

"I traded a saddle for a still," Boyd replied. "But he said it was his."

"It wasn't. It's mine," Claude informed him.

"Get it," Boyd declared. "But I've just lost a saddle. Mace has moved to Bebee, and that is too far to go after it. Oh, I don't know how to make whiskey anyway.'

A few nights later, three men came to get the still. They didn't want to risk hauling it in the daytime and being seen by someone who might turn them in.

As luck would have it, Boyd soon heard that Millard Henley, Mace Singleton's brother-in-law, needed two wagon drivers to haul plow tools to Bebee. He had also decided to move there. Boyd and Bob went to see him and got the job. Boyd would be paid with a cotton planter and would get five dollars when they reached Bebee. On Monday morning, they drove their teams and wagons to Buttermilk and loaded up. They had overjets on their wagons to keep the rain out. They were in a train of four covered wagons, but they headed east instead of west.

Millard's son, Hobert, rode with Boyd. Hobert was a nice young man of seventeen, and he was good company.

The second night of the trip, while they were camping out, just west of Conway, a bad cloud came up. The wind grew to a high fury, and the thunder and lightning became worse and worse. The wind-swept rain fell in sheets and whipped the canvas cover of the wagon, threatening to rip it away. The two men's hair almost stood on end.

Hobert was so frightened he was almost in tears. He thought his father should come and get him. His father and mother were in one of the other wagons. When no one came to get the young man, he groaned, "Nobody don't care nothing about me."

This amused Boyd. He didn't blame Hobert's folks for not venturing out in this wind, rain and lightning.

The storm soon ended. No one was hurt, and no damage had been done. Boyd was greatly relieved. He had been afraid they were going to be struck by lightning or blown away.

When they reached Bebee, the first person Boyd saw was Mace. When Mace saw him, he turned pale. He hadn't expected to ever see Boyd again. He knew the cat was out of the bag about the still not being his.

"I came to get my saddle," Boyd said, in a tone of voice that wouldn't be called friendly. When Mace didn't say anything, he continued, "Claude Blankenship got his still, and I came to get my saddle."

Mace stammered, "I'll tell you how you can get your money back. Turn Claude and his still into the law, and they will give you a reward."

"I'm not that lowdown!" Boyd retorted. "If I don't get my saddle back, I will make enough trouble that I may be sent to the pen, but I'll take somebody with me!"

He walked away. Mace hadn't answered him the last time. After unloading his wagon, he bedded down for the night. He studied over what he was going to do in the morning about the saddle. He fell asleep without reaching a decision. "I guess I will just have to wait and see what happens in the morning," he had thought.

When he looked in his wagon the next morning, his saddle was there. He and Bob went back toward the Iron Ore without seeing Mace again. He forgot to ask Mr. Henley for the five dollars he promised him, and Mr. Henley hadn't mentioned it either. So he lost a few days' wages. The trip to Bebee and back took him and Bob four days.

Chapter 7

NINETEEN TWENTY-NINE

When school was out that spring, Boyd and Lois moved into the sharecropper's house one-fourth mile to the north. The Maxwell family moved back into their main house.

The year was 1929, and their spirits were high as they worked in the fields that spring. Their rent was free, and the land they were working was smoother and not so rocky as that on the mountain.

A lucky break came their way just before crop planting time. Lois's Aunt Dora and her husband, Lawrence, wanted to sharecrop the mountain place. Boyd and Lois would be getting free rent where they were and they would get one-fourth of the crop produced on the mountain.

Boyd helped them move. He had to use his wagon, because they didn't have one. They were very poor. They had been living on Griffin flat, three miles to the east of the mountain, but twice that far around driving the road. Uncle Lawrence had hired out to a farmer, George Griffin, but Aunt Dora wasn't happy there, so she had talked him into moving to the Iron Ore.

When Boyd hauled the first load, the Graves and their children accompanied him to the mountain. Uncle Lawrence wanted him to go back alone for the other load. He didn't want to face Mr. Griffin, since he hadn't told his employer he was leaving.

Mr. Griffin came to the hired-hand's house while Boyd was loading up. He was angry because Uncle Lawrence was leaving. He had hired him for the crop year, and since Uncle Lawrence was such a good worker, he hated to lose him. He berated the Graves all the time Boyd was loading the supplies. Boyd just let him talk, and didn't say much.

After the Graves family was settled on the mountain, Uncle Lawrence asked Boyd to loan him $100 until the cotton was sold that fall. Boyd had to think some on that, because he and Lois didn't have much money to spare. They only had the $125 Mr. Maxwell had repaid Lois. He knew she wouldn't want to loan her money for fear she wouldn't get it back.

He pondered, "But if we don't loan it to him, he won't be able to make a crop. He doesn't have anything to use as collateral to borrow from a bank. All he owns are his household goods and his team of mules. His mules are probably mortgaged. I'll loan him $100 of Lois's money and not tell her about it. Then when he sells his cotton this fall, he will repay the loan, and she will never know the difference."

He knew the Graves were good workers, and he was glad to have them on the mountain place, because it didn't seem so lonesome when he returned up there. They had several children, including two young boys who could help them in the fields.

That spring and summer saw many busy times. The corn and cotton crops got off to a good start and were easier to work than that on the mountain. The garden yielded more than they could eat or can, even though Lois canned enough for two years. The Irish potatoes were good, as were the watermelons, and the sweet potato vines grew so lush, they covered the middles between the rows.

They were now able to go to church at Shiloh on Sunday nights, as well as on Sunday mornings. They always ate lunch with Mr. and Mrs. Maxwell and their children. They then sat around and talked and laughed or sang songs. The Maxwells had a large upright organ all the girls could play, and they would gather around it and sing while each took turns playing. The men listened to the singing, talked about farming, hunting, the stock market, world affairs, and anything else that suited their whims. They gossiped about their neighbors just the same as the women did and maybe more so.

May was decoration month at most of the cemeteries in the Ozarks. People from miles away would come for the all-day services, bringing their dinner with them, and all kinds of flowers to decorate the graves. After the morning service, the men would put tables together under shade trees, and the women would spread tablecloths over them and set out all the good food they had brought. There was always more than enough for everyone to eat. The children would watch with big eyes as they saw different kinds of good food being set out.

There would be platters of fried chicken, beef, ham, and bowls of chicken and dumplings, beans, potato salad, corn, peas, and many other such foods. But the ones that made the children's mouths water were the pies, cakes, cookies, and puddings. There were chocolate, coconut, lemon, vanilla, and other kinds of cakes, as well as pumpkin, butterscotch, apple, chocolate, raisin, and other kinds of pies.

The men would get shade tree limbs and wave them over the tables to keep the flies away. Then after everyone had eaten their fill, they would stroll over to the cemetery and admire the newly decorated graves. Old acquaintances would be renewed. This was the only time some of the people would get to see a few of their friends and relatives. Sometimes they would meet relatives they had never seen before.

At 1:00 p.m. services would resume. A short business meeting would be held. More songs would be sung, poems read, and often a history of the community told; then the afternoon preacher would take over.

The fourth Sunday in May was Shiloh's time for Decoration.

After they had eaten lunch that day, Boyd, Lois, Homer, and Goldie walked to the cemetery. At each grave of their dead relatives or close friends, they reminisced about their lives while upon the earth.

There were Lois and Homer's grandparents, Andrew Jackson Duvall and his wife, Sarah. They had enjoyed long and busy lives, having farmed on Pea Ridge while rearing several children. He had fought in the Civil War, and he and another brother were the only ones of several who had not been killed. He had lost his first wife while she was quite young, and he had been left with a baby girl to raise. He had gone to the Scott's house on Crow Mountain and had told Mr. Scott, "I want to marry your baby so that she can help me raise my baby."

Mr. Scott and his wife had consented, but Andrew's baby girl had died soon afterwards and been laid to rest beside her mother in Pascal Cemetery near Moreland.

They had gone to West Texas in a covered wagon for two years, starved out, and were forced to return to a friendlier climate. They had planted two crops in Texas, but lack of rainfall had doomed them to failure. They had then homesteaded on Crow Mountain near Sarah's folks and had later owned land on Pea Ridge. They may have homesteaded land there and they may have purchased part of it from James Churchill and his wife, who was Sarah's sister.

Two of the graves were occupied by Lois's brothers, who had died in infancy. They had been born without palates in their mouths and they were unable to drink milk without it coming out their noses. There was a third one who had been buried at Pascal cemetery. One of the babies had lived to be eighteen months old, the others not so long.

Leonard and Sewood always made the rounds of as many Decorations as they could, so they could eat their fill of the delicious food. They didn't dress very well, so when Boyd and Bob were dating and going to the Decorations, they were ashamed of their brothers, and they tried to discourage them from going. But Leonard and Sewood went anyway. They weren't going to pass up all that good food.

There were Tate Graveyard, Crossroads, Shiloh, St. Joe, Moreland, Rock Springs, and others. They walked for miles in order to get their fill.

The boys wore overalls that were worn out. They had been cut off above the knees because of the knees having large holes in them. They were without shirts, and most of the time their overalls had only one gallus that would fasten. Their straw hats were frayed on the outer edges. They were always barefoot in the summer. Tom Sawyer and Huckleberry Finn had nothing on those two Iron Ore Mountain Gray boys.

Years later, after Leonard and Sewood were dead, a man by the name of Elmer Standridge, who had moved here from Texas, told me the first time he met the two boys was at a Decoration west of Gravel Hill at the Saint Paul cemetery in the nineteen twenties. The two boys had walked eight miles in order to eat dinner, sixteen miles round trip.

Chapter 8

THE DEPRESSION COMES

The protracted meetings began in August, but Lois and Boyd didn't go. She was going to have a baby. She had worked all spring and most of the summer, and the baby was due the last of August. It was hard on her, but she had felt that it was necessary.

He came the 26th of August, 1929, and she was attended by Doctor Linton, a kind and gentle man from Hector. The baby was strong and healthy. They named him Jyles Maxwell. Lois was kept busy changing diapers and seeing after him. She had to wash clothes every day. The wash pot down at the spring often had a fire under it to heat wash water.

All of Lois's folks made over Jyles. He was only the third grandchild for Mr. and Mrs. Maxwell. They had been very happy when Boyd and Lois had given him Maxwell for a middle name.

That summer after the crops were laid by, Boyd got a job at the rock crusher in Oak Grove. The new highway between Atkins and Oak Grove was now being graveled. The $50 he earned by cotton picking time was very welcome money, because of the lack of money at that time of year. The $90 he received for his timber he sold on the mountain also helped.

A tragedy occurred that summer to Bob Martin, one of the gravel haulers. His truck didn't have doors, and one day he fell out and was killed.

The first bale of cotton that fall sold for $.29 a pound--$145 for a 500 pound bale of lint, and the seed sold for more than enough to pay for the ginning. Then the bottom fell out of the market. The stock market crash caused everything to go way down in price. The rest of their cotton only brought six cents a pound, which was not enough to pay their expenses. The seed and fertilizer had been bought on credit at pre-stock market crash prices.

Uncle Lawrence wasn't able to repay Boyd the $100 he had borrowed from him. After he paid his expenses and bought food for his family to keep them from starving, there was no money left. Lois had to be told about her money being loaned out.

My, was she angry! She was so upset about the money being gone that she had worked so hard for and done without things in order to save, and also about the bad market for cotton. Their dreams and hopes had been dashed; all the work they had done had been wasted and they had very little money left.

Lois got out of picking cotton that fall because of baby Jyles, but she was still kept busy doing housework and caring for him. By November Boyd had all the cotton and corn gathered and picked; then he kept busy getting wood, milking the cow, feeding the hogs, and doing such other things.

Norma, Lois's youngest sister, got married that year to a neighbor named Vilage Duvall, so Earl and Opal were the only children left at home with Mr. and Mrs. Maxwell.

One Sunday that winter when all the Maxwells and their in-laws were sitting by the fireplace, Mr. Maxwell called Boyd and Lois into another room. "How would you like to buy the Uncle Johnny Farmer place?" he asked them. Before they could answer, he continued, "I have paid $600 on it, and still owe the bank $1400. If you want it, I will let you have it for two thousand dollars. You can pay me after you have paid the bank off."

"What about Homer and Goldie?" Lois asked. Homer and Goldie were now living on and farming the place that Mr. Maxwell was talking about.

"Homer and Goldie don't want to go in debt to buy it. I am going to have to sell it to someone or the bank will foreclose on me. If you want the place, I will help Homer build a house on my land."

So Boyd and Lois moved again for the third time during their two years of marriage. This time they were one-fourth mile south of Mr. and Mrs. Maxwell, just across the open field.

The house they were moving into was much better than their sharecropper's house. It was painted white and was larger. It too had a fireplace for heating. There were eighty acres of land in the new farm—forty that joined the Maxwell's and forty on the south side. Forty acres of this land was similar in texture and composition to Mr. Maxwell's, so it would also be easier to work than that on the mountain.

Boyd decided to plant thirty-five acres of cotton and nine acres of corn in 1930, because they would need more money in order to make payments on the farm. He hired his cousin, Ernest Gray, to live with them and work for them until the crops were laid by, since Lois would have to take care of Jyles.

Ernest was Boyd's Uncle Charlie's son, and he was twenty years old. He lived at Bells Chapel, southwest of Atkins. He was a good worker, never complaining, though Boyd worked him from daylight until dark during the busy season. He had to loan Uncle Lawrence $75 more that year, which he had to borrow from the bank. He hoped 1930 would be a better year. If so, Uncle Lawrence could repay him and Lois all he owed them. In May they received a very hard, beating rain that lasted all day and all night. The ground was soon packed after it began and most of the water ran off down the streams toward the Arkansas River.

They were able to finish working the garden and thin and plow the corn and cotton before it rained again, which they were very thankful for. But by the time they finished in June, the ground was getting dry. They hadn't had time to worry about the lack of moisture before, but now they began to search the sky for signs of a cloud.

But each day was the same. The big faucet in the sky had gone dry. The sun seemed to shine hotter each day. After a while the weather became the number one topic of conversation wherever one went—at the store, the church, or in town. Arkansas was a predominantly rural state then. Almost everyone depended on the soil for their livelihood, and how well the crops did depended upon the weather. Even most people in town depended upon the soil, if only indirectly. The merchants bought and sold farm products and they sold their goods mostly to farmers. If the farmers went under, so would the bankers, merchants, and others. So everyone in Arkansas worried about the weather that summer of 1930.

Chapter 9

A VISIT TO THE DENTIST

Lois was often bothered with toothaches. That summer she had a bad one that wouldn't go away. It hurt for a few days. She thought it would finally quit hurting, but the pain went on and on. She had Boyd hitch up Rhody and Jude to take her to the dentist in Atkins. When they were ready to go, Homer decided he wanted to go with them. After they had ridden about a mile down the road toward their destination, they spied a squirrel running up a large oak tree.

"Whoa!" Boyd called out to the team. "Let's go get him!" he shouted to Homer. They didn't have a gun, but there were lots of rocks laying around on the ground they could use. While teenagers, Boyd and Ben had gone squirrel hunting with rocks when they didn't have any ammunition for their guns. They had gotten quite a few squirrels that way, but mostly they had used rocks to jump squirrels out of the tree and let the dogs catch them.

They didn't have dogs that day, but they wanted to try anyway. Grabbing up handfuls of rocks, Boyd got on one side of the tree and Homer on the other. They threw and threw, intending to get that squirrel. They hit it time after time, but not in the head. The squirrel held fast to the tree limb it was on. When it did get hit, it only winced some and moved around to the other side of the limb.

In the meantime, Lois sat in the wagon getting hotter and hotter. Her toothache was killing her, and the hot mid-morning sun wasn't helping. Oh, she was getting angry! She was having to hold Rhody and Jude, and they were becoming impatient. The horseflies were eating them up. They were stomping and twisting in their harness, trying to get away. Jude's back foot went over the trace chain as she kicked at one that was biting her. Lois felt so sorry for the two mules.

"How could two grown men make such a fuss over a silly squirrel?"

Finally, after what seemed like an eternity, Boyd and Homer gave up and returned to the wagon. Boyd was saying, "If we had brought our dogs, I could have climbed the tree, jumped it out and let them catch it."

"Yeah, and you would have really had yourself a prize if you had caught it!" Lois groaned.

When they reached Atkins, Homer went about his business, while Boyd took Lois to the dentist. They hadn't brought any money, since they didn't have any. They would have to ask the dentist for credit. But the first thing they saw on the door of his office was a sign which read, Jim Shanton DDS "NO CREDIT."

"Oh no! What will we do now?" Lois groaned. "I've got to have something done for my tooth!"

Boyd thought for a minute. "Let's go in. I'll talk to the dentist."

They entered the waiting room and waited.

In a few minutes he opened the door of his office to let the patient out he had just finished with. "Next," he called.

Since there were no other patients waiting, Boyd told him, "We don't have any money, but my wife has to have something done for her tooth. It has been killing her for several days."

"Why haven't you brought her here before now?" the dentist asked.

"We didn't have any money, and we kept thinking it would quit hurting."

The dentist frowned, hesitated a moment, then replied, "Well, bring her on in and let me look at it."

Lois climbed into the dental chair and opened her mouth for the dentist to examine her tooth.

"Hmmm," the dentist said, as he poked around on it and her gums. "Hmm, I can't pull it."

"Why not?" Boyd questioned. He was standing in the door of the small room. He thought the dentist was refusing to pull Lois's tooth because they didn't have any money. He knew he had a legal right to refuse, but he also knew that Lois had to have something done about it—and soon. He felt that the dentist had a moral duty to help her.

"It's too abscessed to pull," the dentist responded. "It might set up infection and kill her. I can't take that responsibility."

"What can be done about it?" Boyd demanded.

"I can drain the infection off. That will relieve the pain. Then after a few days I can pull the tooth."

What a relief it was to hear him say that.

Boyd had some business to take care of, so he said, "I'll be back in a little while," and he left.

The dentist was right about the pain being relieved. As soon as he stuck the needle into Lois's gums, the pain began to ease. He didn't charge anything for all he did, and he wanted them to understand that he hadn't refused to pull the tooth because of their lack of money. He received a great big, "Thank you!" from Lois as she got out of the dental chair.

As the summer passed, and still no rain had fallen, everyone grew more and more concerned. The sun seemed to glare down hotter and hotter each day. The loose soil turned to dust, and the unplowed ground got as hard as a rock. The pasture grass had dried up weeks before. Trees were dying, and the streams went dry, as did many wells. Everything had died in the gardens. Only a few early vegetables had produced anything. Even the potatoes had failed.

Boyd, Homer, and Mr. Maxwell kept their livestock alive by cutting sassafras bushes for them to eat. They were lucky that there were hundreds of them in fence rows and in parts of their fields not worked that year.

Every spring in their pastures dried up except one. It provided enough water for their cows and mules and for Homer's and Mr. Maxwell's cows and mules.

Lois seemed to worry more than Boyd did about their plight. "We'll just have to take the bad with the good," he tried to console her. "Things will turn out one way or another."

She knew that, but it was the "other" she was worried about. "How are we going to pay for this place?" she wondered aloud.

"I don't know," Boyd admitted. "We may have to let the bank have it and move back to the Iron Ore Mountain."

Those were the last words that Lois wanted to hear. The one thing in the world that she didn't want to do was to move away from her beloved Pea Ridge.

Things were going just as badly for the Graves on the Iron Ore. Their crops were failing too. They wouldn't be able to repay Boyd and Lois, and they would have to leave the mountain. They had done their best, working hour after hour in the fields, but there was just no way to foresee the stock market crash, and now the drought.

Boyd didn't hold a grudge against Uncle Lawrence. In later years when Boyd owned a car, he sometimes visited his relatives in Bigelow. Since Uncle Lawrence was raised in Perry County near Bigelow, Boyd sometimes took him along, so he knew Boyd held nothing against him.

Chapter 10

THE DROUGHT CONTINUES

Jyle's birthday came and went. His was only four days after Boyd's. He was a shining light in the darkness for his mother and father, always bubbling over with happiness, and couldn't help but infect them with it, in spite of the economic gloom that hovered over them.

The depression years were in full swing. It was bad enough before the drought hit, but the drought was the knockout punch for those already staggered by the depression.

The Republican leaders were tightening the screws on the money supply. This was exactly opposite of what the nation needed in order to make an economic recovery. The Republicans said they were doing it in order to prevent banks from making bad loans.

Whatever the reasoning, this caused such a reduction in the money supply that most people couldn't borrow any. The few people who had money were afraid to lend it for fear they wouldn't be repaid.

Most of those who owed debts couldn't repay them. If the lenders wouldn't extend their loans, the borrowers lost their mortgaged property. In the rural areas, this was usually their house, land, farm equipment, and livestock. Many people who didn't owe money couldn't pay the taxes due on their property, so the state auctioned it off on the courthouse steps. Half the hill land in Arkansas was auctioned off, either for taxes or to pay off mortgages to banks.

Most of the few rural residents who had cars couldn't afford to buy gas, unless they had jobs such as mail carriers or doctors. Most of the cars remained parked in yards, or were sold. Mr. Maxwell had to sell his.

When September came, it still hadn't rained. The cotton had made a little, but not enough to pick in a normal year. But this was not a normal year. There was no other work available, so they might as well pick it.

Boyd and Lois took their cotton sacks and started picking. The few bolls were small and knotty, so a few pounds a day were all they could get. When they finally had the wagon loaded, they had picked over 12 acres. This would have produced six bales in a good year. Three small bales were all they made on the 35 acres. It sold for six cents a pound.

It didn't take long to gather the corn, as there were only a few small ears scattered here and there. Boyd parked the wagon in the middle of the cornfield and then took a tub and went around filling it up. When it was full, he emptied it into the wagon, refilled it and again emptied it. After he had the corn gathered, he had nine tubs full from nine acres.

In late September, it finally rained. Though it was too late to help the crops, it did enable them to sow turnips. A record crop of turnips was sown that fall in Arkansas.

How many people were kept from starving to death by that September rain, we'll never know, but there must have been plenty. People ate turnips for lunch and they ate them for supper all fall and winter, and until the gardens were producing the next spring, they were still eating them, because that was the first crop in the garden.

Lois's Uncle Johnny Farmer told that he had eaten so many turnips, when he had his blood tested, it was over half turnip juice.

After frost, what few persimmons the persimmon trees made were relished by some people. One man said he broke his arm while eating breakfast, when he fell out of a persimmon tree.

Edible wildlife didn't have a chance that winter. Opossums were delicacies. The only compliment the people had for President Hoover was that he sure caused rabbits to taste good. They called them 'Hoover Hogs.' Men went hunting that fall and winter who had never hunted before in their lives. Their women folks made them.

That winter was as unusual as the summer had been. Plenty of moisture was in the ground, yet there was only one light frost. Grass had started growing after the rain in September, and it stayed green all winter. Even without hay or corn for their livestock, they made it through without losing any from starvation. The livestock were actually in better condition than they had been at the end of summer.

The people could hardly believe their good fortune. They kept expecting the weather to turn cold, but it never did. It was a godsend, as if they had received manna from heaven.

But the chickens couldn't eat grass, nor could the hogs. As a result, they didn't get many eggs or much meat that winter.

The Merchants and Farmers Bank in Atkins where Boyd had done business had been closed by the government in 1929. It was rumored that it had made an illegal loan, and was caught by the auditors. Since Boyd didn't like the other bank in Atkins, he had taken his business to Russellville to the People's Exchange Bank. He had borrowed the $75 he loaned Uncle Lawrence, as well as money for himself to buy seed and fertilizer.

The People's Exchange Bank closed during the summer of 1930 and Boyd received a letter from the Federal Reserve in Kansas City, telling him to make prompt and final settlement. He wrote the Federal Reserve back, telling them he wouldn't be able to pay them because of the drought, but that he wouldn't have to borrow any money that next year. He told them if they had to have a final settlement now, they would just have to foreclose on him.

Why he wouldn't have to borrow money next year, he didn't say, because he hadn't figured that out yet. But he did know that he wouldn't be able to borrow from them anyway.

Soon he received another letter with information that the People's Exchange Bank might reopen, but if it didn't, they would deal with him.

The bank did reopen soon, and it sent word for Boyd to come in. The President, L.M. McClure, was very understanding, and he said he sympathized with his situation. Almost all farmers were in the same predicament.

He didn't want Boyd's farm. If he took it, he would just have to sell it to someone else on credit. He might as well keep Boyd as a customer, since he was honest and a hard worker.

"I can extend your loan," he offered. "If you can pay the interest."

Boyd replied, "Yes, I can." He knew his family needed what little money they had from the sale of cotton, but they would manage somehow, and he would keep his good credit rating.

Old Jude went for payment on the cultivator he had bought from Jack Sisney—Will Godby, merchants in Atkins. He had bought it for Uncle Lawrence, but Uncle Lawrence couldn't pay for it.

Chapter 11

JUST GETTING BY

The Maus-Berkemeyer General Store in Atkins had a good business, and Boyd enjoyed trading with them. One day Mr. Maxwell asked to borrow six dollars from him for Opal to get a permanent. He didn't want his father-in-law to know he was broke, so he told him he would get it for him when he was in town the next day.

In Atkins, he bought some groceries from Mr. Maus and paid for them with a check. "Could I make this out for six dollars more than the groceries cost?" he asked Mr. Maus. Mr. Maus said it would be all right, so he had the money to loan Mr. Maxwell.

The next time he was in the store, Mr. Maus produced the hot check. Boyd pretended to be surprised. "Could you hold that check for me a few days?" he asked.

"Sure we can," Maus replied. Boyd loved him for that. He would get the money to repay him some way. Maus and Berkemeyer were Catholics, while he was Baptist, but he thought they were very good ambassadors for their church.

The Pierce-Blalock store opened in Atkins, and he started trading with them some. Soon he received a statement saying he owed them for a sack of wheat shorts, which he knew he hadn't bought from them on credit. The next time he was in town, he went into their store.

He told Pierce, "I have a bill from you for some wheat shorts and I don't owe you for any."

Pierce said, "I sent that bill to you in order to balance the books."   Boyd left their store without buying anything. He didn't think much of that excuse, and he was determined not to trade with them anymore. He started doing business with Richard Burris, who operated a store a mile north of Atkins. He hadn't quit Maus-Berkemeyer, but he hated to ask them for as much credit as he needed.

One day he sent some cream to town by the mailman, Check Davis, and he told him to leave it at the Burris store. Burris would buy it and credit his account for it. Two weeks later, Boyd went to Atkins again, and dropped by the Burris store to pick up his cream can. Burris told him he didn't recall any cream in his name being dropped off there.

He left the Burris store and went on to Atkins and stopped by Pierce-Blalock's. His empty cream can was there. As he picked it up, he said to Pierce, "I want to get the money the cream brought."

"I already paid you for it!" Pierce nastily replied.

"No, you didn't!" Boyd shot back at him.

"Well, you're not getting any money from me!"

Boyd didn't say anything. He was pondering what to do next.

Suddenly Pierce went to his cash register and drew out two dollars and gave them to him. He took them and left. The cream was worth a dollar more, but he would take what he could get, not wanting any trouble over such a little amount of money. There were several customers in the store and he didn't want to cause a scene. Pierce had told Mr. Maxwell he kept a club under the counter to use on troublemakers. Boyd knew they would never get any more of his business. Pierce-Blalock didn't stay in business long. Pierce was making so many people angry, they quit getting much trade.

The residents of Pea Ridge didn't let the depression and the drought keep them from going to church. In their time of trouble, they felt they needed God more than ever. The building at Shiloh where church was held was also used by the community school and by the Masonic lodge. It had three rooms, two downstairs and one upstairs. Only one room on the first floor was used by the church congregation.

One Sunday the pastor announced that a certain gentleman had been called to preach, and he would deliver his first sermon there that night. Everyone was surprised that the man, Sam Surton, had been called. Although he was a good man, he wasn't much of a talker. But he had a son who was a pretty fair preacher.

Boyd and Lois wondered how Mr. Surton would do. They would find out that night. There would be a large crowd present, they were certain, because everyone enjoyed watching and listening to a new preacher give his first sermon.

That night after the singing and devotional service were over, the pastor arose and announced. "We'll now turn the service over to brother Surton."

Boyd could see that the new preacher was embarrassed, as his face was flushed. He hadn't testified during the devotional service. As he reluctantly stepped into the pulpit, it was as plain as day to everyone who was watching that he was scared to death. He couldn't say anything. He squirmed, looked at the ceiling, then behind him. He cleared his throat, as he tightly gripped the sides of the pulpit. Then he clasped his hands together.

Everyone was staring at him. Surely God would give him something to say. Many others who didn't talk much found words when God called them to preach.

Suddenly Mr. Surton exclaimed, "I feel just like I feel!" His face was as red as a beet.

Once again he was silent. Again he squirmed, looked at the ceiling, glanced behind him and clasped his hands together, as he desperately tried to think of something to say. He then repeated, "I feel just like I feel!" His face got even redder.

The congregation was taken aback. Someone giggled in the rear of the church house, but was quickly hushed. It would be very rude to laugh.

The pastor was amused. He walked into the pulpit and stated, "Well, I guess Brother Surton feels just like he feels."

He then proceeded to preach the sermon he had prepared, just in case it was needed.

Back on the Iron Ore Mountain, Mr. Gray, Sewood, and Leonard were barely getting by. They hadn't canned enough the year before to get through a dry year, not as dry as 1930. Ben and Nora had canned a lot for their big family and they had enough that they gave them some, enough to keep them from starving. Boyd and Lois also helped out.

Many years after Mr. Gray's death, Leonard told the story of how they almost lost their crop that year while pitching horse shoes, when they should have been in the fields hoeing and plowing cotton. But he surmised that even if they had lost their crop, it wouldn't have made much difference, because they lost it anyway, due to the drought.

They cut a lot of stave bolts on the mountain, which were used to make staves to ship north, where most of the moonshiners were in the big cities. They had money in Chicago and New York. They were also able to sell some wood to those in the towns of Russellville and Atkins. Wood for heating cost less than natural gas, so in 1930 some of the citizens returned to heating with wood even though they were connected to the natural gas line.

The railroads also had money, though not as much as they had in past years. They bought crossties to replace rotten ones, and Mr. Gray used his broad-axe to make them. He hauled them down the mountain by wagon to Atkins and Russellville, where he sold them.

Ben went into the woods and gathered pine knots and other pine kindling to sell to anyone who would buy. It was hard to starve those Grays out. They were tough and they were not afraid of hard work.

Many years later, William Gray, Boyd's cousin, his Uncle Charles's son, told me about walking behind Mr. Gray one day as he was hauling crossties down the mountain road. The chain that was used to hold the wagon back had broken, and William had run and grabbed the wagon wheel and kept it from wrecking and possibly killing Mr. Gray, as well as the mules he was driving. I had heard the story several times from my dad, but had never met William until then. When I talked to him, he was in his seventies. He had been only a boy when he stopped the wagon.

I knew William would be back to see Dad, because Dad didn't have long to live, so I wrote a poem about the incident, and gave it to him the next time he came back. His wife said he carried it in his billfold until his death. Here it is:

William Gray

A little team of mules one day trod down a lonely mountain road.

One wagon wheel was tightly chained to slow the travel of the load.

The driver, Mr. John Franklin Gray, was sitting up there very high,

The crossties that he was hauling would bring a handsome price.

His nephew William walked behind; at sixteen he was quite a lad,

For the strength in his small body was more than most men he knew had.

They had nearly reached the bottom of the Iron Ore Mountain that day.

Then he could stop the wagon team, get down, and take the chain away.

But then the snapping of a link threw sudden terror in their hearts.

The wagon down the mountain sped; faster and faster it did charge.

Young William knew too well the plight which lay at the next frightful bend,

For just beyond was a ravine; the mules would plunge over its rim.

So running fast, he caught a wheel; it threw him for a somersault.

Jumping back up, he tried again; if he should fail, he knew the cost.

This time it held; the wagon stopped. Bare heels dug in the pebbled ground.

Just how he managed such a feat, no explanation could be found.

The mules' front feet were at the edge of the ravine, fear in their eyes.

They didn't know what had gone wrong, or who it was that saved their lives.

The years will come and years will go; Old memories slowly fade away.

But let's not forget the noble deed of that brave hero, William Gray.

Randall Gray – 1980

Chapter 12

LOSING THE FARM ON PEA RIDGE

In April of 1931, Lois was due to have another baby. When the time came and she needed a doctor, Boyd walked to Moody Maxwell's house to see if he would go for Doctor Linton. Moody, who was Lois's first cousin, was the only neighbor who owned a car. When Boyd reached Moody's house, he knocked on the door and Moody opened it.

"Moody, Lois needs a doctor," he explained. "Could I get you to go after Doctor Linton?"

"Boyd, I don't have any gas," Moody replied. "Come out to my car and I'll show you."

"No, that won't be necessary. I'll take your word for it," Boyd replied. He didn't let on, but he supposed that Moody had some gas put back somewhere. He had probably gotten tired of everyone asking him to go after the doctor and other places. Since Mr. Maxwell had sold his car, everyone had been calling on Moody.

Boyd pondered about what to do next, then he decided to walk the three miles south to where Ray Webb, the mail carrier, lived. Since Ray had a steady job, he wouldn't be so short on money for gas.

Ray gladly went for the doctor but since they were only three miles from Atkins, Boyd had him go there for one, rather than travel thirteen miles to Hector for Doctor Linton. As it turned out, this was to be the only child of theirs that

Doctor Linton didn't attend at birth. This baby was a healthy girl and they named her Bobbye Jean.

Lois didn't get to help in the fields that summer and fall, so Boyd had to hire some help again. He was able to borrow enough money to put in another crop, but he didn't try to grow as much cotton as in 1930, not being able to borrow enough money for fertilizer and seed and for a full-time hired hand.

Everyone hoped it would rain more this year and the price of cotton would be higher. If it wasn't a better year there was no way they could keep from losing their Pea Ridge farm.

Uncle Lawrence and his family were gone from the mountain. They had given up share-cropping, and he had become a hired hand again. Boyd's brother Bob was living up there now.

Boyd seemed to work harder and harder in the field, if that was possible. As he toiled through the long days, he often wondered if he would get any pay for his work that year.

One day that summer he and Lois visited his father on the mountain. His Uncle Bob, who his brother Bob was named for, was living with Mr. Gray. He had been farming in the Petit Jean bottoms, near Danville, a few years back, when the place he had been renting had flooded, and all his crops washed away. When it seemed that he and his wife might starve, he had worried so much that he had lost his mind.

His wife Minnie had gone to live with their daughter, Pauline Bright, near Blytheville, and he was taken to the mental hospital in Little Rock. Mr. Gray had ridden the train with him to the hospital and he had joked to his relatives, "This is the first time I ever heard of one crazy person taking another crazy person to the asylum."

After a few years Uncle Bob had been released and he had gone to live with his brother. Boyd and Lois wondered why he hadn't gone to live with his daughter and wife. Perhaps they didn't have any room for him and his wife too, since they had a child.

When they got ready to go home, they asked Uncle Bob to go with them and visit for a few days. He readily agreed to this. On the way home, Boyd asked him, "How do you like living with Papa?"

"I don't like it much," he answered. "They don't want me to do anything but sit around, and John gripes all the time."

"Why don't you stay with us?" Boyd asked him.

"Mr. Maxwell wouldn't like that." was his answer.

"He wouldn't care." Boyd assured him.

"What about Homer and Goldie?"

"They wouldn't mind. Anyway, they wouldn't have anything to say about it."

Boyd's Uncle Bob Gray, Jyles and Bobbye in 1931

So Uncle Bob became part of Boyd and Lois's family. He was sixty-two years old and he was white-haired and stoop-shouldered. Sadness showed in his eyes. After a lifetime of hard work and hospitalization, he owned nothing in the world except the few clothes he had with him. He was living apart from his wife, whom he loved very much, though the choice was neither his nor hers. Lois felt sorry for him, knowing the heartaches he had gone through and she would do all she could to make him feel welcome in their home. In the days that followed, she and Boyd treated him as well as they knew how. They didn't ask him to do any work but he helped at different things anyway, and they let him. The crops were laid by, so he didn't help in the fields until fall, but he did other little jobs around the homestead.

He was a lot of company for everyone. Jyles became very close to him. His watching after Jyles and Bobbye while Lois was doing her housework was a great help to her.

They were able to attend the protracted meetings that summer for the first time since their marriage. They went to revivals at Shiloh and Saint Joe, a church which was two miles to the east. There were several people converted to Christ and some wayward souls were renewed up.

The crops once again yielded plentifully, including the garden. It had rained several times during the summer. But the price of cotton was still only six cents a pound. By putting it into the government pool, Boyd was able to get nine cents, though they still didn't earn enough to think about making the payment on their Pea Ridge farm.

Lois was disillusioned with farm life. "Pity the farmers," she thought and she vowed that if she had anything to say about it, none of her children would grow up to be farmers.

She had thought thirty dollars a month for teaching school wasn't much, but at least she had received as much as she expected.

With farming, their hopes would be high in the spring, but they would slowly fade as the summer passed. For the last three years, she and Boyd had gotten very little other than their food and aching bodies for all their endless hours of hard work in the fields.

She knew her dream of staying on Pea Ridge was shattered. The bank would foreclose on their farm there and Mr. Maxwell would lose the $600 he had invested in it.

He was a practical man and he couldn't afford to give them free rent anymore, having four other children and a wife to worry about. So it would have to be back to living high on a mountain for them.

Chapter 13

MOVING BACK TO THE MOUNTAIN

That fall after the crops were in and the cotton sold, they were on their way. Uncle Bob was with them. He was now very much a part of their family.

About 1923

Joseph Robert & Velma Duvall Gray

Bob and Velma had to move in order to make room for them. They couldn't find a place to rent on the mountain, so they moved to a farm on Gravel Hill near the Confederate Reunion grounds.

Boyd and Lois hated to see them go. They wished there had been a vacant farm close by but there wasn't.

Boyd had to work harder on the move back to the mountain than he had when they moved down, because they not only had more things to move, they had to move quickly in order to make room for the new buyers for the farm they were leaving.

The milk stock was driven on one trip. He hired two boys to help him, because they were accumulating a nice little herd of milk cows and heifers. They now owned two grown cows and ten large heifers that would freshen in the spring and be ready to start giving milk. He knew that driving them would be quite a chore. The grown cows could be led, so he roped the gentlest one and hoped the others would follow as he led her toward the mountain.

The boys had the biggest job because the heifers wanted to explore the countryside as they walked along and the boys had to herd them back to the main road. Boyd took turns with them so they wouldn't get so tired but he figured that by the time the cattle were safely on their farm on the mountain, each one of them must have traveled at least twelve miles, double what it would have been if they could have just walked straight, instead of having to drive the herd back into the road.

In the spring when the heifers freshened and started giving milk, they could separate the cream and sell it. They had already been selling cream from the two grown cows but after the heifers freshened, they would have much more to sell.

Ben and Nora still lived on the Iron Ore but Mr. Gray and the two boys had bought eighty acres on the west bench of the mountain and moved there. That bench was the largest of the several benches on the mountain, so it was called the Little

Mountain. The main part, or the Big Mountain, was where Boyd and Lois and Ben and Nora lived. No one lived in the house vacated by Mr. Gray now, as it was getting pretty well run down.

Later on, Ben and Boyd heard that a moonshiner was going to move there. They didn't want one that close by, so they burned the house. They knew it wasn't worth any money.

Mr. Gray's present residence was only a mile down the trail from Boyd and Lois's but by the road it was two miles. Either way it seemed like five to Lois because the path and the road were rough and steep.

Both Boyd and Lois felt relieved to be out from under the pressure of paying for the farm they had left. It hadn't been worth even close to the $2000 they had contracted for, because everything had fallen in price so much since the depression began. But Lois had thought they could keep her father from losing the $600 he had invested in it, and Boyd had gone along with her on it. It just hadn't worked out that way. They had surely given it their best shot.

That winter Boyd started on a milking shed as soon as time allowed. He built it twenty by thirty feet, then he put a large corral around it, using pine poles for the cross pieces. He peeled and let them dry before nailing them to the posts so they would last longer.

Every time Boyd came home from the new Barham store on the highway, at the foot of the mountain on the northwest side, Uncle Bob would ask if he received a letter from his wife and daughter at Blytheville. Sometimes there would be one, which would make him very happy. Lois would write a letter back for him. She could tell he would like to be able to go live with them and he always seemed disappointed when the letter didn't say anything about him coming.

When cold weather came, Uncle Bob built some rabbit gums (traps) by nailing four three-foot long boards together. He enclosed one end and put a trap door on the other. The trap door would fall and trap the rabbit inside when the rabbit went in to eat the corn left as bait and rubbed against the trigger stick. With his several gums, he caught at least one rabbit almost every day. The rabbits made great eating and when

Lois cooked, she also put flour gravy and biscuits with it and everyone thought the meal was delicious.

He also caught quail with his quail traps. Quail were plentiful in those days because of the clovers, peas, corn, and other food. There was also lots of sage (sedge) grass in old fields they could use for cover. He used old house shingles to make something like a pyramid and placed it over a hole he dug in the ground a foot in diameter and several inches deep. He made a small opening at the base where the quail could follow the trail of corn into the hole. After quail went inside, they always looked up and they couldn't find the opening through which they had come in.

One day he came upon one of his quail traps that had an entire covey of quail in it. He couldn't believe his eyes. When he took them into the house, he was beaming with pride. He was so happy to be able to contribute something toward putting food on the table. Each day Boyd and Lois grew to appreciate him more.

That fall and winter Boyd often went hunting with Ben, as they had all their lives, except when Boyd and Lois were on Pea Ridge. All the larger game animals, like bear, deer, and turkeys were long gone from the Iron Ore, but there were still lots of squirrels, rabbits, opossums, raccoons, and groundhogs.

They also went foxhunting. Ben was the foxhunter and had the hounds. Boyd just accompanied him. There were several foxes on the mountain and they loved to hear the dogs as they followed them. Ben could listen to the hounds run all night, then eat breakfast and follow the plow or cut wood all that day.

Boyd and Lois no longer visited Pea Ridge every Sunday as they had in 1928. With Jyles and Bobbye, it was just too hard on them. She dreaded the next year—1932. She would once again have to hoe cotton in the rough and rocky soil. They would also have cows to milk. She had Uncle Bob babysit for her, so she would be able to help with milking and with work in the fields now.

Chapter 14

THE STORM

Early the next spring the heifers freshened, so Boyd and Lois were kept busier than ever. They arose at four each morning and worked until late at night. In the mornings, before going to the field, they had to milk the cows, run the milk through the separator and feed the skim milk to the calves and hogs

After that, when Boyd plowed or did other field work, he didn't quit any earlier than he had before they had twelve cows to milk.

He would have to walk a mile down into the 'Cove', a bench on the east side of the Big Mountain, and drive the cows up. The cove was railroad land that had never been sold, so Boyd pastured it just like it was his. He didn't have to pay rent on it.

The coal-oil lantern hung in the shed and threw out its feeble light until long after dark. By the time they had finished at the barn, and had eaten supper, it was 11:00 pm. Their supper was leftovers from dinner. Lois always cooked enough extra to have plenty for supper.

They came, they looked and they saw,
These lovely, wild, rugged hills of Arkansas.

They dreamed of how, when aided by the hoe,
The ax, and plow, the lands bountiful would flow.

They cleared the fields, plowed the land, the grain
they sowed.
They milked the cows, fed the hogs, the hay they
mowed.

The winter found them clearing land, hauling rocks
away,
Planning next year's labors and hoping they would
pay.

They worked so hard for the future that would
come,
For future generations yet unborn.

Though their muscles ached and the days were so
long,
They never gave up, but kept moving on.

The years went by, the work went on,
But then the disillusions slowly come

For though they'd worked their fingers to the bone,
Their efforts seemed in vain, but they worked on.

Randall Gray-1980

They didn't plant as much cotton that year as before, but they had to put in more corn in order to have feed for the cows. Lois helped in the fields half of each day that year, while Uncle Bob kept the children. Then she went to the house while Uncle Bob headed to the field and worked. But her workday was far from over. Housework had to be done and

Jyles and Bobbye cared for. There was the washing of clothes and the changing of diapers, as well as cleaning house and cooking and washing dishes.

After Boyd got the cows up, she left the children with Uncle Bob and helped milk again. Uncle Bob must have marveled at the long hours they put in, but if he did, he never let them know it.

The money they received for the cream really helped out. For the first time, they had a regular income. When the five-gallon can was full of cream, Boyd would carry it on his back down the narrow pathway to the Barham Grocery, where he left it to be taken to Russellville and sold. On his return trip up the mountain, he would tote a fifty-pound sack of flour or other supplies. His lantern showed the way along the lonely and gloomy path as it twisted and turned, trailing around trees, stumps, and large rocks.

Whippoorwills called to each other as he hurried along. Now and then a hoot owl hooted, or a screech owl screeched, sending a chill up and down his spine. He often heard the rustling of leaves as some nocturnal animal scurried to get out of his way. Sometimes a snake could be heard as it slithered into the darkness. He knew that many eyes were watching him, ready for flight if he should come their way. Shrubs brushed against him and he pushed them aside. His straw hat was snatched from his head by a tree limb and flung out of sight. He traced it down with his lantern where it lay among some rocks. He picked it up, placed it back on his head, and continued on.

He was always happy when he reached the two large boulders the path went between at the top of the mountain, and the faint glow of the light in his house came into view. He knew that Lois, Uncle Bob, and the children were inside, waiting patiently for his safe return.

To the south, all up and down the Arkansas River Valley, the lights of Atkins, Morrilton, and the scattered farmhouses looked like twinkling stars as they glimmered in the distant world where they seemed to be. Boyd knew that the people down there, all snug in their homes, had no idea their lights could be seen from so far up in the Ozark Mountain foothills.

One afternoon just before milking time, the weather suddenly started looking rainy, and then the sky turned very dark—almost as dark as night. It got very stormy looking. Boyd grew so worried that he hurried into the house from his work. He knew that dozens of people in Arkansas were sometimes killed by tornadoes. They didn't have a storm cellar to go to, so they would just have to brave the storm from inside the house.

Then they saw the tornado coming across the field from the southwest, destroying everything in its path! It was carrying broken limbs, boards and dust with it! And it was heading straight toward them!

Rushing to the center of the house, they crowded under a heavy table. This might keep them from getting their heads caved in by a flying rock or board. They fully expected the house to be destroyed with them in it!

One of the west window panes had been broken a few days before and Boyd had boarded it up to prevent rain from coming in until he could get another pane. Suddenly there was a loud crash in the front room, as the boards flew off the window and crashed against the opposite wall. The storm had arrived.

Boyd looked around at Uncle Bob. The old man was staring out the open window. "Pray, Uncle Bob, pray!" Boyd yelled.

"It's too late for that," Uncle Bob said. "The storm is already gone."

Boyd went to an east window and looked out to try and see the funnel cloud but it was out of sight. My, but it was on a fast track! He could see that it had leveled the small barn between the house and the milk shed. It had also blown down several large oak and pine trees.

The Grays were very thankful. The tornado would certainly have destroyed their house if it hadn't leapfrogged over them. Boyd knew he would have to build a storm cellar soon because they might not be so lucky next time.

When he was in the Barham store the next day, he told all who were there about the narrow escape they had from the storm, and about the damage done.

A man spoke up and said, "I'll buy those trees from you. I have a sawmill and I can make lumber."

Boyd gladly accepted his offer, as he could use the few dollars the man would give him. The trees would decay anyway. He had no use for them, except for wood. They were much more valuable for lumber than for burning. He had plenty of scrubby trees to cut for wood.

In a few days the sawmill owner had the trees cut into logs and hauled away. All that he left were the bottoms of the trunks and the roots sticking into the air. By each trunk base and mass of roots was a huge hole the tree roots had recently occupied.

Jyles was two and a half years old now, and he was into everything. He was a curious little fellow, and had a lot of exploring to do. He liked to play in the yard, especially around the tree trunk bases and roots as they lay on their sides. As he sat astraddle one, he would pretend it was his horse. He would climb over the roots sticking into the air, and he would imagine that the open holes were his caves. They became his favorite spots.

One afternoon he had just come into the house after playing in the hole next to the house, when Lois happened to look out the window and saw the tree trunk suddenly become up-righted. "Oh my Lord!" she cried out to Uncle Bob, who was sitting in the front room in a rocking chair with Bobbye on his lap.

They walked into the yard and took a look at the tree trunk base. Lois shuddered. "What if Jyles had been in the hole when the tree trunk had straightened up! He would have been killed!" She had to sit down, as she suddenly grew weak all over. She was trembling. If Jyles had been killed, she wouldn't have wanted to go on living.

When Boyd came home from working in the field, she told him what had happened. He was almost as unnerved as she was.

They didn't let Jyles play in the yard for a while, because he couldn't be trusted to stay away from the tree trunks and roots. They knew a little child doesn't understand danger, and he often wants to do something even more if he is told not to do it.

Boyd tested the other trees to see if any of them could be put upright, but none could. They were too heavy for him to lift and he didn't have time now to dig them out the rest of the way, so Jyles would just have to be kept away from them. Then Boyd decided to hitch the mules to them and pull them back into their holes. This worked, although it took him half a day to do it by himself. He would hook one end of a big chain to the part of the roots that was in the air and the other end to the double tree and the single trees that the mules were fastened to. The mules easily did the job but they had to pull hard.

In a few days Boyd started the storm cellar. He hired Lois's brother, Earl, to come from Pea Ridge to help. Earl was a big strong lad of seventeen, so with both of them working, it was finished in two days. They dug the hole, lined it with rocks and covered it with logs. Then they dug a ditch to carry off the water when it rained. The cellar was only a small, crude dugout in an embankment, but it would serve the purpose for which it was built.

Lois was very happy and she was no longer so afraid of storms—if they could make it to the cellar in time. During the following years, they never had an occasion to use it, but it was a comfort just to know it was there. They weren't ones to run out there whenever a little rain cloud came up and no storm ever came again. But the cellar was very good insurance just in case of another storm.

Earl was fascinated with the Iron Ore Mountain. Although he had been up there before, he seemed more impressed with the pretty scenery than ever. He said, "I wish I owned this whole mountain."

Boyd laughed. He was pleased that Earl liked the mountain, but he wouldn't want to give up his small part of it. He knew Ben or his father wouldn't want to part with theirs either.

Earl stayed with Boyd and Lois and attended school at Hector later on. He had dropped out of Atkins school for a while and helped Mr. Maxwell on the farm. But later on, he decided he had made a mistake. So he went back. Then he graduated and attended Arkansas Tech for two years, majoring in agriculture. Tech was only a two-year school then, so he transferred to the University of Arkansas, where he graduated. He taught school for a year then was drafted into the army for World War II. After the war, he worked at the State Health Departments in Little Rock, Missouri, California and Tennessee. He spent his last twenty-five years working in Nashville, Tennessee. His wife died in nineteen eighty and he died in nineteen ninety-eight, in a retirement home in Virginia, where his only child, Debbie, lived.

Uncle Bob's folks at Blytheville continued to ask Lois by mail how he was getting along. She kept them informed of his improving mental and physical health. The first of June they received the letter they had been dreading but were expecting. His daughter and son-in-law were coming to get him.

They were happy for Uncle Bob, but sad for themselves. They had grown to love him, as had the children. What would they do without him? Who would keep the babies while Lois hoed cotton and helped Boyd with the milking?

A few days later, his daughter Pauline and her husband Curtis came for him. They spent the night there. The next day when they were ready to walk down the mountain to where they had left their car, Uncle Bob hugged Boyd and Lois and the children, then told them goodbye.

"Don't go, Uncle Bob," Jyles begged.

"I have to," Uncle Bob replied. "But I'll be back. I'll come visit you every summer. Now you be a good boy and mind your mother and father."

"I will," Jyles said. Tears were running down his cheeks.

Lois cried too, as they were leaving. It would be so lonely without Uncle Bob.

In the coming years, the Brights brought Uncle Bob to visit them often. He had told them about how good Boyd and Lois had treated him, and they appreciated them for that.

Chapter 15

THE GOAT

They were in a quandary as to how to care for the children and still allow Lois to help milk the cows and help hoe the cotton. There were several acres of cotton left to hoe.

They decided to leave Jyles and Bobbye in the house by themselves. Lois put everything Jyles might get into out of his reach, and she gave him strict orders that he was to take care of his little sister. She and Boyd both hated to leave them by themselves, but they didn't know what else to do. It was hard to hire 'hoe-hands' on the mountain and they had very little money to do it anyway.

For a few days everything went along just fine. When Lois reached the house at noon and again late in the day, Jyles and Bobbye would be as she had left them.

Then one morning, Jyles came up to the field where she was working. "I didn't do nothing," he said softly. Lois wondered what he was up to. Then he repeated, "I didn't do nothing."

Suddenly she realized that something bad must have happened at the house. Taking Jyles by the hand, she hurried toward it. When she reached the edge of the yard, she heard Bobbye crying. Rushing into the house, she quickly saw that the baby's eyes were bleeding.

"Jyles Maxwell!" she demanded. "What have you done to her?"

Jyles began to cry. She finally got it out of him that he had put something in her eyes. He showed her where he had found it in the bottom of the safe. It was lime. She had overlooked it when she put the things away.

Quickly splashing water into Bobbye's eyes, Lois soon had the bleeding stopped, but her eyes were very red. She kept splashing water into them, all the while praying that her little girl wouldn't have to go through life in blindness. Bobbye's eyes were all right after a few days and Boyd and Lois were greatly relieved. They had certainly received a scare.

After that, they took the children to the field with them and kept them in the wagon. They couldn't get as much work done because it took some time to catch the mules, harness and hitch them to the wagon and drive to the field, but they knew it was necessary.

They still had to leave the children in the house while they were milking, but Lois made sure she didn't leave anything out when she was putting things away.

One day Marhall Patterson, one of Boyd's friends who lived in a hollow on the east side of the mountain, came to visit. His father-in-law had built Boyd and Lois's house in 1901, and his wife, Ona, had spent her younger days there.

Marshall and Jyles soon became good friends. When Marshall was ready to leave, he said, "Jyles, if you will go home with me and stay a day or two, I will give you a baby 'billy –goat'."

"Can I, Mama? Can I?" the boy begged. Lois knew Marshall was only teasing. He didn't have time to look after a three-year old boy, so she didn't let him go. Then a few days later, here came Marshall down the road leading a baby billy-goat. My, Jyles was happy! He knew who that goat was for. It was for him! Running to meet them, he didn't know which one to hug first, Marshall or the goat, so he hugged them both.

Jyles had many happy times with his billy. He played with him like he was a puppy dog, and he wrestled with him for hours at a time. He pretended he was another goat, and they would butt their heads together. He led him around the yard, and he dreamed of how he would train him to pull a wagon when he was bigger. Maybe he could get a little red wagon for Christmas.

Billy-goat liked to sneak up on anyone from behind and butt them. He didn't hurt them because he was so little, and they thought it was very funny and cute. Jyle's parents knew it was only a matter of time before he grew too big for that kind of play, because he could hurt someone, especially a child. As he got bigger, Jyles would sometimes sit Bobbye on his back and let her ride as he walked around the porch.

The weather slowly grew hotter that summer, and they had to leave the doors and windows open so air could blow through the house. Since there weren't any screen doors, this allowed Billy to have the run of the place, both inside and out. It wasn't so bad during the day, but at night he would run through any time he took a notion. He didn't wake the children. They slept too soundly, but Boyd and Lois woke up, and it was hard for them to get back to sleep.

In August, Maude, Boyd's sister, came up from Little Rock, and she was spending the night with them. She was going to spend a few days up there. Well into the wee hours of the night, here came Billy prancing through the house, just as if he owned it. "What on earth is that, Boyd?" Maude asked.

Boyd laughed and said, "It's only that billy-goat."

"He almost scared me to death!" Maude laughed back.

They knew they would have to do something about Billy. They tried tying him up on the outside of the house, but that didn't work. His baaing all through the night kept them awake even worse than his running loose, until Boyd turned him loose.

Lois talked to Jyles about him. "Jyles, you know we can't put up with that goat any longer. Your daddy and I have to get some sleep so we can work the next day."

After a few days, she and Boyd finally convinced him to give the goat back to Marshall, promising they would get him a tricycle for Christmas if he would—one just like his cousins, Joella and Berwyn had. So he reluctantly agreed to give up his billy goat he loved so much.

Chapter 16

BUSIER THAN EVER

One day that August, Irene and Corene, Ben and Nora's twin daughters, came by their house with an eight-foot long rattlesnake they had killed. Lois shuddered when she saw it. What if one of them was bitten by a poisonous snake that large? They would likely die before they could get to a doctor. That was one reason Lois would like to get off this mountain. Ben took the snake to the Confederate Reunion to show everyone, since it was one of the largest ever seen around there.

Sometimes Boyd took Lois and the children in the wagon down to the foot of the mountain, where Mr. Maxwell met them in his car. They would go home with him to stay a couple of days while Boyd returned to the mountain to care for the livestock.

They didn't go to church anymore, except on those occasional visits. That was another reason for Lois to want to get off the Iron Ore. She had always gone to church before and she wanted her children to attend also.

Boyd did his banking in Russellville all the time now, and most of his trading. Since Russellville was the county seat, he had to go there to pay their taxes. They were due even when the crops failed. The town had a hospital and more doctors and dentists than Atkins. It was growing faster than Atkins, also.

One day at Russellville as he passed a side street, he could see a one-horse wagon parked on it. The wagon was enclosed and had pictures and decorations on its sides. A large crowd was gathered around it. Boyd parked his wagon and team and walked back to get a closer look.

A pretty girl was singing a song about "The Great French and German War." After she finished, the man who called himself Dr. McGraw passed out bottles of medicine to the crowd.

"Ladies and Gentlemen!" he shouted. "This tonic was specially prepared for me in the great city of New York. It is good for arthritis, rheumatism, lumbago, backache, and sore and aching muscles. It will cure a headache, stomachache, indigestion, and any other malady that you may have. The amazing thing is that the price is only 49 cents, and it is guaranteed. You can't beat that."

Several of the men who were gathered around started reaching into their pockets for money. Some of the others were being urged by their wives to buy it. One of the wives said, "It will be worth buying just to see if it is any good. You heard the man say that it was guaranteed. It might help my rheumatism."

Boyd left. He knew better than to buy that worthless junk. It was probably nothing but alcohol and colored water. He had heard of these quacks who peddled their worthless stuff and then left town by the time the buyer learned of its uselessness.

The cotton and corn weren't as good that year as the year before, because it was dryer, but they were better than they had been in 1930. The cotton only brought nine cents a pound again, so it barely paid for the seed and fertilizer.

The garden was good though, and they had plenty of milk to drink. The milk cows were now their salvation. Though the cream didn't sell for a lot of money, it was regular income. The calves and hogs sold were a big help too. The skim milk made very good feed for the calves and hogs.

Boyd stayed busy even after the crops were laid by putting up feed for their livestock. He cut all the corn-tops he could, tied them into bundles after they dried and hauled them to the barn. He had no way of putting up hay, and no meadow land even if he had. But the corn-tops made fodder that took its place. He also brought most of his cottonseed back from the gin and fed it to the cows. Cottonseed meal bought at the farm supply store was added to the corn and corn fodder to provide protein.

As Christmas drew near, Lois knew Boyd wouldn't be able to go with them to Pea Ridge because of the milk cows. He would take her and the children to the foot of the mountain to meet Mr. Maxwell as usual.

On the night before Christmas, Jyles and Bobbye were all excited. They weren't allowed to open their presents until Christmas morning, so they went to bed thinking about the big day that lay ahead. At midnight Jyles woke them. "Can I open my presents now?" he begged.

"Let's let him," Boyd told Lois. "He won't sleep anymore anyway if we don't."

They lit the lamp, chunked up the fire and watched Jyles open his presents. There were candy, nuts, apples, and oranges. He didn't eat them though. He grabbed the big bundle he had been yearning for all week, knowing it was for him. When he tore the wrapping paper off, he yelled, "Oh boy, a tricycle!" He had been wanting one ever since Joella and Berwyn Don had gotten theirs. And he hadn't forgotten the promise made to him when he gave up his goat.

He began to ride his tricycle, going around in a circle. Since Boyd and Lois didn't have the heart to make him quit, they went back to bed. Bobbye was still sound asleep. She would get her presents in the morning. They didn't get any sleep for the rest of the night, because Jyles kept riding his tricycle around and around. There was no sleep in his eyes. Bobbye got her little wheelbarrow the next morning. She was as happy as Jyles was with his tricycle.

After Christmas and the New Year had passed, one morning Lois noticed a hole that had been burned in Bobbye's dress. "Jyles, how did that get there?" she questioned.

"She caught fire last night, and I put it out," he calmly replied.

It had happened when Boyd and Lois were milking. Lois had told him over and over what to do in case he or Bobbye did catch fire. With the open fireplace, she knew there was always that possibility.

A few weeks later, when they were again milking, they heard screaming and yelling from the house. The milk shed was only a hundred yards from the house and Boyd quickly raced over and saw smoke billowing from a clothes shelf in the bedroom. Jyles already had the flame stopped, so the house hadn't caught fire. Boyd got the smoking clothes and carried them outside. "What have you been doing, Jyles?" he demanded.

"I was looking for my truck," the boy answered. "I dropped the match, and the clothes caught on fire."

Then a few weeks after that they had finished the chores and were getting ready for bed when Lois heard something, like a child crying and yelling. The sounds were coming from the milk shed.

"Boyd, listen! Do you hear that? What is it?"

They both listened. "Why, it's Jyles!" she exclaimed. "We left him out there. We forgot about him being there!"

"I'll go get him," Boyd sleepily said. He was so tired he could hardly move. Jyles kept crying as Boyd hurriedly dressed, and he continued even after Boyd reached and lifted him into his arms. He was angry!

"Why'd you leave me out here?" he asked between sobs. "Didn't you know I was out here?"

"We forgot, we were so busy," Boyd sheepishly answered. "You don't usually go out there, so we just forgot. We were thinking that you were in bed."

The boy quieted down when they reached the house. Lois was up getting a snack of milk and cookies for him. While he was eating, Boyd said, "Jyles, I want to tell you something that happened to me when I was a few years older than you. Right out there by our milk barn, a brush arbor stood where they used to have church. Ben and I decided to go up there one night while a revival was going on. A crowd was there, having come from all over the mountain and from down in the valleys.

Ben and I sat in the back by ourselves. After a while, the bench we sat on got harder and harder, and our eyelids began to droop. They got so heavy we couldn't keep them open. We finally laid down on the bench and fell asleep. Sometime later we woke. It was dark as could be. All the lanterns had been taken home by the people who had departed. They hadn't even bothered to wake us. I shook Ben awake, and we hightailed it out of there."

Jyles laughed. So he wasn't the only one who had been left out in the dark.

One day that winter, Boyd killed a groundhog (woodchuck), and he decided to have a little fun with Jyles, since the boy had never seen one. He left it at the well and went into the house. In a few minutes, he told Jyles to go draw a bucket of water. Jyles got the water bucket and started out the back door to the well. When he saw the large groundhog, he yelled, "A cat!" and ran back into the house. He forgot about the water.

Boyd said, "Let me have the bucket, and I will get the water." He expected Jyles to go with him, but the boy didn't. He drew the water, set it inside the door, and went back to the well. He got the groundhog, sneaked around to the front porch and left it by the door. Then he returned to the back of the house and entered.

In a little while, he told Jyles, "Go out on the porch and bring in a stick of wood."

Jyles obeyed, as he always did when he was told to do something. When he opened the front door and saw the groundhog again, he exclaimed, "Another one!"

Chapter 17

THE PREACHER VISITS MR. GRAY

Boyd and Lois often had company. Ben's children were old enough now to run all over the mountain, and they were not afraid of anything. They were in and out of Lois and Boyd's house all the time. They were all older than Jyles, with the youngest one, Avanell, being two years older than him. She sometimes stayed overnight with them.

Bob and Velma sometimes returned to visit them and the other Grays. One day they left their oldest son, James, with Ben's family to visit for a few days. James was Raymond's age. He was very shy and seldom talked, except to answer when asked a question.

The first night of James's visit, while they were eating supper, he kept looking at the large opening into the loft (attic). The loft didn't have a door, so anyone could see up there a little. Since it was always dark James thought it looked spooky. He didn't say, but Ben and Nora could tell by the way he acted.

Suddenly he looked up from eating and asked, "Has anyone ever died around here?"

"No, I don't reckon," Ben said. He wanted to laugh, but he would save that until after James left.

Mr. Gray, Leonard, and Sewood still lived on the Little Mountain. They had a hard time, just like most people around, but they enjoyed themselves, going to church, riding horses, pitching horseshoes, and reading books and magazines. Mr.

Gray would often be reading something, and he would say, "Listen to this." and he would proceed to read the article. He had a bicycle and he rode it everywhere, except when the basket on the handlebars wouldn't carry as much as he needed. He rode it to Pea Ridge one day where Bob was now living and he took turns giving rides to Cecil and James. He carried them around and around the house.

Leonard couldn't read. He couldn't talk plain, so even though he attended school at Oak Grove every day Sewood did, he didn't try to learn. Mr. Gray had told him, "The teachers won't be able to understand you, so don't try." Lois had been his teacher one term and she said she didn't think Leonard was all there. But she found out differently after she married Boyd. He was a very smart person. She told me a long time after she had taught there that one day Leonard had thrown an apple brought from home all the way across the classroom to some girl and she hadn't gotten onto him, because as I was saying before, she thought he was a little off.

Leonard was comical. He could tell a funny story as well as anyone, but it was hard to understand him. One of Leonard's favorite ones was about some friends, Arthur Johnson and his boys from Oak Grove, who were visiting one day. At lunch time, the oldest boy, Archie, ate as if he was starved. Someone laughed at the way he was eating. His dad joked, "Son, you eat just like an old hound dog. You eat fast, take big bites and eat a long time."

Archie responded, as he kept eating, "Breakfast is my heartiest meal." Everyone laughed, because they weren't eating breakfast. They were eating lunch. Another story that Leonard told was about the Sunday night one summer that he, Mr. Gray, and Sewood walked down the path to the church at Caglesville. After services were over, Mr. Gray made the mistake of asking the preacher to go home with them. He wasn't expecting the preacher to accept, but to his surprise, he did.

Leonard and Sewood couldn't believe that Mr. Gray had invited the preacher. They knew their house wasn't very well kept, and that bedbugs were all over the room where he would be sleeping. Going on ahead, the two teenagers straightened up the bedroom, and they tried to get all the bedbugs out of the bed, but in Leonard's words, "All we accomplished was to stir them up."

This was summertime, and the weather was hot. Sewood and Leonard made their beds down on the front porch where it was cooler, and Mr. Gray slept in the front room in a bed that didn't have bedbugs, so the bedbugs hadn't been bothering him. That night they could hear the preacher tossing and turning and scratching something awful.

They knew the bedbugs were after him. Apparently he didn't get much sleep that night, because he could barely hold his eyes open the next morning while he was eating breakfast. He left soon afterwards, and he never darkened their door again.

That summer Boyd and Lois were visiting their neighbors, Tom Arnold and his wife. They lived between the Rockhouse and Uncle Bud Davies, where Annie Miller had lived when she had helped Lois hoe cotton. Lois and Mrs. Arnold talked about their gardens and about canning. Lois said, "I wish there was a way to can beef. We have a calf big enough to kill, but we'll have to wait until cold weather, or it might spoil."

"I can beef by putting the jars in the oven," Mrs. Arnold told her.

"I would be afraid to try that," Lois replied. "I'd be afraid it would spoil."

"You get Boyd to kill the calf and bring it to me, and I will can it for you," Mrs. Arnold offered. "You have him to bring the jar tops and lids. I won't charge much for doing it."

Boyd killed the calf and took it to the Arnold home, then went back and got it after she had canned it. He was very careful with the jars of beef, putting sacks under and around them to keep them from breaking.

When Lois saw the canned beef, she was as happy as she could be. It looked delicious. There were forty quarts, enough to last a few months if they didn't eat too much at a time.

"I will have to get Mrs. Arnold to show me how to can beef," she thought. "I'll bet that anyone could put up pork the same way."

For a little while, they ate beef every day. Since they hadn't eaten any lately, they enjoyed it tremendously. It was delicious.

It was a week later that the bubbles started rising from the beef in the jars. Lois had seen spoiling meat before, so she knew what was happening. She had a sinking feeling inside. A whole calf was gone to waste. It was their last calf, since they had sold all the others except one. That one they had given to a sick man near Oak Grove. He was unable to work. They had also paid Mrs. Arnold to can the beef.

Chapter 18

THE DOCTOR CLIMBS THE MOUNTAIN

Betty Sue was born in October of 1933. She was named for Boyd's mother. Later on when she was a little girl, Leonard told her that someday she would be called "Aunt Betty". She grew very angry. She didn't like it one little bit. As she got older, she laughed about feeling that way.

When they needed the doctor, Boyd rode Old Rhody down to Mr. Gray's. He asked Leonard if he would ride the mule down to Grady Barham's and get him to go to Hector for Doctor Linton. "If you will, I can get back on the mountain and stay with Lois and the kids."

Leonard rode Rhody down to the store and asked Grady if he would go to Hector and get the doctor. Then he waited for him there. He only hoped that Doctor Linton wouldn't be on a call. When Doctor Linton finally arrived after what seemed much longer than it really was, he told him, "Doctor Linton, the mountain road is too rough for your car. You'll have to leave it here and ride Old Rhody up to Boyd's."

Doctor Linton grumbled when he saw that he was going to have to ride a mule. "Is she gentle?" he asked.

"Oh yeah." Leonard replied.

"Won't she buck?"

"No, she's gentle as a lamb," Leonard laughed.

Doctor Linton gave him his black bag to carry, and he climbed into the saddle.

"What's he got to complain about?" Leonard thought, as he walked on ahead. "At least he gets to ride while I have to walk."

He noticed that the doctor didn't hold Rhody's reins, but let them rest across the pommel of the saddle. The tall, rawboned mule was following Leonard as he walked swiftly up the narrow, rough road.

"Oh well, it doesn't matter," he thought. "Rhody is so gentle that she would never spook or run away with him." So he didn't say anything and continued on.

On the side of the mountain, they came to a large mud-hole filled with water. It was in the middle of the road, so not wanting to get his feet wet, he stepped around it. Rhody, who was matching him stride for stride, and was practically breathing down his neck, followed.

"Whoa!" the Doctor suddenly yelled, startling Leonard. Rhody stopped. He looked around. The limb of a large Oak tree had caught Doc under the chin, and if Rhody hadn't stopped, would have dragged him off. Leonard stepped back and grabbed Rhody's bridle and backed her up.

Doctor Linton was angry, "This old mule would live a hundred years to get somebody killed," he growled.

Leonard couldn't keep from laughing. "Doc, you had better hold the reins from now on so she will stay in the road," he grinned.

Lois got out of picking cotton again that fall. She now had a four-year old, a two-year old, and a small baby to care for. Boyd had to hire some help to pick cotton, but he picked most of it himself in order to save money.

Jyles was now the caretaker for two and a half year old Bobbye. Wherever he went, she followed. He looked after her like a mother hen with her little chickens.

He now slept with Boyd, while Bobbye slept with Lois. The baby had her own little bed, which was at Lois's bedside. Lois would wake up at the least little sound from her or Bobbye. Betty never had any more than the usual problems of a baby. She would get hungry or thirsty and start crying at times, or would have to have her diaper changed.

One day Jyles was playing near the cook stove and he touched his bare arm against a hot part. The arm got blistered pretty badly. Lois put some of Mrs. Maxwell's homemade salve on it and bandaged it up, so it wasn't hurting that night when he went to bed. During the night he woke Boyd up with his yelling. "Get off! Get off! Get off!" Boyd was on his blistered arm, having rolled on it while asleep. Jyles quickly added, "And stay off!"

Chapter 19

THE WILLIE HUDSON FAMILY JOURNEY

The William (Willie) and Victoria Hudson family was making it pretty well in eastern Oklahoma between the towns of Holdenville and Lamar in the year 1932, where they farmed, growing cotton and corn just like their Arkansas neighbors did.

Willie's folks had come from the Ozark Mountain Wilderness of Arkansas when he was a small boy. His grandfather was the hunter who had discovered "Diamond Cave" back in the old days when his dogs had run some bears into it. He and his brother Andrew had gone into the cave, while someone stayed outside with the light. The two had found the dogs dead inside the cave and they had killed the bears.

Diamond Cave had later become a well-known tourist attraction. I ventured into it several times when I was young, being led through it by a trained guide. The early settlers thought they had found diamonds in it, thus the name "Diamond Cave", but they had turned out to be only quartz. The guide showed us the roof of the cave, which was blackened from the smoke of the many torches early explorers had carried. He said people had been back in it for seven miles, but no one had ever explored all of it. The cave finally closed down as an attraction after much larger caves were discovered and developed.

When you drive through Harrison's "Main Street", if you watch closely, you will see several signs on businesses with the name "Hudson". Those Hudsons are cousins to the Hudsons in our story.

It had been hard on the Hudsons in the mountains after most of the wild animals had been killed off, and they had come west looking for a better life. They had often played with the Indian children in Oklahoma, so they sympathized with them when the whites treated them so badly. Some Indians lived in houses just like white people there did, and some lived in tepees. They treated the Hudsons well, just as well as they did the other Indians.

Willie and his wife had a family of six in 1932. There were three boys, eighteen-year-old Otto, fourteen-year-old Arthur, and six-year-old Arvil. The three girls were Ina May-seventeen, Ella- sixteen, and twelve-year-old Etta.

Mr. Hudson used mules for farming. Their hooves were smaller than horses, and they didn't step on the corn and cotton as badly as horses did. He had one riding cultivator he could use for plowing the cotton and corn, and one walking cultivator. "You are young, and you don't get as tired as I do walking in the loose ground," Mr. Hudson told Otto.

On their rented property, Mr. Hudson and Otto could plow several acres of land in a few days because the land was smooth and didn't have rocks. So they had fifty or so acres of cotton, besides the corn, which they grew to feed the mules, hogs, and milk cows.

They got their drinking water from a cistern. It was built so it collected water that ran off the roof of the house. That saved them from having to dig a well, which could go dry in a bad year.

But early in 1933 the twenty-foot deep concrete cistern started leaking and it went completely dry. Mr. Hudson lowered Otto down and he could see the crack that had developed in its floor. They went into town and bought some cement to repair it. Otto was again lowered into it, this time with the wet cement they had mixed. He patched the crack and Mr. Hudson pulled him up. They had to haul water for family use from any source they could find until the cistern was refilled.

In the meantime, Mr. Hudson and Otto were putting in crops.

It rained after a few days, and they again had drinking water from the cistern. But soon the water started affecting Mr. Hudson's health. He lost his appetite and ached all over, including inside. The water the family had been drinking was milky-colored, because the cement that Otto had patched the crack with hadn't had time to cure and harden.

He went to the doctor in town, and the doctor told him what the problem was. He said, "You have got to quit drinking that cement water. Get your water from a well, a creek, a spring, or a branch. Anywhere but from that cistern!" It was strange that Mr. Hudson was the only one in the family the water had affected.

After a while he couldn't walk. He was becoming skin and bones. The corn was laid by when he got sick, and the cotton only needed one more plowing, but there was too much for Otto to take care of by himself. The other boys were too small to help.

So Mr. Hudson told Otto to hitch his team of mules to his riding cultivator and bring it to the porch. Its seat was level with the porch, so Otto and Mrs. Hudson could scoot him onto it. After they did this, he took the plow lines and drove to the field and plowed until eleven O'clock, while Otto plowed as much as he could with the other cultivator. Then he went to the house where Otto and his mother helped him inside to eat and rest for two hours.

At one O'clock it was back onto the cultivator and back to the cotton field until five O'clock, when he quit for the day. He and Otto got the cotton laid by that way.

As summer turned to autumn, Mr. Hudson improved in health a little, but not enough to help with the harvesting of the crops. Mrs. Hudson and the children had to do most of the gathering of the corn and the picking of the cotton, but they hired what help they could get.

In the mail they were getting the Kansas City Star, a weekly newspaper that many rural residents of Missouri and the surrounding states subscribed to, and they saw some land for sale near Shirley, Arkansas. Mr. Hudson had often heard his folks talk about Arkansas, and he decided he wanted to go there and try to buy that land.

That fall after the crops were gathered and the cotton and corn sold, they got rid of what farm equipment, household items, and other things they couldn't take with them. They rigged up two covered wagons to carry all their remaining possessions on their journey. There must have been a lot of excitement among the children and adults alike as they loaded their goods and anticipated the long trip ahead of them. Early one frosty morning in early November, they turned the mules eastward toward Ft. Smith, and they were on their way. A horse was tied on behind one of the wagons.

The children were excited as they traveled along, but the slow plodding of the mules soon turned to boredom as the miles slowly added up. They could pick out a tree far ahead and try to predict how long it would take to reach it. It would ever so slowly seem to come toward them. Then after they passed it, they would look back occasionally and see how far they had come from the tree. This went on for mile after mile as they made their way toward Arkansas.

They camped on the trail. Mrs. Hudson and the girls cooked the meals while Otto took care of the mules, with Arthur's help. They had to help Mr. Hudson down from the wagon, even though he was slowly improving. The mules were fed with grain they had brought along.

A few days later, they entered Arkansas. They camped on the outskirts of Ft. Smith, where they bought a Dutch oven. It helped with their cooking. As their journey continued, they decided to stay on the south side of the Arkansas River and follow Highway twenty-two into Dardanelle, because they could save several miles that way.

They traveled through Charleston, Paris, and other smaller towns. The road was paved part of the time, but only one lane and it was graveled part of the time. When it was paved, they drove one mule on the pavement and one mule beside it. They bought supplies and more feed for the mules as they went along. They had plenty of money and their family never went hungry. This was an exciting time for the children. They hadn't camped out very much and they enjoyed the chance to do it.

At Dardanelle, they turned north and crossed the Arkansas River Bridge. The bridge ran from southwest to the northeast for a quarter of a mile. It was the longest bridge the children had ever seen, except for Otto and it was hard for them to believe a bridge could be that long.

North of the river at Russellville, they again headed east until they reached Pottsville and they camped for the night at Galla Creek, where the old iron bridge still stands. They were now half-way to Shirley.

Mr. Hudson had been slowly improving in health, though he was still skin and bones. His appetite was much better, and he was gaining strength every day. Ever since they had left their home in Oklahoma, someone had always helped him down from the wagon, but after they stopped the wagons in Pottsville, he told everyone to stay back—that he was going to get down by himself. Everyone watched as he struggled to lower himself enough that he could put his foot on the wagon wheel hub, then the rest of the way to the ground. His family urged him on, and they gave him a great big round of applause when he made it. He was grinning from ear to ear. So was his wife and children. That was the last time anyone had to help him up or down.

The next day their journey continued, as they passed through Atkins and finally Morrilton. From there they headed north again on Highway Ninety-five. After leaving Morrilton, the terrain became hillier, and after fifteen miles or so, they were in the mountains. Another night on the gravel road, and they finally reached Clinton. What a welcome sight! They still had to go northeast through Shirley, but it was only nine miles away.

At Shirley, Mr. Hudson had improved in health enough that he was able to go into a store and ask for directions to the farm he had seen advertised in the Kansas City Star.

"You don't want that land," a man told him.

"Why not?" Mr. Hudson asked.

"That land is no good. It is sunken land." He meant that it was swamp land.

A very disappointed Mr. Hudson returned to his family and told them what he had just learned. What to do now was the question. They spent the night there. Then the next morning they headed back toward Oklahoma, with the intention of looking for land between Shirley and there.

This time, instead of going through Morrilton, they turned off north of Cleveland, and traveled through Jerusalem and Appleton. One mile southwest of Appleton, they camped under a bridge at Clear Creek. It was a perfect camping spot; they could tell that many people had camped there in the past.

During the night the rains came. Apparently it had been raining for a while up in the mountains where some of the tributaries of Clear Creek originated, because sometime after midnight the creek started rising. It wasn't long before it was full, and its banks were overflowing. Otto woke up when the water started getting his bedclothes wet, and he alerted the others. Everyone got to their feet and put the bedclothes in the wagons. Otto hitched four mules to a wagon and drove them back up into the road; then he took them back and got the other wagon. The trail from the camping area to the main road was too steep for just two mules to pull a wagon up it.

Christmas day was spent camped out between Caglesville and Moreland. The trip from Oklahoma to Shirley and then to Moreland had taken almost two months. Two children had their birthdays while on the road and two others had theirs a week after Christmas.

The next day as they came to the small village of Moreland, Mr. Hudson entered a store and asked if anyone knew where he might be able to rent some farm land. A man told him there was a place on Buck Mountain he could probably rent. He found out that a man by the name of Jim Akins owned it, and he rented it to the Hudsons.

They lived there for a year. Then Mr. Akins wanted them to move to another place he owned on the ridge between Moreland and Oak Grove. He said they were much better farmers than the ones who lived there now, and it was a much better farm than the one on Buck Mountain. They farmed that land for several years. After their sons and daughters were all married and had moved off, they bought a farm on Buck Mountain, where he and his wife lived until their deaths.

So that is how the Willie and Victoria Hudson families came to be residents of Pope County. They were all hard workers, and they contributed greatly to the economy and social life of the county. Otto married Uncle Ben Gray's daughter, Irene, and all except Ina Mae raised families here. She married Arvil Mackey, and they moved to California, where she lived to a ripe old age of eighty-three. Otto is now the only one of the family who is still living. He is ninety-seven years old. Irene died from a brain tumor in 1990.

Ella married Raymond Kinslow of Caglesville; Arvil married Raymond's sister, Lucy Mae; Etta wed R.L. Patton near Hector; and Arthur married Cloe Singleton, daughter of Ernest Singleton, who used to live on the Little Mountain near Sewell Ford. He lived near Center Valley until his death.

Raymond Kinslow was my first superintendent when I taught school, and Otto's granddaughter and three of Arthur's grandsons were in my classroom at Hector School. Arthur and Ina Mae are the only two that I don't remember seeing, but I'm sure I did when I was very young.

Chapter 20

THE EXPLOSION

Boyd hired Sewood to stay with them and work in 1934 until the crops were laid by. He paid him $12 a month and room and board. Sewood was a good worker and he enjoyed being with the children. He helped with the milking and everything. One day when it was time to go down into the cove and get the milk cows, it was pouring down rain. It had been raining for a few hours, and it didn't look like it was going to quit any time soon. Boyd was doing something else, and Sewood knew he couldn't look to him to get the cows. So he said, "It is a bitter pill to swallow, but it is what the doctor ordered." He then put on the slicker (raincoat), walked out into the pouring rain and headed down into the cove where the cows were, a mile away.

Sewood was twenty-one years old at the time, and he was getting restless on the mountain. He was a good looking guy, and the girls had been making eyes at him for a few years now.

He attended churches around. There were no shortages of revivals in the communities around the Iron Ore and he took advantage of them. He was even invited to 'Play Parties', and there were no shortages of them either. These were like square dances, except there was no music. Most of the local churches frowned on having dances with music, but they didn't seem to have any problems with the youngsters having dances without music.

One night after walking several miles to go to one of these parties and then going back up the mountain, it was so dark he could barely see the way. He had gone up the path in order to save a mile or so of walking, but before he reached the top, he wished he had taken the long way.

He had on his white shoes, which were the rage at this time. He missed the path once and stepped into an old stump hole that had been left there when a fire had come through and burned the stump. His foot went down to the bottom of the hole about a foot or so, and he grumbled to himself for not having a light. He pulled his foot out of the hole and was thankful he hadn't hurt himself.

After he reached home, thirty minutes later, and sat down to pull his shoes off, he was astonished to see the shoe that had gone into the stump hole. It was covered with black soot—his beautiful white shoe. It took a lot of doing to get that shoe looking white again. It never did look as pretty as the other one.

Lois left the children in the house that year while she worked in the field nearby. She was always careful to put everything that might be dangerous to the children out of their reach. One day she heard Jyles and Bobbye crying at the house. "What can that be?" she thought. "I had better go see."

Hurrying as fast as she could, she soon reached the house and opened the door. She was shocked to see Betty in a five-gallon cream can with only her head sticking out! Jyles was trying to get her out, but he hadn't been able to. That was why he and Bobbye were crying.

Lois had to work and work to get her out, but finally did. She thought she had put everything away, but had left a five-gallon cream can on the kitchen table.

"Jyles, what were you trying to do?" she asked him. He and Bobbye had stopped crying. They were greatly relieved.

"We were trying to put Betty in the can and shut her up in it," the boy confessed. "But we couldn't get her head in to put the lid on."

Lois was aghast. "What if they had been able to get the baby's head in and got the lid on and left it? She would have been smothered to death!"

"What would happen next?" she wondered.

She wouldn't have to wait much longer to find out. 'When it rains, it pours' the saying goes, and that was the way it was with their family. It seemed that they had one crisis after another.

The garden was again good that summer. They had ordered a new pressure cooker from Sears, Roebuck, and Company and Lois could hardly wait for it to arrive. When it finally did, it was just in time for her to start canning. She could now put up all kinds of vegetables, beef and pork. They would no longer have to wait until cold weather to kill a calf or a hog. Their family was the only one Lois knew who had a slow cooker.

She was in a hurry to use it. She picked the first okra, washed it and put it in the new fruit jars they had bought. She made sure the jars were sterilized, wanting everything to be just right.

She watched the cooker on the stove as the pressure built up inside it. She added more wood to the fire to keep the pressure up. When it was time, she released the pressure valve until the pressure inside the cooker went down; then she took off the lid and set the cooker on the floor.

It was a hot day, so the kitchen door was open. She hadn't read the directions where it said never to put the hot jars where cool air could get to them. Jyles was gone to a neighbor's house on the Little Mountain with Marie New and her son, Ernest. The News were their latest neighbors to the south. Boyd was in town and Sewood was no longer working for them, since all the crops were laid by.

Lois had ten and a half-month-old Betty in her arms when she went to check on the Okra, while Bobbye was at her side. She stooped down to admire the jars, and to see if they were cool enough to be put away. The okra looked delicious in the new clean jars.

Suddenly, without any warning, one of the jars exploded! Okra and hot juice flew everywhere. The girls started screaming. Bobbye ran behind the door, but she was too late to escape the scalding juice. They were terribly burned. Blood was pouring from Betty's face where a piece of broken glass had hit her.

Lois wanted to scream, but she couldn't. She had to keep calm because of the girls. She wiped the blood from Betty's face, which was bleeding badly.

Betty had a deep ugly gash an inch long on her cheek. Lois splashed cool water all over the girl's necks, arms, hands, legs and feet where they were scalded. They wouldn't stop crying. "If only Boyd would come," she thought.

As if sent from heaven, Marie and Jyles came walking up a few minutes later. "What happened?" Marie asked. Jyles started crying. He wasn't old enough to understand what had happened.

Tears streamed from Lois's eyes as she told about it. "And I was so proud of my new cooker."

She hadn't noticed her arms before, but suddenly when they started hurting, she looked at them. They were scalded as badly as the girls' arms were.

"Take Betty to Mr. Gray's house and get him to take her to Dr. Linton's," she told Marie. "I'll keep putting cool water on myself and Bobbye."

Marie pressed a cloth against Betty's cheek to stem the flow of blood as she hurriedly carried her off the Big Mountain toward Mr. Gray's. She breathed a sigh of relief when she reached his house, finding him at home.

Betty wasn't crying at all, although Marie knew she must be hurting. She supposed the baby would resume crying at any time.

When she told Mr. Gray what had happened, he exclaimed, "I knew that old cooker was going to kill somebody!"

Taking Betty, he hurried on toward the store. Just as he started down the Little Mountain, he met Boyd, who was returning from town. He explained to Boyd about the accident and he gave Betty to him. Boyd carried her in his arms on down the mountain and had Grady Barham take them to Hector, where Doctor Linton sewed up Betty's cut as well as he could.

Word was sent to Mr. and Mrs. Maxwell. Opal climbed the mountain and brought some more of Mrs. Maxwell's salve. The salve had twenty-two natural ingredients, with the main one being pine resin. Mr. and Mrs. Maxwell got busy making more.

Lois's burns hurt terribly. She knew what pain the girls must be in. She was thankful their faces had been missed by the scalding water. Not only was Betty's face affected, but her hand, leg and foot on her right side were burned. They left permanent scars. The left side of her body was not touched.

Opal smeared the soothing salve over the burned places and wrapped them to keep from being exposed to the air.

Bobbye and Betty cried most of the time. They couldn't sleep until exhaustion would mercifully close their eyes. Even in their sleep they would make pitiful moaning sounds as the agonizing pain wracked their little bodies.

After two days of doctoring Lois and the girls, they were out of salve, so Boyd took them to Mr. and Mrs. Maxwell's. They would have plenty of additional salve made by now. He left them there and returned to the mountain.

Mrs. Maxwell was a good nurse. She not only knew how to doctor, but her kind and soothing voice was almost as good for her patients as the salve was. It seemed that just when the pain eased it was time to change the dressings. The dressings would be stuck to their skins and when it was pulled loose, the pain was just as bad as before.

The girls' screams and cries as the dressings were removed would haunt Lois for the rest of her life. If only she could do something to ease their suffering. But there was nothing she could do. She was helpless. All she could do was pray that God would help them bear the pain.

After several days, the dressings could be changed without the girls screaming. Then after two weeks, they were recovered enough to go home. Boyd returned to the Ridge with his wagon and team and carried them back to their mountain place.

Betty was the only one who had permanent scars that were noticeable. She had a large "F" branded on her right cheek. After it healed, a piece of flesh an inch long stuck out from the scar.

Lois told Boyd, "We're going to have to get that cut off."

Then one day Betty fell off the bed and hit her cheek. She started crying and Lois picked her up to comfort her. The piece of flesh was gone. It had been sheared off just as well as a doctor could have done it, and it wasn't even bleeding.

After Betty graduated from school in 1951, she moved to Little Rock and attended business school to become a secretary. She had an operation to remove the "F". It was very painful, but worth it. Only a thin straight line remained.

Boyd's brother, Bob, and his wife Velma, moved to Oklahoma near Quinton in 1934. Velma's mother and father had moved out there earlier. The drought and depression had hit them as hard as it had most people. When their house burned, they decided to go somewhere else and make a new start. Uncle Bob hired a man with a big truck to take them. His son, Cecil, who was seven years old at the time, recalls how he slept under a cow that was standing up while on the way out there. The truck bed must have been quite large for it to haul a cow, the household goods and their family. They had some farm equipment also.

A letter Bob's father, John, wrote him in late August, 1935 has been preserved. It reads:

Bob, Velma, and kids,

We were so happy to hear from you. Everyone here is fine. Things are tough, but we are making it. How are the kids? We miss all of you.

Son, we are so worried about you, Velma, and the kids. We know things are really bad there. I feel that you took your family out there because of Velma's dad,

George. I feel he pressured you to come to Okla. Son, please, if you want to come home, let us know. We will come up with the money to send you if you will come.

Love to all,

Your Dad

Since this is a history book, I am going to put a letter in here that Velma's sister wrote to her in August, 1935. The letter is in its entirety.

Mr. and Mrs. Bob Gray

Dear sister and bro.

Will try to answer your card. Sure was glad to hear from you all. This finds us all well, only Clodene has a bad cold. We have been going to church at Pottsville and being in the night air she took a bad cold. Are you all done working? Think we have just begin. I have got done hoeing cotton, but I am working at something every day. I made a new dress this week. Helped a women can corn yesterday. Going to wash this morning, help another women this evening and I guess we will can some for me tomorrow. Leonard is working every day for a man. He likes about a day being done plowing. You sure can get a job here. He will get about 9 dollars this week if nothing happens besides what he works for himself. When he gets done working, in hay, he will have a job working on a farm. Leonard cut about 8 hundred bales of hay one week and helped bale some of it. How much fruit have you all got canned? I have some over 102 qt. I think I will get all my jars filled this week. We want to go to St. Joe Sunday if we can get a way to go. I don't think I ever had as much to do in my life at this time of year. How many hens have you raised? I have sold 24 fryers. I have over 20 more young chickens and one hen setting. Tell the kids that Clodenes little lady dog, little tiny about a week old kitten. How are you all doing out there now? We may make enough corn to get by on. Some of our cotton is awful little, some pretty good. Will make pretty good if we get a rain pretty soon. But we sure are needing a rain. Say Velma, this is the only card I have got from you that you have answered. Our mail carrier is awful bad to get mail misplaced. I guess it got lost. Sure would like to see you all. Looks like as long as Leonard can get a job he will have to see after what little we have. Clodene sure does talk about wanting to see you all. I saw Ben Gray not long ago and he said they had a sorry crop, I had better close.

With love

From Annie, Leonard, and Clodene

Bob never saw his father again. Mr. Gray died before his family moved back to Arkansas in 1937. They located on Linker Mountain and then near Russellville. Later they bought a farm on Tyler Road between Russellville and Pottsville, where he and Velma lived until their deaths.

Chapter 21

BEN GRAY'S FOX HUNT

Ben Gray was an avid fox hunter in the mid-thirties. He had several fox hunting friends in the area, and they often hunted together. Men and boys from miles around walked up the Iron Ore to hunt with him, because they knew he always had some good stories and jokes to tell while they were sitting around listening to the dogs run. He was a great story and joke teller and he had a good memory. If he heard a good story or joke, he would file it away in his mind forever, for when he wanted to tell it. He usually added his own twist to whatever it was. His twelve-year-old son, Raymond, was now old enough that he had started accompanying his father on those hunts.

There were two kinds of foxes in the Iron Ore Mountain area, the Gray fox and the Red fox. The Gray foxes were plentiful, but the Red foxes were getting pretty scarce. They had either been run out of the area or killed out. The hunters liked the Red fox best, because it ran much longer than the Gray fox, without going into its den or up a tree after three or four hours. A Gray fox could climb a tree, while the Red fox couldn't, unless the tree was leaning way over.

After hearing about some Red foxes being seen in the mountains north of Appleton, Ben and some of the other hunters decided to try their luck up there. So one summer day as the sun was sinking low in the sky, he and Raymond drove around and picked them and their dogs up for the big hunt. There was Tom Duvall and his son, Jack, from Oak Grove,

Roy Byrum from Buck Mountain, and several other men and boys. Ben's old worn out, flat-bedded, half-ton Chevrolet truck had five-foot sideboards on it, so there wasn't any danger of anyone falling off or of the dogs jumping off.

They drove six miles east on highway124 to Appleton, then headed north and drove up White Oak Mountain for five miles to the old Cook place where the Red foxes were supposed to be. The Cook homestead was abandoned, so they had it all to themselves.

Ben parked his truck in a small open field, then while the other men and boys were unloading the hounds, he raised the hood and unhooked one of the battery cables so no one could steal the truck. Where they were going to release the dogs was a little ways off and he wasn't taking any chances on getting it stolen. The truck wasn't worth much, but riding in it was a lot better than walking.

After the dogs were turned loose, they soon struck the trail of the fox and away they went. The sound of their barking and yodeling was like music to the hunter's ears. Each hunter's dog had a distinctive sound, so he could recognize his dog's voice. First one dog and then another would be in the lead, and the lead dog's owner would beam with pride when his was ahead. The fox had no trouble staying in front of the pack, so there wasn't much chance of being caught. Any time he wanted to, he could go into his den and be safe, because the dogs couldn't dig him out and the hunters didn't want to. The last thing the hunters wanted was to kill the fox. The Red foxes were getting too scarce as it was and all they wanted was to listen to their hounds as they chased them. If the fox did go into his den, Ben would sound the fox horn to call the dogs and the hunters would either go home or go to another area and try to jump another fox.

The fox made a large circle about a mile in diameter, as it returned to the area near where the dogs had jumped him. Then he did it again. This went on all through the night. Sometimes he would lead the dogs out of hearing, as he would run into a nearby hollow. Then the hunters would get a little worried about losing their dogs. It did sometimes happen, but the dogs would usually turn up at someone's house. Hopefully the occupants would send word about the dog being there. They could get information from the dog's collar. But way back in the Ozarks, there were very few houses, so that presented a problem.

This night the fox kept running, never going into his den. He would get far enough ahead of the pack that he could take a breather, and then when the dogs got close, he would take off again. Sometimes they would lose his trail; then they would sniff around until one of them picked it up again. The chase would again resume.

Not all of the dogs stayed in the chase. A couple of them gave up and dropped out. After a while, they came slinking back to where the hunters were. One of them was limping, favoring her right paw. Their owners were not so proud of them.

"Why, you sorry son of a gun!" her owner declared. "When I bought you, you were supposed to be a stayer. I'm taking you back to where I bought you!"

"Better look at her foot before you criticize her," another hunter offered. "She might have something in it."

Sure enough, when the dog's owner lifted her foot and checked her, she had a small brier in it. He pulled it out with some pliers and said "Babe, I owe you an apology. You rest here awhile. Then maybe you will feel like going back out there."

The other hound didn't have anything in his foot. He was just exhausted. Although disappointed, his owner didn't criticize him because he was just a big puppy.

The hunters enjoyed themselves as they sat around listening to the dogs. After a while, someone suggested that Ben tell a big one, and he got started. They talked, laughed, and listened all night. Some of the other men even had a few stories of their own to tell.

As daylight came the next morning, Ben blew his fox horn and called the dogs. It had been quite a night, and everyone was happy, although tired and sleepy. All the hounds came in and were loaded into the truck. But when Ben tried to start his truck, it wouldn't make a sound. He forgot about having loosened the battery cable. "I don't know what's wrong," he said. "It looks like you'll have to push me."

Everyone piled out of the truck and proceeded to give him a shove. The truck started and ran for a few seconds. Then it died. Ben tried it again, with the same result. He tried it several more times, as they pushed him along, and it started every time, but it wouldn't keep running.

Then his memory kicked in, and he remembered about having loosened the battery cable. He stopped his truck, lifted its hood again, and reconnected the cable. Then he cranked the engine. The battery turned the engine over, but the truck wouldn't even try to start.

After a few tries, he said, "It looks like I've played it. Now I've ruined the coil. I'll have to walk to Appleton and buy one from Arlie Morris and get him to bring me back up here and put it on." Arlie Morris had a garage in Appleton, and he also sold auto parts.

As he walked down the mountain toward Appleton, he kicked himself mentally for being so stupid. He noticed that none of the others had volunteered to come with him to keep him company. "I don't blame them," he thought. "This is my own doing, and I need to be the one to suffer."

After he left, the others found a shade and relaxed. It would take Ben over an hour to reach Appleton, and about twenty minutes to buy a coil and get back up there—that is, if he didn't have to wait on Arlie to finish up a job for a customer. When an hour had passed, a highway crewman came by, and after learning what had happened, he offered to hook onto Ben's truck and pull it down the hill to Appleton. His truck was much larger than Ben's and higher off the ground. He took out a long chain and hooked the two rigs together.

Since Ben was gone, it would be up to twelve-year-old Raymond to steer the truck down the mountainside. He couldn't drive, and he had very little experience guiding a vehicle. He could barely see over the steering wheel, but he was the only one who was willing to try.

The men and the boys got into the truck bed again and stood up, facing the roadway ahead of them, holding onto the front boards. Two of the men, Tom Duvall and Roy Byrum, elected to stand on the running boards and hold on to the doors. The windows were down, so they had no trouble doing that.

There was one little problem Raymond had forgotten to tell the road crewman about, and it was too late when he thought of it—Ben's truck didn't have any brakes! When Ben had driven it down a hill, he had used the gears to slow it down. But Raymond couldn't use the gears, because the engine wasn't running. The workman towing him didn't look back, because he had to keep his eyes on the curvy road, so he thought everything was hunky-dory behind him.

As the two trucks picked up speed, Raymond saw that he was going to run under the larger tow truck, so he veered off to the right and took to the ditch. Luckily the ditch was shallow, and as Ben's truck ran across it and up the embankment on the other side, it slowed down. Then the long chain hooked to the tow truck jerked his truck back into the road. As it again headed for the tow truck, Raymond steered it into the left embankment, then back into the right one again. This went on all the way down the mountain—to the right, then to the left. To the right and back to the left again.

In the meantime, the riders in the back of the truck were scared to death. They looked on in horror as their lives flashed before their eyes. They knew they were going to die. Tom Duvall and Roy Byrum jumped off and took rolling somersaults down the mountain side. Raymond saw them out of the corners of his eyes. Later on he laughed about it, but at the time, he didn't think it was funny.

It was all the riders could do to hang on to the front boards and keep from being tossed around like rubber balls. Two of the boys lost their grips and they fell to the floor among the dogs. The dogs did their best to stay on their feet, but just as they would get on them, the truck would lurch in the other direction and throw them off their feet again. There was a mess of boys and dogs as they were slung against each other and the sides of the bed—first one side and then the other.

After what seemed like an eternity, but was really only a few minutes, they reached the bottom of the mountain, and the highway worker slowly stopped. He had finally taken a quick peek in his rear-view mirror and to his surprise, saw what was going on. At that time Arlie Morris drove up in his pickup with Ben sitting beside him. Ben was amazed when he saw his truck setting there. Arlie put the coil on and the truck started right up.

After a while, Tom Duvall and Roy Byrum came walking down the mountain road from where they had jumped off. They were both scratched up and bruised, but otherwise, they were unhurt. Tom did have a big hole in the seat of his overalls.

Wow, was Raymond glad to get that adventure over with and so were the others. All they talked about on the way home was the ride and their narrow escape. They all got home alive that day, but it was a long time before they quit talking about that wild ride down White Oak Mountain, and they never did forget it.

Chapter 22

STORY TIME

Jyles often asked Boyd and Lois to tell him stories. He liked fairy tells and ghost stories, but he especially liked true ones about the Iron Ore Mountain and Pea Ridge. One rainy day he begged, "Tell me another story about the Iron Ore Mountain."

Boyd asked him, "Did I ever tell you about the man who was whipped by the vigilante committee for not feeding his family?"

"No," Jyles answered, with anticipation in his voice. "Tell it."

Boyd began, "When I was a small boy, there was a man who lived here on the mountain northeast of where Ben now lives. We weren't very well acquainted with him, and we didn't really pay that much attention to him and his family. Besides, we had troubles of our own, with my mother sick with T.B., and then without a mother after she died.

When Doctor Jones from Moreland was called to check on one of the man's babies, and the baby was dead when he arrived, he noted that the infant was skin and bones. He thought he knew what had killed him—starvation, and he spread the story around the neighborhood. Everyone knew the man was lazy and wouldn't work. A vigilante committee was formed, went to the man's house, took him outside and whipped him."

"Let that be a lesson to you!" one of the committee members shouted. "That will teach you that you'd better provide for your family! And don't forget that we might be back!"

The man offered no resistance because he didn't have the energy. He hadn't felt like working. Now he didn't feel like fighting. It wasn't long afterwards that he died of T.B. He had been sick all these months, or perhaps years and no one knew it. Those who had whipped him must have felt very badly."

"Did Grandpa help whip him?" Jyles asked.

"Oh no," Boyd declared. "We didn't know anything about it until after it happened. All the members of the committee were from down in the valley. Not a person will admit being in the vigilante committee, but we heard rumors and one of your mother's kinfolks was in that rumor."

"I'm glad that Grandpa didn't help," Jyles stated. "Mama, you tell me one now," he continued.

Lois replied, "Let me think." Then she began, "When I was sixteen and Homer eighteen, we went with our cousins, Verlin and Roy Davis, in a buggy to a revival at Moreland. Homer drove the mules that were hitched to it. After church was over that night, we started home. As we rode along, we sang songs, told stories, and joked. Homer was having such a good time that he didn't pay much attention to his driving.

Suddenly one of the buggy wheels ran off the high bank of the road and we overturned. We fell all over one another as we tumbled to the ground.

"I'm killed!" Verlin groaned.

We started laughing when we saw that no one was hurt or the buggy damaged. Homer and Roy lifted the buggy back on the road and we continued on. This time Homer paid more attention to his driving.

Roy got married and moved to Jerusalem, Arkansas. He was killed by lightning during a storm in 1927. He and several others were in the cellar. He was holding a little baby when he was hit. All the others with him were knocked unconscious, but he was the only one killed. Even the baby survived. I was teaching school there and a little girl came across the field in the rain that night and told us about Roy."

Lois thought of another short story. "When I was a little girl and was going to school at Shiloh, one of the large boys, Wiley Duvall, wrote on the blackboard, 'x*#$ Kay Akins'. Mr. Akins was the teacher. He promptly whipped Wiley.

After school, Opal and I were walking with some others behind Mr. Akins while on our way home. Suddenly, Wiley, Walter Bewley, and another large boy jumped from behind some bushes and attacked Mr. Akins. They got him down and were thrashing him when my cousin, Check Davis, picked up a big rock and hit Walter Bewley in the head with it. Walter dropped like he had been shot. He was out like a light. The fight was over. Mr. Akins and the boys carried Walter to his house a mile away. It was a long time before Walter recovered."

Boyd had a story to tell next. He began.....

"During the Civil War, most of the honest young men around here were gone away to battle. Outlaws who were called "Bushwhackers" roamed the countryside, looting, burning, and killing. A gang of them would ride up to a farmhouse and demand whatever they wanted—horses, cattle, corn, money, chickens, hogs and other things. Anyone who opposed them was usually killed.

One day a young man, Johnny Jimes, who opposed the local gang of bushwhackers, was at home with his elderly father when he happened to look out the window and see several rough-looking men on horseback heading their way. He knew they were looking for him, so he darted out the back door and crawled into a large hollow tree that had fallen and was laying at the edge of the back yard. Only a minute after he reached his hiding place, the outlaws rode into the yard and rushed into the house.

"All right, where is Johnny?" the leader of the gang demanded.

Johnny had been in a fight with the leader's brother in the village of Caglesville an hour ago and he figured they would come after him as soon as they gathered reinforcements, but he didn't think it would be this soon.

"I don't know. He hasn't been here today." Johnny's father answered.

The outlaws didn't believe Mr. Jimes, so they searched the house, including the loft and under the floor. Not finding Johnny, they proceeded to force the old man to tell where his son was. They tied him up and pulled his fingernails out one by one, trying to get him to talk, but it did no good. Then they pulled his toenails out the same way but they could get nothing from him. They took him outside, tied him to a tree and piled brush around his feet.

Johnny was watching all this from his position in the hollow log. He wondered if one of the outlaws would spot the log and decide to search in it. He eyed the leader through his rifle sight and he was ready to squeeze the trigger, but then, he had second thoughts. He would only be able to get one of them, for they would be upon him before he could get his rifle reloaded.

Taking a good look at the outlaws, he saw that he knew all of them. Before the war, they had been decent men. The war had done this to them. He watched as they set fire to the brush around his father. He couldn't look as the flames grew higher and higher and the smoke slowly suffocated Mr. Jimes.

Suddenly the outlaws ran for their horses, as if they had just become aware of the awful thing they had done, and disappeared over the eastern horizon just as quickly as they had come.

Johnny scrambled out of his hiding place and quickly kicked the burning wood and flames away from his father. He cut the ropes that bound him to the tree and he gently carried him into the cabin and laid him on the bed. But it was too late. His father was too far gone and he died a few minutes later without regaining consciousness. Johnny vowed that he wouldn't rest until the day he had killed the last one of his father's murderers.

Not long afterwards, the Civil War ended and returning soldiers put an end to the bushwhacker gangs. Each member that was still alive went his separate way. Johnny hunted them down one by one and killed them, not bothering with the law. To him, he was the law.

It wasn't long until word got around to the remaining ex-outlaws that the members of their gang were being killed. They tried to run away and moved to other places, some even as far as other states, but Johnny stayed on their trail. He learned where one of them was living on a farm and sneaked into his barn one night. He lay awake all night, waiting for him to milk the cow the next morning.

At sunup, he saw him coming. The man opened the back door of his house and started toward the barn, carrying his milk pail with him. Johnny knew the man he was about to kill was now a respected citizen. He took his wife and children to church and worked at honest labor on the farm. But this thought never once deterred him. He had a job to do, and to him, his father wouldn't rest in eternity until his murder had been avenged.

As the farmer neared the barn, Johnny whistled to him. He quickly looked up to where Johnny was standing in the barn loft. A startled look came across his face when he saw the rifle pointed at his chest. He knew who Johnny was and he knew why Johnny was there. He also knew what Johnny was about to do. He only had a couple of seconds to reflect on his past life and about what was to happen before Johnny shot him.

Johnny slipped quietly away without being seen by the dead man's family. They must have wondered why anyone would have it in for such a good man—enough to shoot him. Johnny was never punished for his actions. There were a lot of men not punished for their actions at the time of the Civil War.

After the war, one man was sitting in a chair in his house on Pea Ridge and someone shot and killed him through a window. No one ever knew who shot him, or why they shot him, but his folks thought it might have been for something he had done during the war.

On Buck Mountain during the war, some bushwhackers called for an old man to come out of his house. His wife begged the man not to go, but he told her they wouldn't hurt an old man like him. But when he came outside, they shot him down like a dog."

Boyd said, "Now Lois can tell you about the panther chasing her grandpa and his brother when they were boys." So Lois began.

"Grandpa Andrew Jackson Duvall and his brother George were sent to get the milk cow late one day. They had trouble finding her, even though she had a bell on. Finally locating her in a gully, they started after her, but suddenly Grandpa saw a large panther watching them. It was crouched under a nearby bush. It had been watching the cow, but now it focused its attention toward the boys.

Grandpa motioned to his brother, George, and they froze, afraid to move. "Come on", George told Grandpa and they slowly moved up the gully away from the panther. Each time they moved, the panther crept toward them. Finally, they could stand it no longer, so they started running. The panther continued to close in at its own leisurely pace, but the head start they had might be enough to escape.

When they reached the head of the gully, they were trapped. The walls were too steep and too high to climb. Then the older brother, George, had an idea. "You help me up and I'll reach down and help you up." So grandpa helped George up. Then George reached down to help him, but just then, from his position facing Grandpa, he saw the panther closing in. He panicked and he let go of Grandpa's hand. Grandpa fell back into the gully, while George started running toward home as fast as his legs could carry him. When he reached there, he told his folks that Grandpa had been killed by a panther.

The men and boys at the house grabbed their guns and started back to the gully. Soon, to their relief, they met Grandpa. He was running as fast as he could and he was all out of breath as he told them how he had managed to somehow scramble up the bank of the gully.

It was getting dark, so they were not able to find the panther to kill it. They did shoot their rifles in the air a few times to try to scare it off. This they must have succeeded in doing because the cow was in her stall in the barn the next morning.

The panther apparently left that part of the country because the next morning the hounds were not able to trail it far enough to tree it.

When Lois finished the story, she looked over at Jyles to see his reaction, but her son was fast asleep. He had filled up on popcorn and dropped off. Boyd carried him to bed.

Chapter 23

JYLES STARTS TO SCHOOL

Sybil DuVall, Lois's cousin who was fourteen years old, came to live with Boyd and Lois in the spring of 1935. Her mother, Lois's Uncle John DuVall's wife, had met with a tragic accident four years earlier and had died as a result. Her family and a friend and her two children had been traveling by wagon and team from church one night west of Atkins, when a car came speeding out of the darkness and crashed into the rear of the wagon. The wagon was reduced to splinters and all of its occupants were thrown out of it. Her mother, who was sitting in the back with her feet hanging out, had been hurt so badly she had died a few days later in the hospital. The driver of the deadly car was very sorry about what he had done. He said lights from a car coming from the opposite direction had blinded him and he didn't see the wagon. The wagon didn't have any kind of light. The man came to see Aunt Tempie while she was in the hospital before she died.

Now Uncle John was distributing his three boys and three girls among his relatives. He had tried to keep them together for a while, but he hadn't remarried, and he gave up on that. Sybil had been sent to live with Lois and Boyd. She was a very good girl and helped with the children, milked the cows, and helped in the fields. She turned the cream separator and did anything else she was asked to do.

That summer she walked two and one-half miles down the trail to Oak Grove and attended school. Since she didn't know the way down the trail to Oak Grove, Boyd went with her part of the way the first time. She made it all right on the way down, but as she was climbing back up the mountain, she turned off on the wrong fork of the road. It was a logging trail that led up into the hollow between the Big Mountain and the Little Mountain. After following it for thirty minutes, she came upon Leonard and some other timber workers and she told them she was lost. Leonard went with her back to the right path and showed her the way. The next day when she came to the main road, she put a pile of rocks there so she would know where to turn off from then on. Never again did she get lost.

Sybil left before cotton picking time that fall. Her father decided to get his family back together. She had really been a big help to Boyd and Lois and they had grown to love her. Lois was going to have another baby, and she was sick a lot, so Sybil had really helped out.

That fall Jyles had to start school. Lois wanted him to go, but she dreaded for him to have to make the trip up and down the mountain every weekday, especially during bad weather. When school began, he left with his new lunch pail and went north the half-mile to Ben's house. Then he walked off the mountain with Ben's children. Corene and Irene, the twins, were now thirteen years old; Raymond was eleven, Ruth nine, and Avanelle seven. So Jyles had plenty of company going and coming. They caught the Hector school bus at the Barham grocery and got off there after school.

Jyles loved school and he was a big hit with the teachers and children. He wasn't at all shy. Someone told Lois when the first grade teacher needed someone to deliver a message to the principal or to another teacher, she always called on Jyles, because he was always so outgoing. But when his report card came home a month later, he had a C on conduct. When Lois asked him why, he didn't know. So she sent a note by him to the teacher and asked her why. The teacher sent a note back home saying Jyles was a very smart boy, but he talked too much in class when he wasn't supposed to. He could carry on a conversation as well as a grownup could, but it wasn't easy for him to sit quietly in the classroom.

He soon learned he would have to walk the road up and down the mountain alone much of the time. Ben's children didn't go to school regularly. He didn't like to go by himself, but he wasn't afraid, because he had been up and down the road and the path so many times.

One day when he was walking home, he heard a strange noise coming from behind some bushes, a sound like he had never heard before. It sounded like some wild animal! He knew it might be a bear or a panther. All kinds of strange thoughts ran through his mind as he stood there. He had heard tales many times of them killing people. He kept listening. The noise had stopped, but then it came again. He didn't know what to do. Whatever it was lurked between him and the way home.

Just then he heard a laugh, and a grinning Sewood walked out from behind the bushes. "Don't you ever do that again!" Jyles told his uncle. "You almost scared me to death!" Sewood laughed, but he never scared Jyles again.

As winter approached, Mrs. Barham told Boyd if the weather was ever bad, Jyles could stay overnight with them. Boyd and Lois were pleased with the kindness of the Barhams and they were very thankful for them and their family. They were neighbors to be proud of because they would help anyone any way possible.

Boyd traded with them regularly and he had them send or take his cream to town. Their store was small and there were a lot of items they didn't carry, but they would pick up anything at town that was needed for the families around.

One day soon after Mrs. Barham invited Jyles to stay, he failed to come home from school. When the sun was almost down, Lois told Boyd, "I'm worried about Jyles. You had better go see about him." So Boyd walked north to Ben's house and asked him if his children had gone to school that day.

"No, they stayed at home to work today," Ben told him. "Why? Is anything wrong?"

Boyd answered him and went on his way to the Barhams. Arriving there after dark, he knocked on the door of their house. "Mrs. Barham, have you seen Jyles?" he asked.

Mrs. Barham laughed, "Yes, he wanted to spend the night with us. He said it was all right with you."

"That rascal!" Boyd declared. "His mother is worried sick about him. She thought something bad had happened to him. He is only to stay with you if the weather is bad."

Jyles had already gone to bed. He was sleeping between two of the older Barham girls. Boyd explained to him that he was to stay only if the weather was bad. After that he didn't stay except when he was supposed to.

Mrs. Maxwell gave Lois one of her long brown woolen coats to cut down and make an overcoat for Jyles. Lois had to darn it in places, because moths had eaten some holes in it. She put patches on the inside in the darned places so the thread wouldn't pull out. They didn't show from the outside. She planned to put a liner in it, but before she had time to, it turned cold one night and the next morning Jyles wanted to wear his new coat to school.

She told him, "I'll let you, but you make sure you don't let anyone see the inside of it." When he got home from school that night, he told her he had worn the coat wrong-side out all day.

Lois exclaimed, "Jyles! Why did you do that? I am so embarrassed. What will the teachers think about me?" She put a liner in the coat before she let him wear it again.

One day Raymond suffered an attack of appendicitis and he was suffering terribly. He wouldn't give in to let them take him to the hospital. His side had been hurting for a few days, but he still didn't want to go. Boyd grew impatient with him. He told Ben he wouldn't sit up with him, but he would help take him off the mountain to go to the doctor. He went on back to his house.

Ben soon came down the road and he said Raymond had decided to go to the hospital. "How will we take him?" Ben asked. "He can't walk."

"We'll make an old time stretcher," Boyd replied. "Like they do in the army." Nora brought out two quilts and they found two poles and made a stretcher for Raymond. His appendix was hurting so badly that he could barely stand it. Though he was a tough boy, he groaned and took on as Boyd and Ben slowly began their two-mile descent off the mountain, handling him as gently as possible.

Halfway down the mountain, Raymond suddenly grew easy. The men continued on their journey. They knew what had happened. His appendix had burst.

They carried him to the Barhams and left him there until they walked to Faye Cagle's house and asked him to take Raymond to the hospital in Russellville. Luckily they made it there in time to save his life. It took a while, but Raymond recovered and was as healthy and strong as ever.

Twenty-year old Sewood left the mountain that fall to go to work for Charley Hudlow, who lived and farmed two miles west of Moreland. He never returned to the Iron Ore to live. Mr. Gray and Leonard were left by themselves.

One day after Christmas, Mr. Gray had a visitor, an insurance salesman. He had climbed the Little Mountain to try and sell him some burial insurance. Mr. Gray didn't want any, and he told him, "I don't have any money."

"I'll tell you what I'll do," the salesman replied, "I'll let you have a year's insurance for two of those hens." He motioned toward some laying hens scratching in the yard.

"No, I don't think so," Mr. Gray answered. "I'm not ready to die yet."

The salesman reluctantly left, having missed the sale after climbing all the way up the mountain.

Mr. Gray didn't tell the salesman he had carried whole life insurance for several years and the insurance company had kept raising the rates until he could no longer afford payments. The company had guaranteed not to raise rates and after twenty years, he would get back a tidy sum of money. What the company did was sell out to another company and they had raised the rates as the years passed, and it looked like they were going to have to pay off. Every year they raised the premiums more. They did the same thing to Mr. Maxwell and Boyd and no telling how many others. In 1935, the government hadn't yet passed a law preventing this. Now Mr. Gray didn't want anything to do with insurance companies.

A few nights later, Leonard was awakened by a strange sound. Listening, he could hear his father gasping for air, then becoming quiet—deathly quiet.

"Papa!" he called, but there was no answer. "Papa!" he called again, louder this time, but there was still no answer.

He was afraid now, afraid his father was dead. Quickly getting out of bed, he lit the coal-oil lamp, then went into his father's bedroom.

Holding the light over Mr. Gray, he could see his father's hollow eyes staring into space, a blank look in them. His cheeks were all drawn in and the ashen color of death covered his features. Leonard listened for a heartbeat, then watched for signs of breathing, but he saw or heard neither. Slowly it dawned on him. He was alone. His father was dead. The house suddenly became a lonely empty tomb. His life was now a vacuum. He had to get out! He had to get to Ben's and to Boyd's!

Still barefoot, he hurried out the door, down the doorsteps and into the yard. There was snow on the ground, which bit into his bare skin as he walked along the narrow road which led to the Big Mountain. His feet cried out to him to go back for his shoes. He reluctantly obeyed. His feet would probably freeze before he reached the top of the Big Mountain. Retracing his steps, he groped around until he found them. The house seemed even more empty now. Feeling terribly alone, he wanted to cry for having lost his father, but the tears would not come.

As he hurried on his way, the icy wind stabbed at his face and hands, though after a few minutes of almost running, the blood flowing through his system soon warmed him. But his feet remained almost as cold as the snow upon which he was walking. He hadn't brought a light, but the reflection of the moon on the snow made it seem almost as light as day. A light would only slow him down.

It was hard climbing the steep part of the mountain because of the snow. He often slipped down and had to get up and start again. After what seemed like hours to him, he reached the top. Ben's house was just around the bend of the road. He woke him and told about Mr. Gray, then they walked to Boyd's. They took the shortcut down the path to where their father lay. They put coins over his eyes to keep them closed, and a sheet over him. Then they sat up the rest of the night in the front room.

Mr. Jonathan Franklin Gray's troubles on this earth were over. He had endured a hard and poverty-filled life, and he had known little but hard work and deprivation. His wife had died of T.B. when she was thirty-nine years old and left him with six small children—ages two to fourteen. He had never known complete happiness since.

Boyd recalled how he had talked so much about going back to Alabama and had often sung about the old home-place back there:

On the banks of the noble Tennessee, where I've spent many happy hours

Wandering around with Lula Love, Alabama's sweetest flower.

She bade me hast to the battlefield to avenge my country's wrong.

She buckled on my sword for me, Dear Willie, don't be long.

Lula's sweetheart she had sent off to war had been killed, and she had never married. The memory of her Dear Willie had been enough to last her a lifetime.

Boyd often wondered why Mr. Gray had sung about the Tennessee River when he had lived in Alabama. Then he looked on a map and saw how the Tennessee River made a loop down into Alabama before it reentered Tennessee and went into Kentucky, where it flowed into the Ohio River.

Mr. Gray was buried in the Hudson Cemetery beside his mother and father. There were no cemeteries on the Iron Ore Mountain. His wife, Betty, had been buried at Bigelow in Perry County where she had died.

Chapter 24

LEONARD COMES TO LIVE WITH THEM

Lois gave birth to another baby boy on February 14, 1936. She called him her valentine baby. Doctor Linton made the dreaded climb up the mountain again. She would never forget him. She thought he was the best doctor in the world.

They named the baby Jerry Franklin. Mr. Gray already had one grandson named for him, Ben's one-year old baby, so they couldn't give him John for a first name. They did give him his grandfather's middle name. When they visited the Maxwell's, Earl begged them to use Zane for a middle name. He was a big fan of Zane Grey, who was one of the most beloved western writers at that time. So the baby got two middle names, Franklin and Zane.

One day Jyles didn't come home from school. As the time for him to come had passed and he didn't show up, Lois began to worry. The weather wasn't bad, so the boy must not have stayed with the Barhams. Could he have decided to do some exploring in the woods and gotten lost?

When Boyd came in from hauling rocks, he went to see about him. First he walked to Ben's house again. His children hadn't gone to school that day either. He then went to the Barhams. They told him he had gone home with Junior Mackey, two miles toward Russellville from there.

Boyd was pretty angry with Jyles. After having hauled rocks all day, he was having to walk nine miles round-trip to get him. Forty minutes later, after reaching the Mackey house, he knocked on the door. "Come in," a woman's voice called. When Boyd entered, he saw Jyles and Junior playing on the floor.

"Jyles, why didn't you come home?" he scolded. "We didn't know where you were."

"I knew where I was," Jyles exclaimed, sounding as innocent as a six-year old boy could.

"Come on, let's go home," Boyd told him.

"Please don't whip him," Mrs. Mackey pleaded.

"I won't," Boyd told her. But he felt like giving him a good one.

Jyles didn't get a whipping, but he received a punishment far worse than that, it seemed to him. When Lois and the other children left for Pea Ridge to spend the weekend, he didn't get to go.

Leonard was living with Ben now. He had moved in after Mr. Gray's funeral. When spring arrived, Boyd knew that Ben had his children to help him in the fields, so he asked him if he cared for Leonard to start staying with him and Lois and working for them.

Ben said, "I don't need him. If he wants to work for you, it will be all right with me."

So that was how Leonard came to be a member of their family. He proved to be a very welcome addition. He not only loved children, he was also willing to help with any task assigned to him. Even though he was crippled, he could do most jobs as well as anyone. He would stay in the field and drive Old Rhody or Nell, the new mare, hitched to a cotton or corn planter from dawn to dusk, and he was as good at chopping cotton as Lois was.

As he ventured around the farm, he seemed as happy as a lark. He was always singing. One of his favorites was "I was seeing Nellie Home" His voice rang out, "It was from Aunt Dinah's quilting party, I was seeing Nellie home. In the sky the bright stars glittered, on the bank the pale moon shone. It was from Aunt Dinah's quilting party, I was seeing Nellie home." Another one of his favorite ones was, "My Bonnie Lies Over the Ocean".

Leonard was also great with children. He loved to play with them. He was just as good with them as Uncle Bob had been, but he also did things with Jyles that Uncle Bob couldn't do, since he was much younger than Uncle Bob.

One morning Jyles left for school as usual, but he no longer went up to Ben's house to go with his children. They didn't go very often, so Boyd and Lois decided to send him down the path. That way he could save a mile of walking. The path went directly west, so he could save time by not going to Ben's. On this particular morning, Jyles returned a few minutes after leaving the house. He had a bewildered look on his face.

"What's wrong, Jyles?" Boyd asked him.

"I'm afraid," the boy said.

"What of?" his father wondered.

"I don't know," Jyles answered. "There's something down in the hollow, and I don't know what it is."

"Well let's go see."

They walked together to the brink of the mountain. Looking down into the hollow between the Big Mountain and the Little Mountain, they could see the most beautiful fog Boyd had ever seen. The top of it started one hundred feet below where they were standing. As it spread across the mile-wide hollow, it was like an ocean, with waves billowing as it rose and fell with the breezes.

Boyd looked at the fog for a minute in amazement; then he thought about Jyles having to catch the school bus, and he explained to him that it was only fog. Jyles was no longer afraid, and he silently walked down the path toward the Barham's grocery store, where he still had time to catch the bus and get in another day of learning.

Occasionally, Opal, Lois's sister, climbed the mountain and visited them. One Saturday she had reached the top and was within a half-mile of their house, when from up in a tree a voice startled her. "Aunt Opal, I didn't know you were coming."

It was Jyles. Opal didn't think about him being in a tree so far from home. He climbed down and walked with her toward the house. As they neared it, they came on Rhody and Nell lying in the shade. Away went Jyles, jumping on the back of Rhody.

Opal was amazed. "That mule will jump and throw him off and hurt him," she thought. But Rhody hardly blinked an eye. She lay there while Jyles sat on her just as if he was riding her, and she didn't move.

The next day Opal and Lois happened to look out a window and see Jyles on Rhody's back. They were under a tree. As they watched, Jyles caught hold of a limb and swung into the tree. A little later he swung down from the tree onto Rhody's back again.

That summer a Mockingbird moved into the honeysuckle vine on the front porch, and each night put the Gray family to sleep with its beautiful lullabies. Night after night he would sing out to all the world that the honeysuckle vine was his turf, and for all others to stay away.

Anyone who has never stood under a tree in the forest or meadowland and listened to a Mockingbird sing has no understanding or appreciation of how lovely the music is, but to Boyd and Lois, Leonard, and the children, it seemed as if they had all the birds of the forest on their front porch taking turns singing. As they lay in their beds with the doors and windows open so the cool mountain breezes could blow through, the music flowed throughout their house on those warm summer nights of 1936.

Chapter 25

THE MOVE OFF THE MOUNTAIN

Boyd and Lois had their eyes on a farm which was for sale at the foot of the west side of the Iron Ore. They both thought it was a perfect place for them. The school bus came within a quarter-mile of the house and the Barham store was not much farther. They would have a good place to buy groceries, and it was close enough to the mountain for Boyd to continue farming up there.

Boyd had promised Lois they would move off the mountain when the children started school. Now Bobbye would be going to school in a year. It was hard on Jyles to walk up and down the mountain each day in the winter and it would be even harder on Bobbye. Jyles had missed several days of school due to bad weather, even when the school bus ran.

They bought the one-hundred acre farm that year for $800, paying $200 down, and they would pay $200 plus interest for three years. They hoped they could make the payments and they could if they didn't have a crop failure.

The house was small for a growing family like theirs, and it was old and unpainted. It only had two rooms besides the kitchen, but it had front and back porches and a large fireplace just like their mountain home. It was also down off the mountain, which Lois had grown to hate because of it being so hard to go up and down.

In the summer of 1937 they moved. It took two trips to haul their household goods and two for the farm tools. They had to put two beds in the large front room and two in the bedroom, just as they had on the mountain. Since the cotton and corn were on the mountain, it was harder on Boyd and Leonard gathering the corn and picking the cotton than it had been when they lived up there, because they had the trip up the mountain each morning before starting to work in the fields. The mules could only go about one-third as fast climbing up as they could on level ground, counting the frequent rests they had to give them.

The pastures were pretty good on the new farm and the fences were good enough to hold the livestock until after the crops were gathered. The barn wasn't very good but it would have to do until later. Most of the corn had to be put in the barn on the mountain and brought down a wagon load at a time later on, as they needed it for the livestock.

After moving off the mountain, Jyles and Ralph Williams, the boy who lived across the field from them, became close friends. They often went home with each other. The Williams were very good neighbors. Whenever Lois had a big job to do, such as canning or making lard, Mrs. Williams would always come to help.

Their chickens were free range, and they had nests in the plum thicket on the west side of the house. They didn't have all that many hens, but they did get enough eggs for the family to eat and even a few to sell to Mrs. Barham at her store. But suddenly they stopped getting any eggs from them. Boyd decided that a Black Snake or opossum must be getting them,

A few days later, when he was in the Barham Grocery, Mrs. Barham asked him, "Did you know that Jyles and Ralph have been coming in here and selling me eggs and buying candy with the money?"

"No," Boyd told her. "So that's what's been happening to our eggs?"

Mrs. Barham went on, "I didn't think anything about it at first, but when they brought them in every day and bought candy with the money, I decided I had better tell you."

Boyd thanked her and went on back to the house. He and Jyles went on a little trip out behind the woodshed. That put a stop to that.

The Barham Grocery was a gathering place for the men in the community. There were a few small sawmills around and men met there to wait on rides to go to the different mills. They even had some marble games, if you can picture that in your mind. One of the Deacons at the Oak Grove church, George Rowland, even played. He was a little man, standing only about five feet-four inches tall, and he was of a small build, but he didn't let that keep him from becoming involved in different things. Leonard said he really had a temper and he would sometimes lose it when playing marbles.

There was no active church at Caglesville, since the Missionary Baptist Church Boyd's father attended had gone dead. There was talk of reactivating it, and making it into a community church (Non-Denominational) so people of all faiths could attend. The Grays were excitedly looking forward to the day when that would happen but so far it had only been talk.

Caglesville had once been a thriving little community called Cagle's Mill with 150 people living in it, or close by. The first house in Russellville had been built with lumber sawed there, as had the famous Pott's Tavern in Pottsville. Ishmael Cagle had run a steam grist mill, either during or after the Civil War. Caglesville had gone down—until in 1937 it had only a few houses and one small store.

Two of Mrs. Barham's daughters, Gladys and Margaret, were at the Gray's house in the early summer and they were talking about how good the wild blackberries were.

"I don't guess I'll get to pick any this year," Lois said. "The kids are all sick."

The next day, here came the Barham girls, each of them carrying a large bucket of blackberries, and they gave them to her. She was so proud of them. What good neighbors the Barhams were!

Mr. and Mrs. Williams' daughter and granddaughter visited the Williams for a few days that winter and the

Granddaughter took pneumonia while there. She was so sick that someone had to be with her at all times. Lois helped with the sitting up. The first night she was walking home after midnight, and with the feeble light from the lantern, she lost the path she was on. She walked and walked and finally came to a fence but she knew she wasn't supposed to cross another one! Then she saw a light, went toward it, and knocked on the door. Wow, was she surprised when Mr. Williams opened it. It was the house she had just left and she was very embarrassed. This time as she went along the path towards home, she was careful not to lose sight of it, and she made it all right.

One day Lois read a story in a magazine about some hillbillies who lived far back in the mountains. One of their small children was sick and they took him to the doctor. When the doctor told the boy to open his mouth and stick out his tongue, the boy only looked at him. After he told the boy again and still got no response, the doctor asked his mother what was wrong with him.

"Talk plain English to him, Doc," his mother said.

"What do you mean by that?" the doctor questioned.

The mother told the boy, "Open up your gobble hole and roll out your lolla-lacker." The boy immediately opened his mouth and stuck out his tongue.

Lois was so amused by the story, she read it to her family and they got a big laugh. Jyles started teaching baby Jerry to stick out his tongue when he told him that. Every afternoon at 4 p.m. when Jyles and Bobbye came in from school, he told Jerry to "Open up your gobble hole and roll out your lolla-lacker", and out Jerry's tongue would come.

Bobbye and Betty by now had become cute and sweet little girls. Bobbye was six and had dark-brown hair—almost black. Lois always cut it so that she had bangs. Betty was four and had pretty blond hair.

One day that fall when all the kids were at home, Mr. Williams dropped by for a little while. After he was seated in a chair, he took his hat off and laid it on the floor. The children were well acquainted with him by now, and they felt very comfortable with him, but they had never seen him without a hat. They hadn't known he was bald-headed and they had never been up close to anyone who was. Boyd's Uncle Bob had a full head of hair, although it was white.

They started staring at Mr. Williams' head. Then Jyles got up enough nerve to put his hand on his bald head and feel it. He rubbed it for a moment, and then took his hand off. Bobbye had to do it next. Then it was Betty's turn. Last of all, baby Jerry had to feel it. Jyles had to lift him up before he could reach it. All this time, Lois was watching Mr. Williams to see how he would react. He just sat there until they had finished and then he grinned and said, "If that doesn't beat anything I ever saw. They've never seen a bald-headed man before, have they?"

Lois laughed, "Now that you mention it, I don't think they have."

Chapter 26

TRAGEDY

On Christmas morning, Boyd and Lois gave the girls dolls, Jerry a toy wagon, and Jyles a pen and ink set. The children were all very excited about it being Christmas, and they were happy with their presents.

Mr. Maxwell came, loaded them into his car and took them to his house to spend the day. He and Mrs. Maxwell had bought all the grandchildren presents, and they had an abundant supply of nuts, candy, apples, and oranges. They always had firecrackers on Christmas, the Fourth of July and other holidays. This was a very happy time for the Gray children. There was always a friendly atmosphere at their Maxwell grandparents and they could play with their cousins, JoElla and Berwyn Don. Norma and her husband, Vil, lived in California now, so they were sadly missed. They had three children but very seldom returned to Arkansas. When they did, it was a very special occasion.

Jyles received a comb and mirror from his grandparents, as did the girls and Jerry. A week after Christmas, Jyles told his mother, "Next Christmas I want you to get me a new suit." He had never had a new suit before, and he was getting to be a big boy. He was now in the third grade.

"All right, we'll get you one," Lois told him. "It's time you had one anyway."

On January 7, Jyles and Bobbye caught the bus at the Barham Grocery. Jyles had wanted to wear his new overalls, but Lois wanted him to save them for Sunday. So he had worn his regular ones. The bus was crowded as usual that morning. The bus driver had to make some of the students sit down. They wanted to crowd toward the front. He was worried about the door of the bus. It was broken, and it would come open if pushed. He had been after them at school to fix it, but they had been putting it off.

When the bus was a half-mile from the school house, the children suddenly started crowding to the front, anticipating getting off, and Jyles was in front of everyone. He was carrying his new lunch pail. In his overall bib pocket was his new ink pen, with the bottle of ink in one of his lower pockets. The boys and girls behind him kept shoving.

Suddenly someone was pushed into him and he had to lean against the door. It came open! He could feel himself falling and he tried to catch hold of something. He grabbed another student. That student was almost shoved out the door too. He caught onto something and tried desperately to hang on but it came loose. It was the student's pencil that he had grasped. He continued his fall.

As he landed headfirst on the rough gravel road beside the bus, Jyles somehow rolled in front of the bus's rear wheels. He felt the bus's tremendous weight as it passed over his belly. The pain was excruciating. His new dinner pail was crushed—ruined.

He didn't lose consciousness. It would have been merciful if he had. The school bus stopped and the driver rushed back to him. His face was as red as a beet. He was moving his head from side to side in agony.

The driver was terrified. What he wouldn't have given for it to have been him lying there instead of the boy. If he could only take his place, but there was no turning around the events of those fateful few moments. What was done was done. If they had only repaired the door of the bus, this wouldn't have happened. If they had only had a rule that the children must stay in their seats until the bus stopped.

He knew the boy was dying, but he tried to put it out of his mind. "No!" he told himself. "He's not dying. He'll be all right."

He gently took Jyles in his arms. A car had stopped. The driver knew that Jyles was hurt, but he didn't know how badly.

"Put him in the back seat," he shouted. "I'll take him to Doctor Linton."

The bus driver placed Jyles in the car and watched it as it moved toward Hector. Then he numbly climbed back into the school bus and drove on to school. He was in a daze. How could it have happened?

Doctor Linton only had to take one look at the dying boy to realize there was no hope. In all of his years as a doctor, he had attended many dying patients and he knew he was seeing one now.

Placing Jyles in the back seat of his car, he solemnly drove toward the Gray's house. There was no use in going to the hospital. Jyles would more than likely be gone by the time they could get to Russellville. He only hoped he would still be alive when they reached the Grays'. It would be less of a shock to his parents if he died in their presence than if he was dead when they first learned about his accident. But even then, the doctor knew it would be almost too much for them to bear.

When he reached the Grays' house, he carried Jyles inside. Lois had seen him drive up and was on the porch, a puzzled look on her face. "Jyles must have gotten hurt," she thought. It never entered her mind that he was near death.

"Doc Linton, what happened?" she demanded.

"Your boy got run over by the school bus," the doctor calmly told her.

"Is he hurt badly?" she asked. She wanted him to tell her that Jyles would be all right. But he didn't.

He only said, "Let's get him inside and into bed."

Lois opened the door and Jyles was carried inside. She was in a stupor. Numbness gripped her all over. "Don't we need to get him to the hospital?"

"Let's wait until he reacts," was the doctor's only reply.

Lois didn't know what to make of that. What did the doctor mean—"Wait until he reacts?"

Boyd was on his way to the store when the doctor passed. He was going through the woods along the path, so he hadn't seen him. When he arrived there, Connie Barham said to him, "I just saw Doc Linton go up to your house."

"Wonder what for?" Boyd asked no one in particular. He knew Connie didn't know.

He started back at once, though he couldn't imagine what the doctor could be doing there. They hadn't sent for him. Maybe Jyles or Bobbye had gotten an arm broken or something like that. It was too early for them to have been playing, he thought. Looking up at the sun, he guessed it to be only about 9 a.m. The school bus gets to Hector anywhere from 8:30 to 8:40. The doctor must have left there by 8:40 or 8:45.

Just as Boyd arrived at his house, the bus driver drove up in the school bus. Boyd met him as he and Bobbye stepped out. Bobbye was crying and the driver was as pale as a corpse.

"Boyd, Jyles fell out of the school bus and I ran over him," he stammered. "I tried to turn the steering wheel in a way to miss him but I hit him anyway."

"You couldn't help it," Boyd tried to console him. "Don't take it too hard."

He went in to see Jyles. Lois and Doc Linton were with him. Jyles was conscious, but very pale.

"Boyd, get him some more water," Lois commanded. She was washing his face with a damp cloth.

"Jyles, why did you get by the door while the bus was still moving?"

"Leave me alone!" Jyles said. "I need some water." Boyd reached his bedside with the glass of water.

Jyles drank it, but it quickly came back up. He wanted some more. It too came back up as soon as he drank it.

Boyd and Lois's faces were grave. It didn't look good at all.

The boy was worried about his new lunch pail that had been smashed. He said, "The bus driver told me he would get me another one."

When Lois had undressed Jyles, she noticed that the bottle of ink in his overalls was undamaged.

It wasn't long before Mr. and Mrs. Maxwell drove up. Boyd and Lois didn't know who had notified them, but it was very comforting to have them there.

Jyles kept wanting water, but he couldn't keep it down.

The Maxwells had brought the looking glass and comb they had given him for Christmas and had been left at their house. Mr. Maxwell gave them to Boyd and he took them in to Jyles. "Here's your looking glass and comb," he told him.

"Put them up," Jyles said. He kept asking for water and Lois would let him drink, but it always came right back up.

Doctor Linton left to go to Pea Ridge to visit a patient, telling them he would stop back by in about an hour. As he was going off the front porch, he told the neighbors who were gathering outside, "The boy is dying."

The water bucket was almost empty and a nest of ants had gotten into the well, making the Grays' water unfit to drink. "You and Papa go over to Mr. Williams' and get another bucket of water," Lois told Boyd.

As the two men left the house, Mr. Maxwell told Boyd, "I'm awfully uneasy about Jyles."

Boyd didn't say anything. He didn't feel like it, but he thought to himself. "I am too, Mr. Maxwell, I am too. This time it has come to me."

They had just returned with the water and were walking up on the porch, when Jyles called out in a loud voice, "Ma, I've got to have something!" Then his voice became a whisper, "Ma, I've got to have something."

Lois ran to the front door. "Boyd, he's dying!" she yelled.

Boyd ran to his bedside, "Jyles!" he called.

Jyles didn't answer. Boyd could see his lips moving, then they were still. He was dead.

Chapter 27

THE FUNERAL

They bought the new suit he had wanted for next Christmas and he was buried in it. He was laid to rest in the Shiloh Cemetery on Pea Ridge. A marble tombstone with a lamb lying on it was placed at the head of his grave.

A large crowd was at the funeral. It was comforting to have so many relatives and friends present in such a time of sorrow. Jyles' teacher, Imogene Tackett, was there, as well as the superintendent of the Hector School, Mr. Odus (Ham) Churchill. He was Lois's third cousin. He blamed himself for not having the school bus door repaired, as he should have. He resigned as the Hector School Superintendent after that year. He told Boyd that he had lost interest in being superintendent after what had happened. In later years, he also lost his life, in a car accident. He was only forty-seven years old.

People told Boyd and Lois that they should sue the school, but they had no desire to do so. They said it wouldn't bring Jyles back, and anyway, the Hector School District was poor and couldn't afford to pay them anything. There was no mention of it, but the school must have had insurance. Even if they had thought about it, Boyd and Lois still probably wouldn't have sued. In 1938 the lawyers hadn't yet gotten so predatory as they were to get later.

The day after the funeral, Lois dug Jyles' marbles up from his secret hiding place in the front yard. He had hidden them under the large cedar tree so that Bobbye couldn't get into and scatter them everywhere, as she had been doing. She also found the letter Jyles had written to his grandparents. It said:

Dear Ma and Pa,

Will you send me my comb and looking glass you got me for Christmas? I need them.

New tears welled up in Lois's eyes. She would never see her little boy again in this world, but she had faith in God and she knew he had a reason for everything. Life must go on, she knew, in spite of the hardships and tragedies of this world. She thought of the song in 1927 after the terrible Mississippi flood that claimed so many lives:

We can't explain the reason these great disasters come,

But we must all remember to say, thy will be done,

And though the good must suffer for other people's sins,

There is a crown awaiting where eternal life begins.

Unknown

Boyd and Lois had to force themselves to do the work that was always pressing around the household and the farm in the days ahead. They still had three small children who needed constant attention and the cows had to be milked the same as before.

Though Jyles was gone, his memory would live on in their hearts and in their memories. They would spend many hours reminiscing about the happy times they had enjoyed with him. The whole family was in a trance-like state for a while. The only thing that could alleviate their pain was time. As time passed, they came to accept the fact that Jyles would never be a part of their family again. They caught themselves wanting to call to him to come and play, to come to dinner, or to get ready to go to school or church or some other place. But over time they found themselves doing that less and less, until finally they came to accept their loss.

Seventy-four years later, as I write this, Jyles' little overalls he wore on the day he was killed still hang in the closet of the house Mom and Dad built in 1942. Whenever Betty comes in from the west coast for a visit, she takes a look at them. Tears come into her eyes as her memory takes her back to those days of long ago.

The Lending of a Child

I'll lend you for a little while a child of mine, he said,

For you to love the while he lives, and mourn for when he's dead.

It may be six or seven years, or twenty-two or three,

But will you 'til I come for him take care of him for me?

He'll bring his charm to gladden you, and shall his stay be brief,

You'll have his lovely memories as solace for your grief.

I cannot promise he will stay, since all from earth return,

But there are lessons taught down there I want this child to learn.

I've looked the whole world over in my search for parents true,

And from the throngs that crowd the land, I have selected you.

So will you give him all your love, nor think the labor vain,

Nor hate me when I come to call to take him home again?

I fancied that I heard them say, "Dear Lord, thy will be done,

For all the joy the child shall bring, the risk of grief we'll run.

We'll shelter him with tenderness. We'll love him while we may,

And for the happiness we've known, forever grateful stay.

And should angels call him sooner than we'd planned,

We'll brave the bitter grief that comes, and try to understand."

Unknown

Part Two

High on a Mountain

Chapter 28

AFTER JYLES

Boyd always built a big fire in the fireplace to heat the house. It didn't have insulation except for dead air between the inner and outer walls, and it got pretty cold in the house, but not as bad as on the mountain. When the kids got sick, Lois put Vick salve on the bottoms of their feet, and either she or Boyd would hold their feet next to the fire to warm them. Lois also put poultices on their chests. Both of these together seemed to help them get better.

The children were not allowed to say "doggone". That was a bad word. They could say "dog bite it", because that was Lois's byword. One day when Betty was sitting with Boyd by the fireplace, she started saying "dog, dog, dog." All of a sudden, "doggone" slipped out. Her daddy almost gave her a whipping.

She said, "I won't say it anymore!" He let her off with a warning.

Boyd's thirty-two-year-old cousin, Lawrence Biffle, often visited them. One day he was helping dig sweet potatoes, and six-year-old Betty said to everyone, "I'm struct on Lawrence." He laughed when she said that.

Once Lois sent Betty to the store to buy something, and when she paid for it, Mrs. Barham asked, "Do you want candy with the change?" Since Mrs. Barham asked her, she thought it would be okay and she took candy. When she returned home with her mother's items and she didn't have the change, Lois was pretty upset. Money was hard to come by.

Lois always had to have her coffee. One morning when she found out she didn't have any, she sent the girls to the store before breakfast to get some.

Two gray-haired white-bearded men came to the house one morning. They showed up without notice. Lois gave them food to eat and milk to drink. Then they sat and talked. They were preachers from Oak Grove, Tom and Doc Johnson. Betty enjoyed listening to them. They stayed awhile, then left.

The girls took a quart or a half-gallon of milk to school to pay for their lunches. One day Betty fell down and spilled hers. She didn't get to eat lunch that day. The quart jar didn't even break.

The children's favorite times were when they had friends and relatives visit.

They loved when their Uncle Earl and Uncle Sewood came. Sewood had moved to Oklahoma, where his father's brother, Uncle Oscar, had moved a few years back. He came to visit a few times, and once he had Uncle Oscar's son, O.J., with him. The initials stood for Oscar John. O.J. swung Betty around and around. She enjoyed that. Once when their Uncle Sewood came, all of them were in the field hoeing cotton, and he came to where they were working. He rode a train to North Dakota one time and worked in the wheat harvest.

He talked O.J. into joining the army for a year in 1939. Before their enlistments were over, war clouds were on the horizon in Europe, and their time was extended.   Sewood didn't get out until 1945, after the war was over, and O.J. never got out. He was killed in Europe in the "Battle of the Bulge", when he stepped on a land mine. Since he was a preacher, he could have gotten out of going into the service. He paid the ultimate price, giving his life for his country and some other countries.

Earl was drafted for the war effort. Many years later, after Sewood and Earl were dead, Betty sent their names to Washington D.C. to be placed on the World War II Memorial. She didn't have enough information on O.J. to send his.

Maybe some of his brothers' descendents in Oklahoma and Texas had sent his name, or maybe the War Department automatically put his name on the memorial, since he had gotten killed.

Boyd and Lois helped organize a community church at Caglesville. As the population of the village had dropped due to so many people moving to California and nearby cities, the Baptist church had gone dead. By having a community church, people from all faiths could attend. They moved the old church about seventy-five yards south so it was on the new highway going east from Caglesville. In 1929 the Arkansas Highway Department had routed the road so it would bypass Cagle Hill, a half-mile north of Caglesville. The hill was too steep for a modern road. By going a mile east and joining the new highway 105 from Atkins, they found a much easier route to Hector. The church building was remodeled after it was moved.

Boyd and Lois and the children walked the mile to church at Caglesville. They didn't have a car and it was more trouble for Boyd to catch the mules and harness them than it was for the family to walk. They carried the small children back home after church when they were too sleepy to walk. The church had a pretty good attendance, at least fifty people. They had a preacher from Hagarville near Clarksville, Claude Overby, as their first pastor. He had held revivals in Pope County and they became acquainted with him that way. He was related to the Barhams somehow.

Several women quilted in the church building one day a week, including Lois. Bobbye and Betty were there with her one day, when someone came in and whispered something to Mrs. Kinslow, who immediately left for home. Their store and post office had been robbed. She thought it was a neighbor kid who had been hanging around the store. He went to church there, as did his parents. His father never gave him any money.

After the law was notified and went to his house. He admitted to stealing the money, which was a very small amount. He was taken to jail and Boyd went with the neighbor the next day to get him out. The boy wasn't punished much, but the scoldings he got from the law officials, from Mr. Kinslow, and from his dad were pretty harsh punishment, enough so that he never robbed anybody or anything else.

A shabby looking tramp came by their house one afternoon when Boyd was away. He needed a bath, because he was very dirty. The kids thought he smelled funny. He asked Lois if she could feed him. She told him she didn't have much, but she could cook some eggs. He replied in a mean tone of voice, "I told you I could eat anything!"

That made her afraid but she invited him in anyway. She got some wood for the cook stove and started heating it. Then she put some eggs on to fry and cold biscuits left over from breakfast to warm up. When he started eating, he never talked, but kept looking around. When he finished, he left without thanking her. She was very glad to see him go.

Their house had a porch all the way across its front. The foundation of the house was so high that Bobbye and Betty made a playhouse under the floor. It was much cooler under there in the summer than it was outside in the yard, even under the trees. When it rained, they would stand on the porch and say, "Let it rain, let it pour. Get in the house and shut the door."

When Betty was old enough to go to school and it was almost time to start, the two girls were so happy they would hug each other and jump up and down in anticipation. They had a friend at school, Virginia Trey, who came home with them to spend the night. It stormed and rained during the night and Virginia became scared and wanted to go home. She didn't get to because Boyd didn't have a car or truck and he wasn't going to drive the seven miles to her house and back with it raining hard and him having only a wagon and a team of mules for transportation.

Soon afterwards, the day Bobbye and Betty were supposed to go home with Virginia and spend the night she didn't show up at school. They were very disappointed and were determined to go to her house anyway. They knew which bus she rode, so they boarded it and asked the driver to drop them off at Virginia's house. When he stopped and let them out, a very surprised Virginia and her mother greeted them.

Her mother had a crippled hand. The house Virginia lived in was very shabby and rundown. There wasn't a man anywhere around. They were obviously very poor. There was no supper that night, and for breakfast it was cornflakes and buttermilk. The girls had never had buttermilk with cereal before, and it wasn't very tasty to them.

As they were leaving for school that morning, Virginia's mother gave her some money to spend at the Hector store. The students were allowed to get off at the store, where they could buy things, and then walk the quarter-mile to school. They got off there and all three of them entered the store. Virginia bought some cookies, which Bobbye and Betty thought she would share with them. But they were out of luck because she didn't give them any.

The girls were allowed to play with their friends, Doris and James Kinslow and several other children in the big sawdust pile north of Caglesville on Sunday afternoons. They always had a good time climbing to the top and sliding down. They also made caves back in the sawdust. It's a wonder someone didn't suffocate, but when the sawdust caved in there was always a boy or girl there to dig them out.

One day their cousins, JoElla and Berwyn Don, came to visit. They played in the pile of cotton Boyd had put on the front porch. They dug holes in the pile and covered themselves with it. The cotton had that new clothing smell and they loved to play in it. JoElla and Berwyn were living in Russellville now. Bobbye and Betty envied them for getting to live in town.   One Sunday there was a baptizing in Isabel Creek at Oak Grove. Homer, Goldie, JoElla and Berwyn Don came by on their way to it. They were in their new car. Bobbye and Betty were allowed to ride in its rumble seat. This was in the back, outside of the interior of the car. JoElla taught them the song, "Mama's Little Baby Loves Shortnin' Bread".

Sometimes when they picked up the mail at the mailbox, samples of chewing gum would be there, sent from Wrigley's in Chicago. The kids always looked forward to that. The Watkins man came once a month. He would open his fold-out case with all the herbs, spices, ointments, linaments, and many other items. The kids were fascinated as he gave his sales pitch. He talked a mile a minute as he showed his wares, lifting each item out of the case and explaining what it was or how it worked. He would give the kids samples of his candy. Lois always bought several things from him. She couldn't refuse after he had given candy to the children.

Their Uncle Earl came one Saturday evening in his new car. He was going to take all of them to see a movie in Atkins. It was "Gone with the Wind". Everyone was enthralled with the movie but since it was so long it was hard for some of them to stay awake.

The next day at church, someone told Lois about seeing her at the theatre and she was very embarrassed. In 1940 some church members thought it was a sin to go to a movie. Brother Kinslow was one of them.

When the kids came into any money, they would head for the store. The Barhams didn't stay in the store all the time, especially during slow days, so when someone would come, they would have to roust them out. Their house was about fifty feet from the store, and when a kid knocked on their door, whoever answered it knew they would be going out there, maybe for a few pennies. It wasn't worth getting out of their "Easy Chair" for that. One day Betty found a nickel and she couldn't rest until she had it spent on candy. Without telling anyone, she walked the quarter of a mile down the road. Her mother was busy and the other kids were asleep, so she knew she could go down to the store and back without being missed.

When she reached the store, no one was tending it as usual for that time of day. She knocked on the door of the Barham house and when one of the young women answered it, she said, "I want in the store." The young woman reluctantly went into the other room and got the store keys and opened the building. Betty spent her nickel on candy and happily hurried back through the woods, eating her candy while on the way home. She reached her house without her mother being any the wiser, and she didn't have to share her candy with Bobbye or Jerry. The Barham lady slowly went back into her house to her "Easy Chair", with her mother and her being five cents richer.

Margaret Barham had a truck and she drove it on a peddling route out of the store. Betty got a ride once with her, to Aunt Opal's on Pea Ridge. She visited her a while, then rode back home with Margaret.

Chapter 29

I WAS BORN

On January 11, 1939 I was born and Grandma Maxwell came to be with Mom for a few days. Doctor Linton was thankful that he no longer had to ride the mule to the top of the Iron Ore and back. His fee was $25. I was weighed on a cotton scale and it said "sixteen pounds". Not tons, just pounds. The word got around and everyone wanted to see me.

Mom said I was back to normal size in a few months, because I didn't start growing for a while. Having weighed so much at birth, by the time I was grown, I should have been as big as Hoss Cartwright on Bonanza, but when I graduated from high school, I only weighed 145 pounds at 17 years of age.

Mom also gave me a middle name of Loraine. That was Aunt Opal's new husband Loraine (Doc) Murdock's name, so I was named for him. Uncle Doc pronounced it Loren but my folks pronounced it Lor-rain. After I started to school, Jerry told all of my classmates that I had weighed sixteen pounds when I was born; also what my middle name was.

The boys there got a big laugh out of both items of information. They said Loraine was a girl's name. Every few years, Jerry would tell about it again and I had to endure more teasing. A good friend, Tommy Arthur, started calling me Loraine all the time. I didn't know what I was going to do. He was bigger than I was and I couldn't give him a whipping.

Finally, in desperation, I called him by his middle name, which was Fay. I didn't think Fay was such a bad name, but apparently he did. He never called me Loraine again. Years later, when Johnny Cash had the song out, "A Boy Named Sue", I was reminded of my middle name. I didn't think the boy named Sue had anything on me. The only difference was that Sue was his first name, while Loraine was my middle name. I also started pronouncing it Loren.

Chapter 30

DAD'S CAR

Dad finally bought an old car. He had trouble learning how to drive it, but he was determined to do so. When mom rode with him, she was literally scared to death. One Sunday after church, he wanted to visit Marshall and Ona Patterson, so we all piled into the car and headed over to the Buttermilk area, then past Tate Graveyard, and finally into Patterson Hollow, which was in the shadows of the Iron Ore.

Later, while on the way home, Dad was driving along, about twenty miles an hour, when we overtook a man walking along the side of the road. As he looked at the man, he steered the car toward him. He was about to hit him, when Mom yelled for him to get back on the road. The man jumped into the ditch.

Later we reached the junction of Highway 105 and 124. A big embankment was on the west side of the highway we were entering. When Dad was supposed to turn south, he seemed to become petrified. He didn't turn but headed right for the drop-off. He finally brought the car to a halt within inches of it. Mom was horrified.

That night he decided to attend Oak Grove Church. Mom was too tired to go and none of the kids wanted to go except Betty. Darkness had arrived when they left home. A few hundred yards before reaching the church, Dad was blinded by an oncoming car and he ran off the side of the road. Betty was sitting on the passenger side and that door came open. She fell out! Dad didn't know she was gone.

After he got back on the road, he said, "That was a close call, wasn't it?" Then he looked over and saw the empty seat and the open door. Wow, was he surprised—and shocked!

There wasn't enough room on the shoulder of the road for him to pull over, and he was afraid to park on the road at the time, when other cars and trucks would be coming their way as they went to church, so he drove on to the church house, parked the car, and ran back to look for her.

All kinds of horrible thoughts went through his mind as he hurried as fast as he could back in the direction where she was. Would she be dead? Would she be badly hurt? He could hardly bear to think of how he would find her.

In the meantime, Betty had fallen into the ditch with rocks, briars, and weeds. She got to her feet and started walking along the ditch onto the road. The night was as dark as pitch. Headlights shined on her, and then a truck stopped. The driver asked her, "Little girl, do you want me to take you home?"

Betty said, "No, I am going to where my daddy is." Dad soon came and found her. Incredibly, Betty didn't have one scratch on her, and her dress wasn't torn or dirty! At that moment, she started believing in guardian angels. She hadn't felt a thing when she hit the ground in the ditch that night. When she was older, she said, "Twice that day I was saved by a guardian angel."

A few days before Christmas that winter, Dad went to the pasture, cut a Christmas tree and put it up in the front room. It reached all the way to the ceiling. It was the first Christmas tree Betty had ever seen that she remembered.

Bobbye happened to see some Christmas presents Dad had hid in the barn and she took Betty out there to show them to her. Betty wondered why Santa Claus had hidden them there. She thought he was supposed to ride his sleigh from the North Pole and bring them down their chimney.

The girls went home with JoElla and Berwyn Don that Christmas. Uncle Homer took them around town and showed them all the Christmas lights. They saw more of Russellville than they had ever seen before. They attended a Christmas program at Harmony, a Baptist church near Russellville.

Chapter 31

THE NEW BARN

Dad had wanted a good barn for a long time, and he talked to the neighbors and kinfolks about it. One day, his Uncle Alvie Biffle, who was married to his father's sister and was Lawrence's father, said, "I have some pine trees that would make excellent logs for a barn. If you want them, I will give you all you want.

Mr. Hopson, a close neighbor, told him he would supervise the building. So Dad went into Uncle Alvie's woods and he was delighted to see dozens of slim pines, which were exactly what he would need for the barn.

He and Uncle Leonard started cutting the trees. When they had enough for a load, he hired a log hauler to take them to the barn site, where they peeled them with log peelers. Dad knew that bark was much easier to get off before the log dried out, so he peeled the load of logs just unloaded. Then he and Uncle Leonard went back to the woods to cut more logs for another load.

They worked at cutting the logs and peeling them for several weeks. The rafters would also be made of small poles, so they had to cut and peel them. Some Oak trees were cut and peeled for the bottom logs. Then they gathered a few loads of rocks, which the bottom logs would be placed on so they wouldn't touch the ground. Three-year-old Jerry helped with the peeling of the logs. He couldn't do much, but Dad let him help anyway. He knew it would be good for him.

Mr. Hopson's plans had three stables to be lined up side by side for the horses and mules. A narrow hall was to go between two of the stables, so that anyone could walk from the center hall to the storage area, which was to be on the west side of the mules' stalls. Across from the stalls, ten feet over, would be a large corn crib, another narrow hall, and a feed room.

The two sections would be connected at the top, about eight feet up, by pine poles, which would have boards put on top of them. Above the boards would be the hay loft. The west side of the barn, an area about eight feet wide, would be for plow tools and anything else Dad needed it for. The east side would have six stables, also eight feet wide, which would be used to milk cows.

The barn would have outer walls on the east and west sides made of regular boards, each one being six to eight inches wide. These boards would be placed vertically. Then finally, the pine pole rafters would be put on for the roof. The top of the center ridge would be twenty-four feet high, and the roof span would be forty-six feet across. From one end of the center hall to the other would be thirty-four feet. When it was finished, it would be one of the best barns in Pope County, not counting the two large red barns at Arkansas Tech. Those had been built at taxpayer's expense.

But first, a lot of work would have to be done and it would take several men to do the job. This was going to be a much bigger deal than back in the old days when the early settlers built a one or two-room log cabin.

Some of the neighbors who helped build the barn were Mr. Hopson, two of his sons, Glen and Elmer, Jimmy Mackey and his son, Arley, Dewey Kinder, Will Williams, and his son, Ralph. Others who helped have been lost in the pages of time, but I'm sure there were several more. We still have the barn and whoever you were, we thank you from the bottom of our hearts.

The logs and poles had all been peeled when they began. The rocks had also been found and carried to the site. There was a beehive of activity around there as the men worked to level the ground so the barn would be perfectly level as it slowly climbed into the sky. After the site had been checked and rechecked to make sure it was level, the actual work of building the barn began.

Stakes were placed at the corners and they were measured to make sure each individual section was square. Some of the workers placed rocks where the logs would be laid, while others started notching the logs to be fitted together. One by one, they were lifted into place. All the logs looked new as they were put together. Many times during the day, the men took breaks to get some much needed rest, and they would admire the good work they were doing. Then at the end of the workday, they would give their day's work a final inspection before going home to eat supper and to get a good night's sleep so they would be ready to continue their work the next morning.

Several weeks later, the barn was complete except for the roof. Mr. Hopson had advised Dad to cover the barn's outside logs with vertical planking to keep them from rotting over time. As the years passed, he knew that Mr. Hopson had given him some very good advice.

Building the roof was the hardest work and the most dangerous. The pole rafters were put on, with the first ones going across from the outside of the mules' stalls on one side, and from the outside of the corn crib and the feed room on the other side. These poles met twenty-four feet up in the air, where they were nailed to a center board between their ends. After these rafters were up, the lathes were put across them.

Afterwards, more rafters were placed from the outside logs to the outer walls of the barn. Several weeks of work were required to get the rafters up. Then the tin roofing was put on last. They also put large doors at each end of the hallway.

Dad was extremely proud of his new barn. He was happy that no one had gotten hurt while building it. Now he had to build a new corral for the horses and mules and a cow lot for the cows. There was no end to a farmer's work.

DAD'S MONUMENT

It was built in the late nineteen thirties
With pine logs that an uncle gave Dad,
And with the help of some very fine
neighbors,
As good friends as a man ever had.

A hall was put in the middle for wagons,
Beside, stalls for horses and mules.
On the other was a corn crib and a feed
room.
Overhead was for hay and some tools.

To the west of the mules' stalls was for
storage,
To the east of the cribs, six milk stalls.
We spent many hours there with the
milking,
In the spring, summer, winter, and fall.

We walked up the path every evening,
Then we walked it again every morn.
We could smell the coal-oil from the
lantern.
It cast shadows all over the barn.

Every cow had a name, and she knew it.
When we called, she would come every
time,
And she'd wait til the cow we'd just
finished
Had gone out, then she'd get into line.

Many times I was kicked by a kicker,
Many times swatted by a cow's tail.
Many times I would have to pour the milk out
When a cow would step in the milk pail.

The cat was always there for a handout
From the stream I would squirt through the air.
It would be there both night time and morning.
To get what that it thought was its share.

Old Charlie, I recall how she would chase us.
There was excitement when she was around.
You'd better have a club when you were near her,
Or she'd butt you, put you on the ground.

Lawrence Biffle once helped with the milking,
And Old Charlie went off toward the pond.
Lawrence followed her, planning to head her.
She turned on him, chased him back to the barn.

We'd feed the horses and mules at the day's end.
"Put six ears in each trough," Dad would say.
"And don't forget to put hay in their mangers.

They have earned it, for they've had a hard
day."

They would soon eat the corn off the corn
cobs,
And the hay then lay down for the night.
Come Sunday, we'd be playing in the
hayloft
With our friends, and we'd have a cob
fight.

On the west side was parked an old buggy.
It was there every year all alone.
Mom called it Dad's ten dollar folly.
She had ever since he brought it home.

He had bought it at the sale for ten dollars.
Never used, he called it his antique hack.
Finally, forty years later he sold it
For ten dollars, his whole investment back.

It's been seventy–three years since he built
it.
My, he worked hard everywhere that he
went.
The log barn will be standing for ages,
And we call it our dad's monument.

Randall Gray---2005

Those horses, mules, and cows were like family to a
small boy. I rode Nell and some of the other horses with the
older kids as I held on behind; most of the time we didn't use
saddles.

Once, when Betty and I were going up the mountain
road, our horse became scared when a panther-like noise came

out of the brush. She started running and we were barely able to stay on her back. Another time we didn't stay on. She went under a low limb and both of us were pulled off. We learned later that Cleo Mackey, Corene's husband, and someone else had scared us.

I went with the older children everywhere they would let me. Once Uncle Leonard and we children were walking to the barn. The horses and mules were standing close to the path. I wanted some excitement, so I walked over to Old Nell, grabbed her by the tail, and yelled, "Get up, Old filly!" She got up all right, and as she did, she kicked me in the belly. It knocked the breath out of me. That was more excitement than I had bargained for.

After we reached the barn, I decided I wanted an apple from the apple tree that grew in the horse corral, so I climbed up to get one. The limb broke and I fell out, landing on my belly. For the second time in just a few minutes, I had the breath knocked out of me. Everyone started laughing—that is, everyone except me. I got to my feet, and I said, "That didn't hurt!" But as soon as I got my breath back, I started crying, not from being hurt, because I wasn't, but just because I wanted to. I suppose I was embarrassed.

Chapter 32

OUR HOUSE BURNS

Donald was born May 2, 1941. Doctor Linton again came to the house, and he was again thankful for not having to climb the Iron Ore. Donald Rex was the name given to him. As he grew, we gave him the nickname of Donald Duck. Uncle Leonard called him Duck. He was good-natured about it, never getting angry with anyone for calling him that.

Walter Tappet lived in the house on the mountain that year and sharecropped part of our land. When it looked like he was going to lose part of the cotton, Dad had Uncle Leonard, Betty, and Bobbye to help him hoe it. He criticized twelve-year-old Bobbye and ten-year-old Betty for not doing enough work. Uncle Leonard told him where to get off. The girls weren't even getting paid.

The cotton and corn were good that year. Mom and Dad were now out of debt for the first time since their marriage. They had been married for thirteen years and they had five living children. Bobbye and Betty were old enough to help with Donald and me. Jerry could just about take care of himself, since he was five years old.

The cows still took a lot of work, with the milking, the running of the milk through the cream separator, and the feeding of the skim milk to the hogs and calves. They were now milking fifteen cows. The income from the sale of cream, calves, and hogs helped supplement what they received from the sale of cotton.

In the fall of that year, one day when the girls were at school, we had just eaten lunch and Jerry and I were playing on the floor. Mom was sitting at the sewing machine and baby Donald was lying on a pallet at her side.

Suddenly we smelled smoke and it was coming from the inside of the house. We looked around and then we looked up. Smoke was coming from the ceiling near where the fireplace flue was. It was getting thicker and thicker as we watched it.

Mom was so shocked, she couldn't move for a few moments. Then she yelled for Jerry to run over to Mr. Williams and tell him our house was on fire, and then run over and tell Mr. Hopson. She grabbed Donald and yelled for me to get outside.

After we were outside, there was nothing we could do but watch our home go up in smoke right before our eyes. The flames shot up into the air, as they climbed higher and higher. They became hotter and hotter. Mom yelled for me to get back. "Get back!"

I'll never forget that flaming house as long as I live. Our house burning and playing on the front porch are my only remembrances of the house.

Mr. Williams came running from across the field. But he was old and he couldn't do anything to help us. Mr. Hopson came running up, and then Grady Barham. He had seen the flames from the store. Mr. Hopson entered the burning building and came back carrying our large cook stove. Grady brought the machine out. But the fire was too intense for them to risk going back inside. So those two items were all that were saved. Our clothes, beds and bedclothes, cooking utensils, chairs, and everything else were lost.

Later that day, when Bobbye and Betty rode home from school on the school bus, they looked out the bus window toward our house, and it wasn't there. The bus driver said, "It looks like you don't have a house anymore. "

The girls were afraid that Mom, Jerry, and I had burned up in the house. They ran down the path toward where the house had been as fast as their legs could carry them. Jerry came to meet them. He told them his cocoon hadn't been killed. He was keeping it until it became a butterfly. After the fire, Mom had taken Jerry, Donald, and me to the Williams house.

Dad was working on the mountain piling up rich compost from the woods when the house burned. He was going to haul the compost off the mountain and spread it on our garden to enrich the soil. Mr. Hopson walked up the trail and told him his house had burned. Dad was aghast. He couldn't believe it. "Are Lois and the kids all right?" he asked Mr. Hopson.

Mr. Hopson assured him that we were okay. Dad was thankful that the girls were at school. He and his friend and neighbor hurried off the mountain as fast as they could. He never did haul the compost and spread it in our garden. It was still piled up there many years later. I'm sure it is still there as of this writing.

Our house was still smoldering when the two men reached it. Coals were still glowing, but there was nothing that could be salvaged. All Dad could do was look. Grandpa and Grandma Maxwell drove up about then in their new car. After the initial greetings were over, and the shock had worn off, they asked Mom and Dad what their plans were for a place to stay.

Grady Barham was still there and he, very generously, told Mom and Dad that we could move into a little house of his and stay until we found a better place for our large family.

How the fire had started in the attic of our house was a mystery. We didn't have electricity, so no wiring could have started it. Since it was warm weather, there was no fire in the fireplace, and it had been hours since Mom had cooked breakfast in the cook stove. Dad said, "There must have been a match in the attic and a mouse must have struck it."

Five years had passed since Dad and Mom bought the house and land and they had never recorded the deed. Fortunately for them, the man they had purchased it from was honest, and he made them a new one. This time Dad wasted no time in having it recorded.

They didn't have insurance on the house, so when they were ready to rebuild, they would have to borrow some of the construction money. The rest they would get from the crops and from the milk cows, plus what Dad could earn working out, such as at a sawmill or in the North Dakota wheat harvest. Farmers in the area were traveling to North Dakota to help harvest wheat after their crops were laid by. They would come back in time to harvest their own crops of cotton and corn.

Chapter 33

ANOTHER HOME

Grady's house was only a quarter of a mile away. We didn't have anything except what we were wearing, but the wonderful neighbors we had in the community immediately came to our rescue. Those who had clothes of our sizes donated to us, and they gave us lots of canned goods and other foods. Mrs. Barham had Margaret to make up all kinds of collections for us while on her peddling route. We received very little money though. There wasn't much in the area.

Grady's house we were moving to was on the road going up on the mountain, and it was only a hundred yards or so from HWY 105, the Atkins to Hector route. The little house only had a kitchen, a living room, a small bedroom, and a small front porch. It was unpainted, like our other house, but it didn't leak, so it kept us dry, and by burning several ricks of wood in the heating stove, it kept us warm in the winter. There were Mom and Dad, Uncle Leonard, and us five kids. We had two beds in the front room and two in the bedroom. There was barely room for seven of us to turn around in either room.

Dad decided not to go to North Dakota that year so he could get started preparing to build a new house. Mom kept at him until he knew there was no putting it off.

After the corn and cotton were harvested, and the cotton sold, he and Uncle Leonard started cutting pine logs to be made into lumber. There were plenty of pine trees on the side of the mountain and on top. A man located a sawmill near where they cut the logs, and someone dragged the logs out of the woods to the sawmill. After they were sawed into lumber, a trucker hauled them to the field where Dad had chosen to dry the lumber. It was stacked in a way that plenty of air could get to it. Then he and Uncle Leonard kept fires going all day and night to dry it out.

A few weeks after Dad and Uncle Leonard first started to work in the woods, the dried lumber was ready to be hauled to a planer north of Dover. The only planer around that shaped the lumber like that in Grandma and Grandpa Maxwell's house was located there.

I had my third birthday while we lived in the Grady Barham house. I slept with Uncle Leonard. One day after he had been working hard all day and I had been playing hard in the grass all day, the chiggers were feasting on me in bed. I kept asking him to scratch my back. Just about the time he would doze off, I would ask him to scratch it again. Finally he started griping. He said, "I have to get to sleep. I have to get up early in the morning to cut logs." But he did scratch my back once more.

It wasn't long before my back was itching again, but I was afraid to ask him anymore. Finally, after a few more minutes and I thought I couldn't stand it any longer, I said, "Uncle Leonard, if you'll scratch my back, I'll have Daddy get you some candy the next time he goes to town."

He relented and scratched my back one more time. He told that story from time to time as long as he lived.

Mom dipped snuff. Men and women had it so hard back then that they had to have some kind of support. Snuff and coffee were about the only vices the non-drinking people had.

One day the girls and Jerry were at school and Mom ran out of snuff. She sent me to get her some at the store. She also gave me a nickel to get some candy. When I reached the store, I roused one of the Barham girls and I wistfully eyed the candy and gum in the glass case. But to save my neck, I could not make up my mind whether to choose gum or candy. The young lady was getting restless, so I had to make up my mind quickly. I picked a bar of candy, and I picked a package of gum. The only problem was, there was no money left over to get Mom's snuff.

I chewed some of the gum while I was going home. The candy bar I put in my pocket. I would save that for later. Right after I left the store, Uncle Ben came along in his truck. He was on his way to the mountain. He asked me if I wanted to ride. I said, "No. Mom told me not to ride with strangers." He laughed, and then went on his way.

I was in trouble when I reached home. When Mom asked me for her snuff, the only things I could produce were the rest of the package of gum I had, and the half-melted candy bar that was in my pocket.

"You get right back down to the store and trade that candy bar for a box of snuff," she demanded. "And don't eat it while you are on your way!"

That was one long trip back to the store. I knew the Barham lady would be mad about having to come back out to the store, and I knew that she wouldn't be very happy when she saw the melted candy bar. I knocked on their door again, and when the same girl came to the door, I asked her, "Will you let me trade this candy bar for a box of snuff?"

I'm sure that if she hadn't known that Mom had sent me down there, she would have refused to exchange the two items. But she reluctantly said to me, "I guess." She said the two words in such a way that the words were much longer then they look on paper.

I took the snuff back to Mom, and I was a very relieved little boy to know that I was "off the hook".

Mom quit dipping snuff after that. She told us years later that after that incident, she decided to spend the money on candy for her children instead of snuff for herself. Our mother was one wonderful person.

That same year I was playing in the yard one day and I looked across the road and saw stacks and stacks of lumber down near the store. Those stacks were seven feet high. My, did they look inviting. I hurried over to them and started climbing. I was way up high. I could see for a long way. This was fun, feeling the breeze blowing in my face.

It was one of the Barham girls that had to go and spoil my fun. She started running across her yard and the highway toward where I was. I couldn't figure out what she wanted. When she came to where I was, she said, "Now you come down here this minute! You're not supposed to be up there!" I reluctantly climbed down, while she got under me and held her hands up toward me for some reason. Later on, she told everybody that she was scared to death that I was going to fall and hurt myself.

"These grownups sure do know how to take away all the fun," I thought.

In Grady's house, five-year-old Jerry liked to stand against the wall behind the cook stove in the wintertime while Mom cooked breakfast. It became his favorite place. He would stand there with his back against the wall and his hands in his overalls above where the pockets were. His hands would be next to his belly. One morning when he went around the stove, he almost put his bare foot on a large black snake that was coiled up back there. It was in the exact place where he usually stood. He let out a shriek that could be heard all over Caglesville.

Mom ran into the kitchen from the living room to see what all the fuss was about. She was as scared as Jerry was of the snake. She didn't know that it wasn't poisonous. She just didn't want a snake in her kitchen and certainly not one so large. While she was gone to get a chopping hoe to try to kill it, the snake made its escape down the rat hole in which it had come in. Mom was very happy to see that it was gone when she got back. The last thing she wanted was a large dead snake in her kitchen. She wadded up an empty flour sack and put it into the rat hole to keep it from returning. She would have Dad nail a board over the hole as soon as he got in from work.

Chapter 34

THE NEW HOUSE

Dad and the two carpenters, John and Rayvelle Hemmer, started work on the new house in 1942. They chose a location one-fourth mile east of the house that burned. It was on Highway 105.

John was Mom's first cousin on her father's side. His mother was Grandpa Maxwell's sister. John had built Grandpa and Grandma's house twenty-six years before, so he had plenty of experience.

Dad hauled rocks from the chimney of the house that burned to use for the foundation of the new house, which was to be 54 feet long and 32 feet wide. He also hauled rocks from the mountain. The house would have a porch across the front and a screened in back porch. There would be three large bedrooms, a large living room, and a kitchen and dining room. The house wouldn't have electricity, so they couldn't put a bathroom in, nor a kitchen sink. Those would have to wait for a few years. As the house slowly went up, Mom often took us kids and walked the one-fourth mile to the site.

Mom would envision what the finished house would look like. She had waited fourteen long years for a new one. Betty had often heard her crying and saying, "We will never get a new house."

Later on, Betty said, "Maybe God heard her cries. Maybe he was the cause of our old house burning down."

Whatever the reason, it did get Dad on the move toward building a new one. It took a few months for the house to be completed. It didn't seem like they would ever be finished. The carpenters didn't have power tools like builders would have later. The house was painted a beautiful white just like the Maxwell house.

A beautiful green asphalt roof was put on. Dad said he had the carpenters use so many nails in the house that he thought it would roll before it would be torn apart by a storm. We had a large front yard and a large back yard, which would be used many-many times by us kids, playing basketball, baseball, croquet, horseshoes, and many other games.

The opening underneath the floor was just right for us small boys to go through and play there. We used short pieces of wood left by the carpenters as cars and trucks. Dad dug a hole underneath the floor to store potatoes. It was an ideal place for them. It was cool and dark. Mom often sent us kids under there for potatoes she would use in cooking. The attic was also a good place for us to play. There wasn't a light but enough light came in from different places for us to see enough to get around.

Before the house was built, Uncle Earl advised Mom to have a hall in the house. She thought he meant a breezeway between two parts of the house like her Grandpa and Grandma Duvall had and she said she didn't want one. Mom had many regrets about not understanding what Uncle Earl meant. They could have easily corrected their mistake, but they never did. After Mom and Dad were dead, Betty remodeled the house and she had the problem corrected.

All of us thought we had died and gone to heaven when we moved into our new home. Now that Dad and Mom are gone, I realize how hard Dad and Uncle Leonard worked to make that new house a reality, and how hard Mom worked to keep the household, with all of us kids, going.

Bobbye's children: Susan, Tim and Tracy, picking Jonquils in the yard of the house that burned.

The house didn't have a well yet, and it wouldn't for a while, so we had to carry water from a well one-fourth mile away on Mrs. Barham's property. There had been a house there in past years, but it was long gone when our new house was built. The well there had much better and much more drinking water than the one at our old house, so we elected to use it. When Mom told one of us to go get a bucket of water, it was quite a chore getting and carrying it back.

Chapter 35

THE OUT BUILDINGS

Dad was always doing something. He had built a two-holed privy before we moved into the new house. That was a dire necessity.

As soon as we moved in, he built a "smoke house". It wasn't really a smoke house, because we never did smoke anything in it, but that's what we called it anyway. It was really just a storage building. Through the years it was used for keeping the meat, the cream separator, empty fruit jars, and many other items. Its dimensions were ten by twelve feet.

Then he built a shed onto the south side. The meat stored in the "smoke house" didn't spoil, even in the summer, because he used "sugar cure" on it. The "sugar cure" had a lot of salt in it, so it did the job, just like salt did back in the old days.

Grandpa Maxwell came and helped him with the car shed. They placed it on one side of the house, and it was just big enough for one car or pickup. Then he started on the chicken house. A chicken house and yard were a must for our family. The chickens would provide eggs to eat, and for Mom to use in her cooking. There would also be some to sell to merchants in town, and to the Barham Grocery.

He put the chicken house one hundred feet south of our house. He built half of it into a room for the hens to roost in at night in order to shut them up so the varmints couldn't get them, and half into a room filled with nests for them to lay in. He made the nests out of lumber he sawed and hay was placed in each one, so the eggs would have soft landings when the hens had laid. There was a small opening between the roosting and nesting areas, so the chickens could walk back and forth between them. In the roosting area, he placed strips of wood a few feet off the ground for them to sit on at night. He made the windows in both sections of the chicken house, so light could shine in, but instead of using glass he put chicken wire over the openings. This would keep the varmints out. Before we children were grown, we had quite a few visits from varmints at night. Varmints have to eat too.

From the large sawdust pile in the woods, he hauled several loads of sawdust and spread it around on the chicken house floor, so the chickens didn't have to walk or sit on the cold ground in the winter.

Then he built a chicken yard, using six-foot-high chicken wire. The yard was forty feet square. The wire was supposed to be high enough to keep the chickens from flying out, but sometimes one did, and someone would have to take a pair of scissors and clip one of its wings. Then it couldn't fly at all until the wing's feathers grew back.

Mom ordered baby chicks from a Sears-Roebuck catalog, but when they came through the mail, most of them were dead. In spite of all she and Dad could do, the rest of them died. They bought some chickens somewhere, and it wasn't many more months before they started getting eggs, only a few at first, but every day there were more. Since the hens were of different breeds, some of the eggs were white and some of them were brown.

Dad brought home a rooster one day. He said he had solved the problem of getting baby chicks. What he meant was that the rooster would solve it for him. That rooster was a beautiful specimen. It had orange and green feathers, which made it the "Cock of the Walk". Anyone who was still in bed by the time daylight came was awakened by his crowing.

But there was one problem with the rooster. He was a flogger. When Dad built the privy and later the chicken house, he hadn't counted on a flogging rooster. He had gone off to work somewhere, and he didn't know about the rooster's vice until hearing about it from Mom's letter she wrote.

The chicken fence had developed a hole in it somewhere and that rooster had found it. Or maybe, he made it himself. We soon learned that he lurked around the corner of the privy occasionally, just waiting for an unsuspecting victim to come along, so he could jump upon his or her back. He especially liked to jump on the girls' backs. I guess he thought they were prettier than the boys were. If he had done his flogging regularly, he wouldn't have been kept around as long as he was.

Mom wrote Dad, "Boyd, we have to do something about that rooster."

When Dad had bought the rooster, he was very proud of it. He had seen some of his offspring, and he knew they were beautiful. He wrote Mom back and told her he wanted to keep the rooster if there was any way possible. He suggested that she have Uncle Leonard get some clubs for us to use on him when he tried to flog someone.

Uncle Leonard got some short boards from the stack that was left over from building the house and that rooster got his come-uppance. He started laying off us after he learned what those clubs could do to him. But after a while, Bobbye got complacent, and forgot to take a club when she visited the privy. She got flogged pretty badly that day.

When Mom saw how the rooster had torn her dress and how he had bloodied her back, she took the matter into her own hands. She had Uncle Leonard club him into submission and then wring his neck. He made some pretty good chicken and dumplings.

Dad didn't get to eat any. Then she wrote him a letter telling that his pet rooster was no more. Uncle Leonard found the hole where the rooster had been getting out and he patched it.

Mom always had one of us shut the chicken house door tightly at night to keep the possums, raccoons, minks, owls, hawks, and other creatures out. But one morning when Jerry went to get the eggs, a big black snake was curled up around one of the nests. He had been helping himself to our eggs throughout the night. Jerry ran back to the house and told Mom and Uncle Leonard. Our Uncle made short work of that snake. Uncle Leonard was a treasure. While Dad was away working, what would we have done without him?

We were getting more eggs than we could eat, and more than Mrs. Barham could sell, so Mom sent the extra ones to the Bill Price Grocery store in Russellville. After Dad returned from the wheat harvest, he took a bucketful to Mr. Price.

Mr. Price asked him, "Are they fresh?"

"Oh yeah," Dad declared. "They just came from the henhouse."

While the grocer was putting the eggs into the egg bin, one of them suddenly exploded, right into Mr. Price's face!

Dad was embarrassed to death. He had just been caught in a big lie, and he had always prided himself for being a very honest person. He knew what had happened— whichever one of the kids had been gathering the eggs had overlooked that egg in the nest, and he had continued to overlook it so long that it had become old and rotten.

Mr. Price reached into his pocket, brought out a handkerchief, and wiped the rotten egg from his face. Then he proceeded to place the rest of the eggs in the bin. He did all of this without saying a word. Dad bought a lot of groceries from him. Apparently Mr. Price didn't want to lose his business.

Dad was gone off somewhere, when early one morning before daylight, there was the most awful squawking I ever heard coming from the chicken house. We were between dogs, (That means we didn't have any.) so there wasn't any barking. It awakened everyone, and Mom yelled, "Jerry, you and Randall go out there and see what's going on."

Uncle Leonard was away somewhere. Where was he when we needed him? As usual, Jerry took the lead in running out to the chicken house, and I was right behind him. We were as scared as all get-out, not knowing if there was a panther or bear or what out there. He had lit a lantern, so we had a dim light to see by, but the shadows thrown out by that lantern were spooky to a small boy.

After reaching the chicken house, Jerry located a large possum skulking in a corner. It was baring its teeth like possums do and its teeth looked as sharp as daggers. I wouldn't have wanted to try to pet a possum, at least not a wild one. It had killed one of our prize hens.

Jerry grabbed it by its tail and carried it outside. We hadn't brought a gun with us, but he found a club about as big as a baseball bat, and after many tries, he broke the possum's neck. If I hadn't seen the hen it had killed, I would have felt sorry for it. But if Jerry hadn't stopped it, there is no telling how many chickens it might have killed. Probably not that night, but it would have been back many other nights.

There were other nights when varmints got into the chicken house and took chickens without being caught. They could dig under one of the outer walls. Jerry set a steel trap in there once, and one of our cousin Raymond Gray's prize foxhounds got his foot caught in it.

Jerry hadn't secured the trap well enough, and the dog dragged it home. Raymond wasn't very happy about that. The hound's foot did get well after a while. The door of the chicken house must have been left open, because the dog couldn't have crawled through a small hole under a wall.

Chapter 36

UNCLE BEN'S TRUCK

Uncle Ben and Aunt Nora still lived on the Iron Ore, but they were talking about buying some land off the mountain. One day he and Raymond were traveling up the Iron Ore, and they overtook two women walking in the direction they were going.

Uncle Ben asked them if they wanted a ride and they gladly accepted. The truck had an old flat bed and the women sat on the very back. But when the truck was climbing the steepest part of the mountain, it died. Since they didn't have any brakes, the truck started rolling backwards. After they had gone down the road a ways, Uncle Ben backed into a bank to stop it. When the truck stopped, the two women were thrown out. They weren't hurt much, just bruised up, but they were badly frightened.

He told them he would have to back the truck down the mountain to where the road was more level, so he could get a running start to climb the steep part. The two women started walking up the mountain.

After he backed down to the level part, he gunned the truck, and it made it over the steep part. He and Raymond soon overtook the women. Uncle Ben asked them if they wanted to ride with them again. They said, "No thanks. We had rather walk."

Another time he gave a lift to a stranger going up the mountain and he asked him where he was going. The man said he was going to a sawmill on the mountain to try to get a job.

"Where do you want to get off?" he asked the man.

"Oh, about where Ben Gray lives," he said.

When Uncle Ben saw that the man didn't know him, he decided to have a little fun. He said, "That Ben Gray is pretty sorry, isn't he?"

"That's what I always heard," the man answered.

Uncle Ben made a few other comments running down Ben Gray and after each comment, the man said, "That's what I always heard."

Just before they reached Uncle Ben's house, the man asked, "What's your name?"

"Ben Gray."

The man's face turned very red, but he was a quick thinker. "You were the cause of that," he said.

A minute later, they pulled into Uncle Ben's driveway and the man jumped out and hurried away from him as fast as he could walk.

Once Uncle Ben had a wreck between his house and Russellville. One of the fenders on his truck was dented pretty badly. The man who ran into him begged him not to call the law. He said, "If you won't, I'll pay for having your truck fixed."

Since it was too late in the day for them to go to a body shop, the man promised that he would meet him at a certain shop the next day. Uncle Ben said, "Okay, but you'd better be there."

He made a special trip to Russellville the following morning and he arrived at the body shop at the appointed hour they were supposed to meet. The man was nowhere to be seen. Uncle Ben found out where he lived and he drove to his house. The man was there, but he said he didn't have any money to fix any truck.

Uncle Ben knew then that he had made a mistake in trusting the guy. The law wouldn't do a cotton-picking thing to help him get his truck fixed, since both trucks had been moved from the accident site without a policeman giving a report on it. He fumed about letting the man snooker him. He would remember that face. He wasn't used to anyone getting the best of him. He thought to himself, "This isn't over yet."

Sometime after that, he was in town, and he met the man walking down the sidewalk toward him. There weren't any people around and he saw his chance. As soon as the two met, he pulled his pocketknife out of his pocket and opened it. He told the man, "Give me your billfold!"

The man was frightened. He had never had a knife pulled on him before. He quickly gave Uncle Ben his billfold. When Uncle Ben opened it, he found a few dollars. He took them, gave the man back his billfold, and went on his way. He didn't get enough money to pay for repairing his truck, but he did get a measure of satisfaction in knowing he had gotten a little revenge on the man.

Chapter 37

NORTH DAKOTA

Dad went to the wheat harvest in North Dakota twice in the mid-forties. Mom, Uncle Leonard and the girls worked hard milking the cows and doing the household work and other chores while he was gone.

The first time Dad went to North Dakota, his way was paid, but he had to sign a paper saying he would stay for at least thirty days. Several neighbors signed up to go also, including Orel Reed, who was married to Mom's cousin, and Dolphis Craig from Moreland. Two or three hours after they left for the first time, Orel's wife, Grace, sent one of her girls to our house to tell Mom our horses and mules had gotten into their pasture.

Uncle Leonard had to take the fence down more than it already was. With the help of Mom and Grace and their older children, they were able to get them back into our pasture. It was quite a job separating them from the Reed horses and mules. They wanted to visit with our animals. After a long time they were finally separated and ours were driven back home. Uncle Leonard then had to put the fence back up.

The men caught a train in Russellville to go to North Dakota. Although the train ran day and night, it took two days to make the trip, because it was slow, and it stopped in every little town. Once a black couple boarded the train and there was only one seat available for them and it was next to Dad.

The man asked, "Would you mind if my wife sat there beside you?"

"No," Dad said. "And I will sit on my footlocker and you can sit here where I'm sitting."

In North Dakota, Dad was staying with a family named Merrick. Their daughter, Myrna, was Betty's age. She and Betty became pen pals. They wrote each other for a long time but they never met. Dad lived in a little building behind their house, but he ate with the family. He said Mrs. Merrick always kept a large picture of a snow scene in the living room in the summer, and she kept a large picture of a summer scene in the winter.

"Mrs. Merrick was pretty clever," he recollected. When a person said something, she often reversed it. One day while they were eating, he said, "I am too light for heavy work."

She added, "And too heavy for light work?"

The combine had not yet been invented and as the reaper cut and tied the wheat, the workers had to stack it on trailers, which were pulled by horses or mules. It was then taken to a thrasher, where the wheat grain was separated from the straw. It was hard work, but the employers treated them well. Besides the three large meals a day they were fed, the women brought them a snack at mid-morning and again at mid-afternoon. They took breaks while they ate. The animals also got a rest, which they needed.

Apparently the Merricks liked Dad's work. They wanted him back the next year and he went.

The second year Dad didn't come back after the wheat harvest. A storm had occurred in the county where he was and thirty-six large barns had been destroyed. He worked during the fall helping rebuild some of them.

Uncle Leonard and Mom were responsible for getting the corn gathered and the cotton picked in Arkansas. They hired some help picking it, and when they had enough for a 500 pound bale of lint, they hired someone with a truck to take it to the nearest gin. But they still used the mules to pull the wagon up the mountain and into the cotton field.

Years later, in the 1960's, the Merricks visited Dad in Arkansas. They had been to Florida and stopped by on their way back home to North Dakota.

Donald married a woman from that area, and in the nineteen seventies they visited the very house of the people where Dad used to work. They showed him the little house Dad stayed in while he was there.

In 1987, when he was seventy-four years old, Uncle Sewood got a hankering to visit North Dakota again, to where he had worked back in the nineteen thirties.

He and Aunt Lillian told me that if my wife and I would go with them, they would pay all our expenses. I told him we would go, but only if we shared expenses. They agreed.

On the way there we enjoyed our conversations. We drove through Missouri, Nebraska, and South Dakota going north. We also visited Canada for a few hours. We stopped at historic markers until everyone but me grew tired of them. When we reached where Uncle Sewood had lived in a little town, he was surprised that there was only one house left where there had been enough of a village to have a post office when he worked there. He wondered why he had received the letters back that he sent to the post office.

Uncle Sewood's belt had a large buckle which had, "Praise the Lord" on it. I teased him about belonging to the "PTL" club, a religious organization led by Jim Baker, the television host who had recently been put in prison for defrauding investors.

Uncle Sewood had a good sense of humor, and he started telling people at places where we stopped for food, gas, or to use the restrooms, that he was making up money for Jim Baker. He would show them his belt buckle.

Everyone he talked to got a good laugh out of his joke, because they knew that was what it was. One well-dressed man in Jasper said to him, "I have this side of the street covered. You will have to get on the other side."

In the house where he used to live, a lady resided who knew some of the folks Uncle Sewood had worked for. I took his picture at the house, and I took his picture in front of the big red barn he had helped build when he was there.

On our return trip back to Arkansas, we came down through Minnesota, Iowa, and Missouri. We ran out of gas as we skirted Kansas City and I had to walk a mile to get some. The first house I came to, a man gladly took me to get some gas and then he took me back to the car.

I was very appreciative for him doing that. Uncle Sewood and Aunt Lillian's car's gas gauge wasn't working. They had warned me before leaving on the trip, but I got complacent and forgot about it.

We could tell that Uncle Sewood was beginning to get a little feeble. He had gone down in health in the last few months. That was why Aunt Lillian had wanted us to travel north with them. He had wanted to drive himself. The next summer I was working in the back yard and Sissie called out the back door that Uncle Sewood had suffered a heart attack and died. He was "One Fine Uncle". Ricky, my youngest brother, and I were pall bearers at his funeral.

Chapter 38

RAMBLING

I'm going to do some rambling now. These stories are so short that I can't have an entire chapter about each one, but the people who told them to me wanted me to use them, so here goes.

Dad built another storm cellar at the edge of their back yard soon after the move off the mountain, and the children loved to play in it. It was built exactly the way the one on the mountain was, which was a dugout in the bank of the road that passed the house until 1929, when the new highway was built.

Sometimes when storm clouds gathered, the family would go in and close the door. The children were always afraid of being blown away and afraid their house might be blown away too. Sometimes when they didn't go into the cellar, Betty would cover her head with bedclothes so she couldn't hear the thunder and lightning.

A man who lived in Appleton started driving a truck to Russellville and back on certain days and he let people ride with him for a fee. The truck was much better than using a wagon and horses or mules, so the days of the horse and buggy were coming to an end. Farmers did still use them locally.

One day Dad took Betty to Russellville on the truck. The bed of the truck was crowded with people, as was the cab. When they reached town, the truck parked on the north side and everyone went their separate ways. They had to be back at the truck by a certain time to go home.

Dad bought a watermelon and burst it open. He and Betty sat outside on the ground and ate it. At noon he took her into a little café and bought them some chili and crackers to eat. Betty thought the chili and the watermelon were both delicious.

Another time Grandpa Maxwell took Betty and Bobbye to Atkins in his car. Betty saw some kids with black faces for the first time. She asked her grandpa why those people painted their faces with shoe polish. He laughed, but he did not explain why the people were black.

In the fall, Mom and the kids who were old enough would sometimes sit under the hickory tree, lay a hickory nut on a rock and crack it open with a smaller rock, then pick the meat out with a horseshoe nail. The nuts were good, but it was hard to get the meat out. One day Bobbye and Betty were there by themselves and they decided to put the hickory nuts on the large flat rock the family used for the back doorstep. The rock was perfect for the job, but after they finished, they forgot to clean it off.

Not long afterwards, Dad opened the back door and headed toward the well with the well bucket. He was barefoot. If the girls had been there, they would have yelled, "No Daddy, no! Don't step on the hickory nut shells!"

But unfortunately they were not there, so Dad stepped on the sharp hickory nut shells and let out a cry like a banshee. He always was one to show his emotions. "Who put these hickory nut shells on the doorstep?" he yelled. No one confessed. The girls weren't as honest as George Washington was when he chopped down the cherry tree. They were too much afraid of what the consequences would be.

Uncle Ben was pretty comical, as all of Dad's brothers were. Once when I was helping Jerry drive the cows from our east pasture to the barn, he was coming off the mountain and we happened to be there at the same time he was. He asked who my girl was. I told him I didn't have one.

He said, "Anyone who doesn't have a girl will have to go to the war."

At that time, World War II was in full swing, and I had heard many horror stories about what was happening in Europe, so I said, "Mama is my girl." He didn't have a response for that, but he did have a good laugh.

Uncle Ben and Aunt Nora's daughter, Irene, had married Otto Hudson and they had a little boy born in 1939, the same year I was born.

They named him Jimmy. I was only two months older than he was. When he was three years old, one day he was playing outside with his little wagon. Irene was working in the house and she heated some water and set it down on the floor. She was going to scrub the floor.

In the meantime, Otto came in from working outside, and his hands were covered with grease. He called Irene to come into the kitchen and pour some soap onto his hands so he could wash them. She went in where he was and about that time Jimmy entered the house where she had been. He was walking backwards while pulling his wagon, and he sat down in the scalding water. They rushed him to the hospital as fast as they could and he seemed to be doing pretty well. He had been there for several days and he was laughing and talking. Then three days later he died. It almost killed Otto and Irene and I lost a playmate. They moved to the house one-fourth mile south of us not long after that.

I often climbed the Iron Ore with different members of our family, sometimes up the path and sometimes around the road. Most of the time when we went around the road, it was either on a horse or in the wagon.

One morning when Bobbye, Betty, and Jerry were at school, Mom discovered that Dad had forgotten to take his lunch with him as he went on the mountain to plow. She sent me up there along the path through the woods. I walked along the same path that hundreds of people had traveled for many years.

Our black dog was with me. He was a medium-sized dog, weighing between twenty and thirty pounds. He wasn't as big as a wolf though, and Dad had spotted a wolf (we later learned it was a coyote) not long ago on the mountain. I thought about that as I walked up the mountain. I had a case knife in my pocket. I got it out and carried it in my hand so I could open it at a moment's notice, if necessary.

As I look back to that time, it seems incredible that a four-year-old boy was allowed to have a knife, but in those days a pocket knife was standard equipment for boys of all ages. We were allowed to take them to school and anywhere else.

We played mumble-peg at recess. But that was before boys started pulling knives on each other. One boy got his teacher down and held a knife to his throat. Another pulled a knife on a classmate when they had an argument. So knives were eventually banned from school.

Dad was working near where the dog and I came out at the top of the mountain, where the path led between two large rocks. He said he saw the dog come out first and he knew that someone else would be coming into view. But he couldn't imagine who it might be. Then I popped out into the field. He was glad to get his lunch. I stayed with him until he quit for the day. As we came off the mountain around the road, I rode on the back of one of the horses. Dad drove them and walked behind. I felt like I was grownup as we came down the mountain.

A few weeks after that, Dad, Uncle Leonard, the girls, and Jerry were on the mountain working, when I decided to go up there where they were and come back with them. I left the house without telling Mom. She was busy with the baby Donald and the housework. I followed the same path I had before. This time the dog didn't go with me. When I reached the mountain top, no one was there. I couldn't figure out where they were.

I walked the half-mile north to where Uncle Ben's house was. He and Aunt Nora had moved off the mountain, but his daughter, Corene, and her husband, Cleo Mackey, now lived there. Cleo came to the front door when I knocked, and he told me Dad and everyone else had already gone off the mountain by the road. I followed the road on the way home, since I was already where it started down the mountain.

On that trip up the mountain and back, I walked five miles, with over a mile being steep terrain. Mom wasn't very happy with me when I reached home. She gave me a good scolding, and she made me promise that I would never again go anywhere without telling someone. Dad didn't say anything. He was probably remembering back when he was a boy and had all kinds of adventures. I'm sure he had lots of them, as much energy as he had.

It didn't take long to forget that promise. The next fall during hunting season, I was playing outside one afternoon, when I heard some dogs barking on the side of the mountain on Sewell Ford's land. The hounds had a squirrel treed about one-half mile from the house. I was drawn to them the same way the rats in Hamelin were drawn to the Pied Piper. I headed across the field and up through the woods as fast as I could walk. Before I reached whoever the hunters were, the echo of an ax started sounding. They were chopping down a tree.

A few minutes later, I reached them, and it was Uncle Ben and his sons, Raymond and John. As soon as the tree started falling, Raymond grabbed his twenty-two caliber rifle and readied to shoot whatever jumped from the tree. Seconds later, a Red squirrel sailed through the air—plump, it sounded as it hit the ground. Without any hesitation, it darted up the hillside. Raymond's gun sounded, and the squirrel tumbled end over end, and then lay still. Raymond had hit it dead center with the squirrel running as fast as it could go. That kind of shooting made a very strong impression on a four-year-old boy. Uncle Ben didn't scold me at all, but he told me I had better get back down to the house before my folks came looking for me.

Dad and Mom were of the Free Will Baptist faith, and Oak Grove, a Free Will Baptist church, didn't have enough deacons. The deacons there asked Dad if he would come to their church once a month and be a deacon. He agreed to be, even though he and Mom hated to miss church at Caglesville. So we now had two churches, and both of them had revivals each summer. When Dad wasn't off somewhere working, we would be going to both of them, since the revivals were at different times.

Jerry became good friends with a boy named J.C. Kinder at Oak Grove. They became very good buddies. J.C. started going to Caglesville some Sundays. He had a little Shetland pony named Betty, which he rode to our house one day. He only lived a mile and a half from us. He and Jerry were in our front yard talking, and I walked outside and was petting "Old Betty". He asked me if I wanted to ride her. Of course I said, "Yes."

He lifted me onto her. Then he said, "Now flank her."

"How do I flank her?" I asked.

Jerry said, "You just kick her in the sides with both feet."

So I kicked her in the sides with both feet. She didn't like that. The next thing I knew, I was flying through the air. After going about two feet above her, I landed on some bricks that had been left there when the flues of our house had been built. My elbows and knees took the brunt of the blows as I hit those bricks, but the rest of my body got their share too. My knees and elbows were both bare. I went back into the house. They say that experience is the best teacher, but that was ridiculous. In the years ahead, Jerry gave Donald and me some learning experiences, some of them pretty bad, but I won't tell about them.

Along about then, a man named Arley Crow moved into the house on the Little Mountain north of Sewell Ford's. He had a little girl named Christine that I liked. She was the same age as me. They visited our house a few times and I played with her. Arley worked in the timber, cutting logs with Dad and Uncle Leonard at times. One day when Arley came walking up to our house, he had a large sack on his back. I said, "I'll bet he has Christine in that sack."

Arley and Uncle Leonard were cutting logs for Tom Kinslow one day. Tom became annoyed with Arley for some reason and he told Arley that he wasn't going to pay him. Arley said, "You are going to pay me too!"

Tom said, "No, I'm not. You can't get blood out of a turnip."

"No, but you can stomp hell out of the greens," Arley answered.

Arley got his money. Soon after that, he moved his family from the Iron Ore to some place in the Ozarks above Hector and we never saw them again. Twenty years later, we heard that Arley had died from a brain tumor. A few years after that, J.M. Bewley, who worked for the forest service, reported that he had seen Christine working in a store way back in the mountains. I wish I had traveled up there to see her.

We raised Irish potatoes to sell some years, and one day when we were digging them, six-year old Donald came to the potato field. I told him to climb the Walnut tree close by and tell Jerry he was crazy. Mom didn't like for us to use that word, but we did anyway. Donald did as he was told, but when he reached near the top of the tree and was about to tell Jerry that he was crazy, he lost his grip on the limb he was on and he started falling. Dad was in another part of the potato field and didn't see Donald climb the tree. Neither did any of our other brothers and sisters.

Dad said, "I heard him crashing down through that tree and he was trying to catch hold of every limb he passed, but he couldn't grip them enough to stop his fall. Then he caught onto one when he was about seven feet from the ground. I ran over to where he was and I reached up as far as I could and told him to drop and I would catch him. But he was too scared to let go. I didn't think I was ever going to talk him into letting go of the limb, but after he became so tired that he couldn't hold on any longer, he fell and I caught him."

Cousins June and Doyle were at our house one day, and we decided to go down to the "Big Tree" to play. It was a huge Catalpa tree north of our house on Mrs. Barham's land. It had three trunks about fifty feet tall and they were great for climbing. We played in it for awhile before we became bored. Then someone suggested that we get thorns from a large Honey Locust tree and make roadblocks across Highway 105.

I didn't like the idea, fearing that we would get into trouble, but the others did like it and they placed thorns on the road from one side to the other. We hid behind trees and waited for a car to come along. Since the road was gravel, cars and trucks only traveled at about thirty miles an hour.

When one finally came along, the driver saw the thorns and stopped. Then he went around them. After a few more cars passed by, and all of them did the same way, I finally convinced the other kids to remove the thorns. Dad would have tanned our hides if he had known about what we had done. I would have been punished too, because I was guilty by association.

In 1947 Arkansas had an outbreak of polio. Everyone was literally scared to death because of it. One morning Mom came into our bedrooms and told us our next door neighbor, eight-year-old June Byrum, had died of polio during the night. Her family lived in the little house where we had lived the year after our house burned! I was eight years old, the same as she was.

What a shock! We had been riding the school bus with her every day as we went to school. She was in the third grade, one grade behind me. Only a few days before, she had come up the road from her house and told Jerry and me to stop throwing rocks toward their house. Her mother had sent her. They didn't know it, but Jerry and I were not throwing rocks at their house—we were throwing them at each other. Every time we had a dispute, rocks were our ammunition.

Another girl at Hector School died of polio. She was a grade ahead of me.

How thankful I am for the vaccine Doctor Salk found for the polio virus. That dreaded disease affected so many people's lives, including Uncle Leonard's.

We had a surprise on November 22, 1947. Dad took us boys to Uncle Ben's house to spend the night. We thought we were getting a rare treat. The next morning Aunt Nora woke us and told us we had a new brother. I couldn't believe it. I knew Mom had been missing church, so I found out the reason.

At school the next day, one of the girls in my class announced that I had a new brother. He was born on November 22, the same day that President John Kennedy would be killed sixteen years later. With all the brothers and sisters he had, he would get spoiled in the years ahead, but he turned out pretty well. They named him Ricky, after the Ricky on "Ricky, Rebel, and Champ" on the radio. His middle name was Boyd, like Dad's first name.

Charley Foster, the man who had caused Sewell Ford to attack Lawrence Biffle, (in a later chapter) became lost in the woods above Hector. He had moved up there to live with his son. He was becoming senile.

Uncle Ben and two other men found him with his feet in a frozen creek. They took him to the hospital in Russellville, where he caught pneumonia and died. Dad and Uncle Leonard lost a good friend.

Jerry, Donald, and I often spent the night at Uncle Ben's house, and his younger children, John, Doyle, and June often spent the night at our house. John was a year older than Jerry, and June was almost a year older than I was. Doyle was a year younger than Donald.

Chapter 39

THE LUMBER HAULER

We had beef cattle on the Iron Ore, and Uncle Leonard and Jerry had the chore of walking up there and checking on them once in a while. They went up there one day and the cattle were out of the pasture. Uncle Leonard tracked them along the road leading off the mountain to the east. The barbed-wire gate had been left open by a lumber hauler.

He was bringing lumber from a sawmill on the other side of the low gap, a bench of the Iron Ore. Uncle Leonard and Jerry found the cattle down in the cove, where Dad used to pasture his milk cows when he and Mom lived up there, and they drove them back up the road and into their pasture. Then Uncle Leonard closed the gate.

The next day, he and Jerry walked up there. The cattle were not in the pasture. The gate had been left open again. They found the cattle and herded them back, and once more closed the gate. About that time, they heard a truck coming toward them from the direction of the sawmill. They hid in the bushes several yards from the road and they watched as the lumber truck approached.

When the driver came to the gate, he didn't even stop. He drove right through the gate, leaving barb wire strung along the road for a hundred feet. They collected the wire and put the gate back together. It took them awhile to do the job, and they were in a pretty bad mood as they walked off the mountain and related the day's events to Mom.

I was excited as I heard Uncle Leonard and Mom discussing what had happened, and what they were going to do about it. I heard Uncle Leonard say he was going to take Dad's twenty-two rifle and wait on the driver to come by and then shoot over the cab of his truck. Mom decided to solve their problem in a more diplomatic way. She found out the truck driver's name, which to her surprise, happened to be one of her former students when she had taught school at Oak Grove nineteen years before.

She wrote him a letter and explained how it caused her family problems when he left the gate open. She also added that she remembered him in school and that he was a good boy then and she knew he would want to do the right thing about the gate. Uncle Leonard and Jerry kept a close eye on the gate for a few days and the lumber hauler never left it open again.

Chapter 40

I START SCHOOL

In 1944 I started to school. I was very excited about getting to go with the older kids, as I had always wanted to be with them. I had hoed cotton with them that summer—a year before Dad usually made us start. I wouldn't take a row of cotton by myself—I would go ahead of the others and hoe on different ones' rows. Dad was surprised that I went with the others until all the cotton was hoed.

Miss Keener was my teacher. She was a very pretty woman about twenty-four years old. June, my frequent playmate and cousin was in the same room. So were two other cousins, Patrick Marable and Opal Reed. Carolyn Barham and Peggy Eakin, who went to church at Caglesville with us, were also in our grade. We liked Miss Keener, but she didn't put up with a lot of nonsense or playing around when we were supposed to be learning.

All the rooms in the elementary school burned wood. There was a stack of wood behind the school that covered nearly as much ground as the school house. We sometimes played back there. Some of the boys liked to find beetles in the wood and scare the girls with them. The janitor would come around ever so often and refill the heating stoves. We would watch him as he silently went about his work.

The lunchroom was a long building, shaped like an old-time dwelling house, one that they called a shotgun house. It was a lot bigger, of course. Bobbye and Betty were old enough now that they could work there a little while each day to pay for their lunches. Behind the lunchroom was a pig pen, where scraps of food were taken. We would sometimes watch the pigs as they ate.

The elementary school didn't have indoor restrooms, even though it had electricity. A hundred yards or so from the school were two privies, one for the boys and one for the girls. There wasn't any way to wash our hands after using the privies. If anyone needed to go to the privy during class, all we had to do was raise our hands and we would be permitted to go. Classes started at 9:15 and had a fifteen minute recess halfway between then and 12 o'clock. We got an hour off for lunch and had an afternoon recess, so very few children needed to go during class. School let out at 3:15.

The school house was a large white building with two stories. Three rooms were downstairs and three upstairs. The playground was huge. The school building was almost in the middle, so we could play all around it. That was before they had playground monitors, so we could fight and carouse all we wanted. The playground had a few swings, a slide, and some seesaws. It had two basketball goals and a little area to play baseball.   One of the boys' favorite pastimes was playing marbles. We always had a few in our pockets. We played so that any marble was ours to keep if we knocked it out of the ring, or, we could give the marbles back to their owner.

Mom told us not to play for keeps, but it was very tempting to play that way, especially when I was a better shooter than whoever I was playing with. Sometimes I played for keeps when Jerry wasn't around to see me. He would always tell Mom.

Once Miss Keener gave us some pictures to color and then stepped out of the room for a few minutes. I had my pockets full of peanuts I brought from home. Dad always grew a small field of peanuts. I had to be a big shot and I showed them to the other boys at my table. John Coyd Garrigus asked me if he could have some. I said, "No, these are for me to eat."

He said, "If you don't give us some, I will tell the teacher on you when she comes back."

I didn't think I had any choice but to give them some. By the time every boy at my table had helped themselves, I had none left. Those boys made quick work of my peanuts, and guess where the hulls ended up? They threw them right on the floor. A few minutes later, when Miss Keener returned to the room, she didn't have to be a detective to know what had happened.

"Okay," she said. "Clean up this mess at once. And while you're at it, I'm going to make some signs for all of you to wear the rest of the day."

I wondered what kind of signs she was talking about. But soon I found out. She already had some poster board cutouts. They were three inches wide and eighteen inches long. In a very few minutes she had written on them, "I ATE PEANUTS IN TIME OF BOOKS." She pinned a sign on the back of each of us boys. I could hear some of the other students giggling, but they stopped when Miss Keener warned them, "Okay, for those of you that giggle, I'm going to pin one of these signs on you, and you can wear it the rest of the day, just like these boys."

That stopped the giggling. But it didn't stop the looks we got, or the smiles. It was back to work for us, and in about fifteen minutes the bell rang for recess. "Are you going to take these off until recess is over?" one boy asked.

"No, you go ahead and wear them on the playground, and you watch how you play. Anyone who loses his sign will have to wear one for an extra day."

All the other boys with the signs on their backs gleefully hurried outside to show their friends from the other classrooms. But I hesitated. What would Mom say when she found out about me having to wear a sign? If I went outside Jerry would be sure to see it and I knew that he couldn't wait to get home and tell on me. I came up with a solution. I would put my coat on over the sign so no one could see it. Miss Keener was out of the room, so she wouldn't know the difference. I had my coat about halfway on when she came back into the room.

"Oh, so you want your coat on before you go outside? It is a little cold out there. Tell you what I'll do. I'll take the sign off your back and let you put your coat back on. Then I'll replace the sign on your back."

We did all that but it didn't solve my problem. I still didn't dare wear that sign outside. So I stayed right there in the room. I did that for the rest of the day. I didn't have to go to the lunchroom, because I had brought my lunch from home. Miss Keener never said a word to me about that. Jerry didn't rat on me either, so Mom never found out about that sign. Wearing those signs probably did me more good than a dozen paddlings. I sure didn't want to wear another one.

Miss Keener got married after that year and she became Mrs. Teeter. She quit teaching at Hector. She had taught there for two terms. I didn't see her again for many years. It wasn't until Dad died and she came for visitation. She did the same when my mother died. She said she wanted to see us again.

I helped get our fiftieth class reunion together at Hector High school in 2006, and I called Mrs. Teeter to see if she could come. I told her I would go get her if she didn't have any other way. Her daughter said she would bring her.

We had a good time that night. She was about eighty-eight years old. She said she still remembered those two years she spent at Hector. It had been sixty-two years ago that she had taught us. She was a good teacher and I learned a lot from her. She died two or three years later and I attended her funeral.

The forest ranger had a daughter who was in our class. The only thing I remember about her was she was pretty and liked horses. Once she rode her Shetland pony to school. They wouldn't let anyone do that now. Her father was transferred after we were in the second grade, and she didn't come back to school. When I graduated from Hector High, I attended Arkansas Tech for a half-semester and I was in a typing class with a Virginia Benson. She liked horses and she was really pretty. I thought that she must be the same girl. But I was shy and never asked her about the past. I'll always wish I had.

Nothing much happened in the second grade. One day during recess I went inside and laid my head on my desk. Miss Morgan, my teacher, came in and asked if I had a toothache. "No, my tooth is just hurting." I said. She laughed but she didn't tell me what a toothache was. She missed a chance to do a little teaching right then.

I was in a play that year. Each class had to put on a play at "Assembly" for the rest of the school. I got to play the prince in "Beauty and the Beast". Virginia played Beauty. I didn't get to kiss her though, at least not on the lips. Miss Morgan had me kiss her on the hand.

In the third grade, I got my first paddling. The school had installed water fountains in the rooms and all of us boys were lined up to get drinks. Our teacher, Miss Roberts, came in from outside, lined us all up and paddled us. She never told us why.

My Aunt Lillian, who Uncle Sewood had married, taught in Hector High and she told Mom that Miss Roberts said we had been stomping our feet. I hadn't been stomping mine, but she probably wanted to make sure she got the guilty ones. I will say this—I needed paddling at times when I didn't get them, so maybe it all evened out in the long run.

Mom had been a school teacher for a few years and she usually took the teacher's side in any controversy. She always said that if the students didn't like their teacher, that meant he or she was a good teacher. She also said that if we got a paddling at school, we would get another at home. She didn't keep her promise on that one though. She didn't give me another one. But as I rode home that day and dreaded to face her that was punishment for me. Jerry told on me, as usual.

We had a fire in our third grade flue that year, so we had a little excitement. But our janitor and Mr. Story, our principal, soon had it out. We waited outside while they extinguished it.

Jerry and John were two grades ahead of our class. John was a year older than Jerry, but he had deliberately failed so he could be in the same room as Jerry. One day the two of them got into trouble with the teacher and she took both of them into the cloakroom to give them paddlings. She paddled John first, while Jerry looked on. Then she started paddling Jerry while John watched. John started laughing, so she gave him another one.

In the fourth grade, we had another Miss Roberts, a sister to the third grade teacher. If anyone who came from the third grade was a trouble maker, she already knew about it from her sister.

I made it pretty well in her class. I only got one paddling that year. Several of us didn't have money to eat in the lunchroom, so we brought our lunch from home. We never had store bought bread at home unless the preacher was coming home with us, so we took biscuits to school. At lunch time we boys would eat in the classroom, while the girls would go into the cloakroom to eat. There were chairs to sit in while eating. The cloakroom didn't have a ceiling, since it had been built after the classroom.

One day, while we were eating, some boy threw a biscuit into the cloakroom where the girls were. The rest of us thought that was funny, so we did the same. The girls didn't think so and they eagerly awaited Mrs. Roberts to tattle on us.

After recess was over, Miss Roberts decided to make examples of us and one by one, she brought us to the front of the class and paddled us while the rest of the class looked on. Not a one of them laughed. They were afraid of what might happen to them. The paddling didn't hurt, since she used only a flat board. When we got a licking at home, it was with a switch. The embarrassment of having to bend over while the whole class watched was enough to make us not want another one. They don't let you give a paddling in front of the class these days. Most of the punishment now is "Time out".

Once Miss Roberts announced to the class that in a few days each one of her students would be required to get up in front of the class and sing a song by themselves. All the class sang together every morning, but sing a song by myself in front of the whole class? Heaven forbid! I couldn't do that! I had never sung a song by myself in my life! I didn't know what I was going to do. I asked Betty, who was in the ninth grade, to come to my rescue. She taught me a song called, "My mama told me if I'd be goody that she would buy me a rubber dolly. But someone told her I kissed a soldier. Now she won't buy me a rubber dolly".

I tried to get out of going to school that day by saying I was sick. Mom said I would be just as well off at school as I would be at home, so that didn't work.

Miss Roberts went by alphabetical order when she called on us to get up before the class. There were five ahead of Gray, three boys and two girls. All of them did a good job with their songs. Then it was Gray's time. Instead of calling on June first, she called on me. I had rather have been put in jail than go in front of the class that day.

After I started singing, before I finished with one line of my song, the students started laughing. I said, "You had better quit laughing!" When I said that, they laughed twice as loud. I don't remember if I ever got through with my song or not because my memory is blank on that, but I doubt it.

June was next. I had heard her sing, and she couldn't carry a tune. She wouldn't go to the front of the class. She put her head down on her desk and started crying. Miss Roberts didn't make her sing and I thought, "If I had known that crying would have gotten me off, I would have cried too."

While we were playing at recess one day, we heard a roar in the sky. Everyone started looking in the direction from which it was coming. As we listened, an airplane came soaring out of the western sky. And it was headed straight toward our school house.

It was a Tech plane. We called them that because the Russellville airport was by Arkansas Tech and every time we passed by the airport we could see the small planes. They were used for crop dusting more than anything else in the summer. As we watched, the plane came nearer to the school house. At the last minute the pilot raised the nose of the plane and missed the schoolhouse by a few feet. He landed in a field about a quarter of a mile east of the school.

All the boys on the playground ran toward where the plane had landed. The playground didn't have a fence around it and by the time the teachers had reacted, we were already gone. When we reached the beautiful red airplane, the pilot had gotten out. He said that he had run out of fuel, so he had to land. We boys couldn't resist touching the plane. Everyone gathered around it.

Then Mr. Story walked up. He was a big man with a great big nose and he was as mad as a hornet! He said, "You boys get right back to the school house!" I ought to whup every one of you!" He didn't though. I guess there were too many of us to whip. I notice that very few school playgrounds are without fences nowadays.

Someone brought a football to school one day and the boys started playing keep away. The boys were fifth and sixth graders, so I didn't get in on the action. I did like to watch. The boys would get on the ground trying to get the football. They would be spread out like the spokes of a wheel, as they fought for the ball. One day there was a boy on the ground I didn't like. He was Veo Condley, a friend of Jerry's. That's probably why I didn't like him. Jerry and I didn't get along very well. They were in the sixth grade.

All the boys on the ground were on their stomachs and I saw a great opportunity. I would give Veo a good swift kick in the seat of his pants with my heavy brogan work shoe, then I would fade into the crowd quickly, and he would never know who kicked him. There was always a crowd of smaller boys watching the ones on the ground.

My scheme went as planned at first. But there always seems to be a joker in every deck. I kicked Veo as hard as I could, then hurried into the crowd.

Veo jumped to his feet. "Who kicked me?" he demanded. Everyone started looking at me. I walked away as fast as I could.

Suddenly an older boy grabbed me. "Here he is, Veo!" he yelled. As he held me in his arms, I could see Veo coming at me—he looked like a giant, and I knew that I was in for it.

When Veo reached us, the boy told him, "He's all yours." as he pushed me to Veo.

Veo put one arm on my shoulder and said, "Let's you and I go for a little walk."

"I'm in big trouble," I thought. "He is going to take me somewhere and give me a good beating." I looked toward the school house. There wasn't a teacher in sight.

After the two of us were away from the crowd, Veo asked me why I had kicked him.

He wasn't as mad now as he had been and he didn't look so mean, so I began to think that there might be a way out of my predicament. "Veo, I didn't mean to kick you," I lied. I knew we were taught at home and church not to lie, but this was an emergency. "I thought you were Jerry. I'm mad at him for beating me up the other night. I sure do hope that I didn't hurt you too bad."

"How could you keep from hurting me by kicking me with those old heavy brogan shoes you're wearing?" he said. "And I'm still hurting. You had better not ever do that again. Do you hear me?"

"Oh, I won't, Veo. I promise you that," I told him, with a sigh of relief. He went back to the school house as the bell rang.

I decided that Veo had let me off because he was a friend of Jerry's. But the way I had it figured, Jerry might have helped him beat me up if he had been asked. Jerry wasn't very fond of me.

We had a good fifth grade year. Miss Pitts was our teacher. She was a little on the heavy side but we loved her. The thing I remember most about her was that she often read stories to us. I believe that was what caused me to start loving to read. I still remember one book she read to us. We started giving book reports that year and I gave mine on Robinson Crusoe.

One day Miss Pitts had to go to the second grade class for something and when she came back, she said there was a mean little boy there and that he had showed out. His name was Ronnie Griffin. Donald was in that class. There was also Ronnie's sister, Nancy. I don't remember exactly how Miss Pitts said he showed out and I don't remember anything about him at school after that, but I do remember Nancy.

Years later, Uncle Sewood's wife, my Aunt Lillian, said that Ronnie had been put back in the second grade from the third and he didn't like the fact that his sister made better grades than he did. Donald said that Ronnie's father was an artist and Ronnie sometimes brought his father's artwork to school.

Ronnie must have moved away after that because Donald said he was gone the next year. Forty-five years later, I was in the bank at Hector. A man named Larry Wells was in there, and he said, "They had a lot of excitement in Russellville today."

He proceeded to tell about a Ronald Gene Simmons going on a shooting spree. I didn't know until later that Ronald Gene Simmons was the one and only Ronnie Griffin we had known at Hector. The word got out that when he was going to school at Hector, he had gone by his stepfather's name and apparently had gone back to being Ronald Gene Simmons later.

As the drama unfolded that day and the next, we heard that he was gunning for everyone who he felt had hurt him in the past. One woman he killed had refused to date him even though he had a family and several children. Another victim of his, if I remember correctly, had fired him from a gas station job.

Before he killed the people in Russellville, he had killed his wife and all his children, their spouses, and their children. In all, he had killed sixteen people. He gave himself up at Russellville and said that he had killed everyone who had ever hurt him. But he even killed babies!

When asked why he hadn't killed himself, he replied that he was afraid he would bungle the job.

At his trial he was sentenced to death. He wanted to die, and he got his wish. He spent his last hours in a gas chamber.

In the sixth grade our principal was Mr. Story. He was married to Mom's third cousin, but back then we didn't pay much attention to that. He led singing in the mornings, and he would pretend to cry when he was singing about "Uncle Ned", a slave who had lost his teeth, his hair, and his eyesight before he died.

We loved Mr. Story. He was kind, but he was firm. Years after I was in his class, I read in the newspaper that when he was young, he had walked from Hector to Oak Grove to teach school. That was fifteen miles a day round trip. Maybe he couldn't afford a horse. They didn't pay teachers much in the old days.

One day two boys, Ronald Trigg and Donald Wooten, who sat together in a double desk, were giggling too much to suit Mr. Story. He walked back to where they were and told them to go to the front of the room and stand in the corners. Ronald immediately went to his corner, but Donald, who was the class clown, took his good old easy time. Mr. Story pulled a paddle out of a pocket and started paddling Donald and he paddled him all the way up to the appointed corner. Donald moved a lot faster after he started feeling the paddle. Mr. Story could hit hard.

He didn't have to give many paddlings. One day a boy from Miss Pitt's class knocked on our door. Mr. Story opened it and the boy told him she had sent him there because he had been throwing paper wads. The boy had a little grin on his face like he didn't have a worry in the world. Mr. Story brought him into the classroom and introduced him. This was his first year at Hector. He had been going to a school out of state. Then he began talking to the boy.

He said, "Your dad came by my house before school started and said he wanted to move to where there was a good school, so you could get a good education. He had heard that Hector had a good school, so he had moved your family here."

As our teacher went on and on, we students watched with great interest. We knew the new boy was a smart-alec—that he thought the people who lived in the Ozark hills were just a bunch of hillbillies and weren't very smart.

The smile the boy had on his face gradually faded and by the time Mr. Story finished talking he had a great big frown on it. As the minutes passed, the confidence gradually diminished and he started to worry. Then Mr. Story reached into his desk and pulled out a great big paddle, much bigger than the one he had used on Donald Wooten.

He took the boy outside, into an open area just outside the door, and we listened as he let that poor boy have it. The fifth grade room was a few feet away also, so the students there must have heard the paddling just as well as we did. Each time he hit the boy, every one of us winced, just as if it might have been us.

That was the last student sent from Miss Pitt's class to Mr. Story the rest of that year, and there wasn't one paper wad thrown in our classroom that school year of 1949-50.

At the front of each desk were two grooves where pencils could be placed so they wouldn't roll onto the floor. Bobby Laymon had an extra pencil, one that was almost new and had a good eraser on it. A student in front of him, Gerald Hurley, would reach back and borrow it every few minutes to use its eraser. Gerald had worn his eraser out.

Bobby had an ink bottle almost full of ink. He took off its lid and dipped the eraser of the pencil in it. After he wiped the excess ink off the eraser, he placed it back in the groove on his desk.

A minute later, Gerald reached back, grabbed the pencil and without looking at the eraser, tried to erase the mistake he had just made. To his surprise, he got ink all over his paper. He put the pencil back, gave Bobby a dirty look, and didn't borrow it anymore.

Chapter 41

UNCLE BEN'S RUNAWAY

We were baling hay at Uncle Ben's one day, when the mules John was raking hay with ran away after stepping in a yellow jacket's nest. John was thrown off and dragged by the teeth of the rake.

We were all watching and were scared to death that he was going to get killed. We had heard of it happening to other people. But luckily for John and for all of us, as the mules pulled the rake rapidly over bumps and holes, the rake teeth raised into the air and he was released.

He was bruised and bloody, but other than that, he was okay. All of us breathed a big sigh of relief. John wasn't very old. He was only four years older than me and I was barely old enough to be helping. My job was only to follow the mule, as it went around and around pulling the lever that worked the hay press. It wasn't long until John was again raking hay.

Uncle Ben wasn't so lucky later that year, 1945. He had some young high-spirited mules which were very wild and easy to spook. They wanted to run at the least little thing. He liked them that way because he could get a lot of work done. Different people warned him that the mules were dangerous, especially when pulling the hay mower he used to cut hay.

He had bought him some hay equipment after moving off the mountain and he baled hay for people all that summer. On this particular day, he and his work crew had been baling on the Louis Curtis farm, and he decided that afternoon to drive his mules to the Fate Balenger place to start cutting his hay. He sat on the metal seat behind the mules and he could mow all day and never get tired. His son, Raymond, and some of the others had been trying to get him to quit for the season because they had been baling hay for several weeks and felt they were about worn out.

He told them they couldn't quit just yet because he had promised Fate he would cut and bale his hay.

The Louis Curtis farm was one mile west of the Rock Springs church and the Fate Balenger farm was about one mile east of it. As he was driving along the dusty road going to the Balenger place, he heard the sound of pounding hoofbeats racing across a field toward him and his mules. The sounds grew louder as they approached.

He looked around and saw two wild-looking mules bearing down on them. They were in a pasture alongside the road and were only looking for company, but he gripped the reins tighter, knowing that his mules might start running at any time.

They did! They took off like a shot out of hades. No matter how hard he pulled back on the lines, he couldn't make them slow down. He thought about jumping off but decided he couldn't do that. His mower would be wrecked and he needed to get that hay cut. The mules kept running faster and faster, finally reaching full speed.

He was barely able to stay in his seat. Every time the mower hit a bump or hole in the road, it bounced high and Uncle Ben bounced even higher. He was thrown from his seat, and he fell between the right wheel and the sickle bar.

He couldn't get loose! The tread of the iron wheel tore his trousers off and it started tearing the flesh from his upper legs and belly. Desperation set in. Putting his right hand between his belly and the wheel, he hoped to keep his insides from being ripped out. All the flesh was torn from the back of his hand, and blood spurted everywhere.

His hand bones were crushed; his forearm bones broke and pierced through his flesh and skin; his elbow joint was mangled and thrown out of place. He prayed to God to help him. He wasn't ready to die; he had a wife and several little children who needed him.

The mules showed no sign of slowing down, but finally, after what seemed like an eternity, he was thrown free, landing in the ditch beside the road. His head slammed against rocks and a stump, where he came to rest, more dead than alive—but still barely conscious.

He didn't know how long he lay there before he was found, because he passed in and out of consciousness. He yelled as loud as he could, hoping that someone would hear him. A woman at a nearby house did, and she came running to see what was wrong. He heard her ask him his name and he was barely able to whisper, "Ben."

His face was too bloody for her to recognize him. Everyone around there knew Ben Gray, but there were some other "Bens" living near there also, so she didn't know which "Ben" this was. She got scared and went back to her house. She didn't have a phone or a car, and she was there by herself, so someone else would have to find him.

Finally one of Jake Garrigus's son-in-laws and another man came along in a pickup truck and saw him. Uncle Ben was able to tell them he was Ben Gray. They loaded him into the back of the truck and drove straight to the hospital in Russellville, just as fast as they dared go.

His pain was so bad he didn't know how he was staying conscious. He was hurting so much that he didn't have any thoughts about regretting having those mules, or that he hadn't listened to people who feared for his safety.

As they were carrying him through the door of the hospital, one of his arm bones sticking through his skin caught against the door, and more pain shot throughout his entire body!

Since Uncle Ben was so near death, the doctors and nurses saw no chance for him to survive, but they had seen miracles before, so they hovered over him, giving him shots to reduce the pain, and blood to replace that which had been lost.

They also washed the blood off his body. Then they started operating, setting his bones and sewing him up.

Even with the pain killers, the pain in his body was so terrible that he moaned and groaned and yelled and took on so much that he could be heard all over the hospital. None of the doctors or nurses or anyone else thought he had a ghost of a chance to survive.

Soon after he was taken to the hospital, Raymond and the rest of the hay crew were notified about Uncle Ben's accident and they immediately quit baling hay. Several of them, including Raymond, hurried to the hospital to be near him. As the doctors operated, people had to hold him down and Raymond had to listen to his cries. It was all he could do to keep from breaking down because he knew that his daddy was suffering so badly.

After a long time, and the doctors and nurses had finished with him for the time-being, and he was left alone for a few moments, he heard the voice of his brother, Bob, outside his door. He heard Bob ask someone, "Is he dead?"

"No," he heard a doctor answer. "He's alive, but barely. If it's the medicine that's keeping him alive, he'll live til morning. If it isn't the medicine, he'll die tonight."

They immediately came into his room and he whispered to them, "I'm not going to die."

"Thank heaven for that!" the doctor exclaimed.

Uncle Ben knew that God wouldn't let him die. If he had intended for him to die, he wouldn't have thrown him free of the mower when he did. It was his faith that God wouldn't let him die that gave him the courage and determination to pull through, plus the fact that he was a very tough individual.

In a few days, when the doctors thought he might live, they operated on his bladder, which had burst. They set all of his broken bones they could. They had waited too late to get the elbow joint back in place on his right arm. They hadn't set it because they were so sure he wouldn't make it. They wanted to cut his arm off at the elbow. "We may as well cut it off," one doctor told him. "It will never be of any use to you."

"Nope," Uncle Ben said. "I want my arm."

"What good will it do you?" the doctor questioned. "You'll never be able to do anything with it, like drive a car or open a door."

"I can use it to slap gnats!" Uncle Ben declared.

The doctors laughed. They couldn't argue with him on that point. He would be able to slap gnats and flies with it even if he couldn't use it for anything else.

All the skin and flesh were gone from the back of his right hand, leaving the bones exposed. When the nurse took the bandages off his hand, he could see that the flesh which was left between the bones was rotting. She used tweezers to pick out the rotten flesh as he watched. The nurse was amazed when he didn't get sick. It was all she could do to keep from it.

The doctors were wrong about Uncle Ben's arm. Although he was never again able to bend it at the elbow, he was able to use his hand and arm for many things. When he drove a car or truck, he put his right hand on the top of the steering wheel to help guide the vehicle. He also used it to load pulpwood billets. Before they had winches to help load them, they did it by hand. He could use his right arm and hand very effectively as he worked.

One day two nurses who were working with him started talking about Doctor Linton. "He isn't anything but a quack," one of them said.

This went all over Uncle Ben because he was fond of the doctor. "I'll tell you right now!" he retorted. "Doctor Linton has more sense than all the doctors in this hospital put together!" Not another word was spoken against Doctor Linton by the nurses.

Many months passed before he was able to resume work. The hayfield and the hay mower had long since been forgotten. When I heard about Uncle Ben's accident, I cried. I loved him. No one thought he would live and I didn't think I would ever get to see him again. After we learned he was going to pull through, we went to the hospital. We didn't get to see him because we were too young. But we had the run of the building while the adults were visiting him. June and John said they wanted to show us something in the hospital basement. They had been to the hospital several times, and they knew it almost like the back of their hands.

We quietly walked down the basement stairs. All the rest of us wondered what they were going to show us. We reached the bottom of the stairs, and John opened a door. Lo and behold, there was a human skeleton and it wasn't plastic. It hung in a corner and it just stayed there grinning at us. I had never seen a skeleton before and I ran out of the room and back up the stairs as fast as I could go. As I was running, I heard everyone behind me laughing

Chapter 42

UNCLE LEONARD

My Grandfather, Jonathan (John) Franklin Gray, died at the age of 65 in 1935. Unless you skipped it, you have already read about that. Since I was born in 1939, I never knew him. But I heard so many stories about him that it seems like I did. All I want to tell about him now are a few things that rubbed off from him onto Uncle Leonard.

Jonathan's (John's) grandfather and great grandfather had been well-off, if not wealthy. They had lived in Alabama, owned slaves, and hundreds of acres of land, but the Civil War hadn't been kind to them and they were left without very much. It is reported by a historian there, Roger McNeese, that John's great grandfather, Jonathan, had once loaned Thomas Jefferson's grandson $2000 in gold coins and had never been repaid, perhaps because of the war. Two thousand dollars in gold was a tidy sum of money before the Civil War. And it didn't go down in value during the war like Confederate currency did.

It is recorded in Alabama that his great grandfather was the cohost at a reception for ex-Presidents Andrew Jackson and James K. Polk in the late eighteen thirties or early eighteen forties. And they had alcohol at those receptions.

Uncle Leonard inherited his liking of alcohol from his father. His father used to tell Mom that he didn't think it was any more harm to take a little drink of whiskey than it was to take a drink of water. He knew that Mom hated alcohol. She had been taught by her father, who said alcohol had almost ruined him.

So after Mom married Dad, there were a few clashes about alcohol. It actually started when twenty-one-year-old Uncle Leonard moved in with Mom and Dad. Uncle Leonard didn't drink much, but what little he did was too much for Mom. Since he was such a good worker, and since he was so good with the kids, she had to put up with him. That doesn't mean she had to like it. Uncle Leonard had to keep his moonshine, wine, beer, or whatever it was hid somewhere around the farm, or she would pour it out.

One day when he was in a store in Moreland with a friend and the friend's three-year-old son, and they were all drinking soda pops, the little boy said, "Leonard keeps his soda pop up in the woods." The men standing around in the store had a good laugh at that. One day in the cotton field, someone saw that same little boy smell Uncle Leonard's little dog's breath, and he told the dog, "Shee-oo, you have been drinking Leonard's old wine."

When I was four or five years old was the first time that I became involved in their clash over alcohol. Mom started sending me around the farm searching for his hiding places. This was while Uncle Leonard was away and while the other children were away also. There were plenty of hiding places close to the house because of little briar patches here and there. There were no brush cutters back then.

One day when Uncle Leonard wasn't working because of rain, he headed down toward the chicken house. He didn't know that Mom was watching. He thought when he went down that way that everyone would think he was going to the privy.

But Mom could see down there well enough to tell if he went into the privy or to some other place. He went to some other place. He disappeared around the chicken house, so Mom couldn't see exactly where he had gone, but she could tell about where he went. She knew that he was going to get a drink.

He came back to the house after a while, as Mom watched him. As soon as he entered the house, she said, "I have to go to the privy." Uncle Leonard didn't say anything, but he kept an eye on her through the window.

When she didn't enter the privy, but kept on going around the chicken house, he knew exactly where she was going. She was after his moonshine. He headed down that way as fast as he could walk, but by the time he reached the chicken house, he met her on her way back to the house. He reached the hole in the briar patch where his moonshine was, and all that was left was the empty jar. Mom hadn't even bothered to put the lid back on the jar.

Wow, was he angry! He had spent the biggest part of a day's wages, received for cutting logs, on that gallon of whiskey. He hurried back to the house and let Mom know what he thought of her for pouring his drink out. That moonshine wasn't easy to come by. His friend had driven him fifteen miles up in the mountains to get that. He told Mom how sorry he thought she was.

All Mom said was, "Well, you oughten' to drink."

I often wondered why Dad didn't take sides when they were fussing with each other, but as I've gotten older, I've come to realize that Uncle Leonard was a valuable extension to our family. He would do anything for anyone in need. He was able to help people, because he made a lot of money for those times, cutting logs and other wood products, in addition to what he made working for Dad , and he didn't have a family to provide for. Of course he would have loved to have had a family, but life had dealt him a low blow when he had contracted polio as a baby.

I also know that Dad didn't think it was such a bad thing to take a little nip now and then. I never knew of Uncle Leonard missing a day's work because of his drinking. I've known him to sit up with sick people many a night and then work hard the next day. That was before nursing homes.

Uncle Leonard didn't just go to work and eat and sleep. He liked to have a little fun just like everyone else does. He ran around with his friends some. He even bought an old car so that he wasn't housebound so much. But he never learned to drive it. He got other people to drive it for him. It wasn't hard for him to get someone because when he ran around with them, he furnished the money for their entertainment.

A young man who lived five miles down the road was glad to chauffer wherever he wanted to go. His brother would drop him off at our house and later on would pick him up. He stayed all night with that person one time. His friend had a sister who was a little odd. Uncle Leonard said he and his friend had come in after a day on the town, so to speak, and that his friend's sister wanted a chew of tobacco. His friend told her, "No."

She told his friend, "I have a notion just to cut your neck!"

His friend said, "Here." He gave her some. He was afraid his sister might do what she threatened to do and she might do it while he was sleeping.

One time when Uncle Leonard and his friend had been running around, they had gotten into an argument about something, and his friend refused to drive him home. Instead, he parked Uncle Leonard's car at his house.

Uncle Leonard was angry. He had watched as other people drove, and he decided that he would drive his car home. His car had a standard shift, but that wasn't going to stop him. He did all right with it too.

He drove up the road toward our house without making a bobble. But when he reached our house, he didn't slow down enough before turning in and he missed our driveway. He was going way too fast when he turned in. He managed to get his car stopped just before he hit the fence that separated our yard from the cow pasture. That was probably the first time, and I know it was the last time, that he ever drove a vehicle.

Just off our driveway out by the highway was my favorite place to play with my toy dump truck I got from last Christmas. There was a bank of soft soil that had been left when the highway was built. My truck was a very sturdy little dump truck, all metal, not plastic like the toy companies make today. I also had a little shovel for scooping up the dirt. I had been playing that day and left my toys. So when Uncle

Leonard missed our driveway, he ran smack-dab over my truck.

He promised to buy me another one. But instead of buying another truck, he handed me the money. When Mom saw him hand me the money, she came into the room and said, "Here, I'll take that. I will use it to buy your Christmas present for this year." The time was November, so I had to wait two months for my replacement truck and it was my only present for Christmas, except for the gifts we received at church and school when we drew names. Those presents weren't very good, though. They were usually handkerchiefs, socks, or yoyos. Mom knew how to stretch a dollar and like I have said before, money was hard to come by.

Uncle Leonard had a good mind. He couldn't read or write. But he could do plain arithmetic in his head. No one ever cheated him. Once when Dad was going to the store he sent for some item and gave Dad a five dollar bill to pay for it. The item cost about three dollars. When Dad returned with whatever he sent for, he gave him the item, but forgot to give him his change.

After they had sat there for a few minutes Uncle Leonard said, "That's the last time I'm going to buy anything at that store if they have gone up that much." As soon as he said that, Dad remembered he had forgotten to give Uncle Leonard his change. He gave it to him.

Uncle Leonard also had an excellent memory. He could recite poems learned in school when he was a boy. Here's one of them:

> Who can keep money and own a car?
> I'd like to know just who they are.
> They can't eat hay and they can't eat corn.
> They'll gobble your money just as sure as you're born.

> In every town through which you pass,

They've gotta have oil and they've gotta have gas.

There's something about them that's always broke,

Just like the owner, and that's no joke.

I had a little money and I kept it in a gourd,

That was before I traded for my Ford.

Now my hands are dirty and my clothes are worn,

I'll never own another, to this I've sworn.

When I come to cross the bar,

Old Saint Peter will own no car.

So carry me over to that peaceful shore

Where the sound of a car will be heard no more.

When Donald was two years old Uncle Leonard took him to town on the bus. They now had a bus going from Appleton to Russellville on certain days. Donald was a very bright little boy at two years of age.

Everyone thought he would be a smart man when he grew up and he proved them right. Uncle Leonard took him into a café and bought some dinner. Then he took him into a theatre to watch a movie. They showed "Double Features" in those days and they had a cartoon and news reel. When the lion came on the screen before an MGM movie started, Donald was scared stiff. He thought the lion was real.

One day when we were eating dinner, Uncle Leonard became ill. His stomach was upset and it had gotten that way very quickly. His face became pale. He rose from the table and told everyone he was going to die. Mom asked him, "Are you ready to go?"

He replied, "No, but I'm going anyway." He headed for the back door just as fast as he could walk and went into the back yard to threw up. His stomach quit hurting immediately. He came back into the house where we were and was grinning from ear to ear.

On one of his log cutting expeditions, he and Lawrence Biffle batched in a little house north of Caglesville down off Cagle Hill. Otto and Irene (Gray) Hudson were living there as renters but they were gone somewhere to work, probably picking cotton. Irene had left several jars of vegetables she had canned from the garden and the two cousins helped themselves. One day after cutting logs until almost dark, Uncle Leonard and Lawrence came in from the woods and they were very hungry. Uncle Leonard built a fire in the cook stove while Lawrence opened a jar of Irene's soup. A few minutes later he told Uncle Leonard to go outside and get a bucket of water. The well was a little ways from the house and Uncle Leonard had some trouble with the well bucket, so he was a little while getting back to the house.

After he reentered the house the soup was piping hot. He set the water bucket down and picked up a spoon and dipped some of the hot soup out and put it into his mouth. When the soup hit his mouth, it was so hot there was no way he could stand it. He didn't want to spit it out, so he swallowed it. Lawrence told about it later. "When he swallowed that hot soup, I could hear it sizzle all the way down to his stomach! I could even hear it sizzle after it reached his stomach! Leonard headed for the bucket of water and started drinking dipper after dipper. I thought he was going to drink that whole bucketful."

Chapter 43

NINETEEN FORTY-SEVEN

By nineteen forty-seven Bobbye and Betty were teenagers. Bobbye was sixteen and Betty fourteen. Bobbye was in the tenth grade and Betty in the eighth.

They had become very pretty girls, Bobbye with her almost black hair and Betty with silky blond hair. They made excellent grades. Mom and Dad were very proud of them. Bobbye had been taking piano lessons for years from Mrs. Ruby, the superintendent's wife. She was the music teacher at the Hector school. Betty was teaching herself to play an accordion she bought with money she had earned picking cotton.

The girls gave me a penny for every bobby pin I could find for them. Money was hard to come by at certain times of the year, so I worked to find one now and then.

Mom also gave us a nickel for every mouse we could catch in our mousetraps. Late one night I heard the trap go off I had set behind the piano. I got out of bed, took the dead mouse off the trap, then reset it. I caught another one before morning. so I made a dime in one night. It doesn't sound like much today, but then it was enough to buy a 52 page Lone Ranger comic book at the Hector Drug Store. I'd like to see someone try to buy a comic book for that today—2012.

A young man who lived a few miles toward Hector happened to be at our house one day. He became very interested in Bobbye's piano playing and both girls' singing. He was a pretty good singer, and he joined them. He started coming to our house almost every Saturday when he thought the girls would be home. His name was Troy Oberture, in his late thirties, well dressed with a good voice. He was crippled.

Troy coming to our house got to be a habit. He never came when the girls were at school, because he wanted to join them in singing. Everyone could tell that he had a crush on Bobbye and she didn't like it. So she made a deal with me— the next time that Troy came, the girls would disappear and I would call out from a back room. "Go home Troy!"

She would give me a quarter for my effort. Wow, a whole quarter! That was enough to buy a new comic book, a candy bar, an ice cream cone and I would still have a nickel left over.

Mom didn't know anything about Bobbye's scheme or she wouldn't have let it go through. She hadn't yet figured out how she was going to discourage Troy from having a crush on Bobbye, but she didn't want to hurt his feelings. Only a few days later, on a Saturday, here came Troy strolling up the road and into our yard. Betty saw him and she notified everyone that Troy was on the way.

Bobbye took me into the middle back room where I would yell out the words, "Go home, Troy!", and we waited for just the right moment. Little brother Donald was there also.

Troy knocked on the front door and Mom let him in. She told him to have a seat and she did likewise. She did her best to carry on a conversation with him. He kept looking around and she knew that he was wondering where the girls were. He didn't say anything about them, but she knew.

In a couple of minutes, Bobbye gave me the signal to yell out. But I was beginning to have second thoughts on what I was supposed to do. What would Mom think? What would she say to me about it? What would she do to me? I really did want that quarter, though. I had to have that quarter. In my mind, I was already reading that comic book, eating that candy bar and licking on that ice cream cone. I had already seen the comic book I wanted at the drug store. It was a Lone Ranger and had a picture of him behind a great big Saguaro cactus, looking around it and getting ready to shoot his six-gun at the bad guy who was shooting at him. I had to have that comic book, and this was my chance to get it.

"Now . . ." Bobbye whispered to me. "Now."

I called out for Troy to go home but I said it in such a low voice that he or Mom couldn't possibly have heard me.

Bobbye told me to say it again, only louder. So I said it again, but not much louder than I had the first time.

Suddenly six-year old Donald said, "This is the way to say it Randall, GO HOME, TROY!" He said it so loud that he could be heard all over the house.

Mom later said she and Troy heard Donald say the words very, very plainly and it embarrassed her to death. But she and Troy sat there like they hadn't heard a thing. In a minute, Troy said, "I guess I had better get on back home." He went out the door and that was the last time we ever saw him.

Donald got the quarter. I had to go back to catching mice and hunting for bobby pins to get the comic book. Later in life, Donald won awards for his public speaking. I guess he got started that day in 1947.

Chapter 44

WE GET ELECTRICITY

In the late nineteen forties, we finally got electricity. Everyone was very excited when the Arkansas Power and Light Company started putting the poles up along the highway. After the poles were up, they started stringing the wires from pole to pole. When they finally reached our house, Dad hired a young man to wire it. Our house was his first project, and when he completed the wiring and turned on the switch, every light in the house went on. Compared to the coal-oil lamps we had been using, it seemed as light as day to us. The young man had to do some adjustments. Then we could turn the lights on and off in each room.

We no longer had to study by a coal-oil lamp. Dad had bought an Aladdin lamp once, which also used coal-oil, and it threw out brilliant light, but any little vibration, and the wick would crack, no longer working so he had given up on it.

Now, all we had to do was buy some appliances. Dad wouldn't spend much money for things like that, but he did buy an electric radio. We could listen to it every night. Many a Saturday night we listened to the Grand Ole Opry with Roy Acuff, Ernest Tubb, Uncle Dave Macon, Grandpa Jones, and many others. Listening to them was better than watching a western movie in town on Saturday afternoon. The men cutting logs nearby got into an argument about how old Grandpa Jones was. One of them said, "I know he's seventy-five years old." Actually he was about thirty years old. I met him forty years later and he was seventy then.

Also every week we could hear "The Lone Ranger", with HiYo Silver and Tonto. From out of the past come the thundering hoofbeats of the great horse, Silver. The Lone Ranger rides again. Return with us now to those thrilling days of yesteryear. There was "The Green Hornet", "The Screaking Door", and several other night programs.

For the women during the day, there were "Larry Noble", "Stella Dallas", "Days of Our Lives", with McDonald Cary, "As the World Turns", and others. Mom would listen to the soap operas every day as she did housework. It was a real treat for her to get to listen, as it helped reduce the boredom of keeping house.

At a certain time every night, religious singing came on. Betty wouldn't let us miss that. The station came out of Mexico so they could use 50,000 watts and be heard over most of the United States. Bill Garrett was one of the hosts. He advertised items we could order. One item was a package of double-edged razorblades. Bill said he would throw in a knife that was worth the price of the razorblades.

Betty ordered them for Uncle Leonard. When they came they were so dull that they wouldn't shave and the knife thrown in wasn't worth a flip.

Uncle Earl was now working at Sears-Roebuck in Little Rock and he bought Mom and Dad a Cold Spot refrigerator. They would pay for it over several months. Now we could have ice cream regularly, without having to turn the handle of an ice cream maker. We could also have ice cubes to use in drinking water. Dad also bought an electric wringer washing machine.

Uncle Earl was very good to us. For Christmas he would get each of his nieces and nephews presents. He also bought some evergreen shrubs from Canada for us, to go around the front porch of our house. Those shrubs were there for many years before they died.

When the rural people of Pope County got electricity, our ice man, Wade Nowlin, lost his job delivering ice. He moved to Arizona and delivered ice there for a while. Then he lost that job. He worked as a prison guard until his retirement, then moved back to Arkansas, which he called God's Country. There were quite a few people who moved back here after retirement, and there were many others who would have moved back if they could have.

Chapter 45

IRENE SCARES DONALD and DOYLE

One day six-year-old Donald and five-year-old Doyle, Uncle Ben's son, were playing with Otto and Irene's little four–year-old daughter, Jana, at the Hudson house. They were in the back yard, while Irene was inside doing housework. After a little while, Donald and Doyle got the urge to go to the bathroom and they decided to go up in the woods. Without telling Jana why they were going, they started, and they told her she couldn't go with them.

That didn't set to well with Jana so she went into the house and told her mother they wouldn't let her go with them. Irene decided to play a little joke on the two boys, so she put clothes over her head and face and followed them to where they had gone.

In the meantime, Donald and Doyle had finished using the bathroom but they hadn't put their clothes back on, when the most hideous looking monster came at them. It had its hands way up in the air and its claws were pointing right at them. It made the most horrible sounds their young minds had ever heard.

Grabbing their clothes, the two boys headed toward the highway, then up the road toward our house as fast as they could go. Donald ran ahead, and yelled at Doyle, "Come on, Doyle."

Suddenly Irene appeared in the yard without the covers over her head and face, she called to them, "What's going on here? What's all the fuss about?"

The boys stopped running and got their clothes back on. They walked back to where Irene was and told her about the monster being after them. She laughed and told them that it was her, that she was trying to teach them a lesson.

Chapter 46

SUNDAY AFTERNOON FUN

We always had fun on Sunday afternoons. We played horseshoes, baseball, basketball, crochet, and anything else that we could. We had watermelon and cob fights. One Sunday J.C. Kinder, Gerald Cooper, and I were in the barn loft pretending it was a fort, and that we were defending it, and John, Jerry, and Jimmy Hallum were on the ground attacking us.

We were armed with corn cobs we had broken off so they were easy to throw. We even had a few we had gotten out of the mud in the hog pen and they were twice as heavy as the others. We were loaded for bear. We saved the hog pen cobs for when we would really need them.

Our attackers bombarded us for a while and we let them have it right back. Finally, John decided that he would storm the fort and he started climbing up the ladder to the loft where we were. We peppered him with corn cobs, but he kept right on coming. He was one tough boy and he was bigger than the rest of us. J.C. hit him right between the eyes with one of the mud soaked cobs, but he kept coming. J.C.'s eyes got as big as saucers. He knew he was in for it just as soon as John reached where we were. I wasn't too worried because John had always looked after me and I knew he wouldn't hurt me. But J.C. couldn't say the same thing.

He and J.C. were friends but this was war. He peppered J.C. good after he reached the loft. That did it for the day. We'd had enough of cob fighting. So we found some other fun for the rest of that Sunday.

Another Sunday afternoon we rode Dad's heifer calves that he was keeping for replacements for not only his dairy herd, but also for his beef cattle herd. There were several of them in the calf pasture by the house, just the right size for us boys, and Dad was busy visiting with Sunday company so he wouldn't be paying any attention to us. He wouldn't have let us ride his calves if he had known. John wasn't there that day for some reason. We herded the calves into the small pen in the corner of the pasture and we started riding them. We used Dad's saddle on some and bare backed on others.

Most of the time we'd get bucked off but we'd get right back on. We finally had ridden all of them except for one big heifer and none of us could stay on her to save our necks.

J.C. came up with a solution. He said, "We'll get her over in one of the barn stalls and Jerry can get on her backwards."

"What good will that do?" Jerry asked.

"Remember, when you hold the tail of a cow up she can't kick?"

"Yeah."

"A calf is the same way. If you'll sit backwards on her, you can hold her tail straight up, and she can't buck."

Jerry didn't much like that idea, but J.C. was a pretty slick talker. He convinced his friend he knew what he was talking about. When we had the heifer in the barn stall, we held her until Jerry was firmly on her back. J.C. handed the end of her tail to him and we kept holding her so she couldn't move until we were ready.

When everything was set, J.C. opened the door of the stall. The heifer darted out into the hall of the barn and headed for the corral gate. We had forgotten to close it! Jerry was pulling as hard as he could on her tail. She didn't buck much, but she sure could run. They passed through the corral gate and headed for the woods.

I had been into those woods many times and I didn't like the thoughts that came into my mind. There were brush, briars, vines, low tree limbs and just about everything else you can imagine, where they had gone. For a few minutes we were too stunned to run after them, so we just watched as they disappeared right before our eyes. Finally we started after them but were afraid of what we would find in the brush.

Just as we entered the woods, here came Jerry. He was all scratched up, his clothes were torn, and his hair was a mess. Blood was running down both hands and some was running down his face.

J.C. asked him, "Well, did you ride her?"

All Jerry said was, "Don't you say a word or I'll beat you up!" He walked slowly toward the house where he was going to get some more clothes. When he looked in the mirror, I'm sure he would be washing up also. J.C., Jimmy Hallum or I didn't say a word because we knew he was very capable of doing what he had threatened to do.

Chapter 47

BB GUNS

I was at Uncle Ben's one day, there to spend the night, when he and John got into a discussion about who was the best shot with a BB gun. John told his dad, "I'll bet I could run down the road, and you couldn't even hit me with a BB gun." The BB gun was a pump gun and it was powerful. John didn't have a shirt on, so he would be taking a chance, but he was one tough boy.

Uncle Ben took him up on it and Father and son were soon ready to have a little fun. What John had in mind was to zigzag back and forth so Uncle Ben couldn't hit him. But he learned a little something about his father that day. There were several of us boys and girls watching the two, and we thought it was going to be very interesting as to what would happen.

Uncle Ben wasn't supposed to start shooting until John reached a certain spot in the yard. He stuck to that rule, but as soon as John reached that spot, he started peppering him. We could hear the impact each time a BB hit John in the back and it hurt me every time it did. I was glad I wasn't the one running. John zigzagged to the left, and he zigzagged to the right, but it didn't do him any good. He might as well have been running in a straight line. Even with Uncle Ben's stiff right arm, he hit John every time. When John came back from the highway in a few minutes, he was very embarrassed. He had red welts all over his back.

Those BB guns were very important to little boys back then, but we had to be careful with them. One boy got one for Christmas and he shot his sister in the eye. I heard that his father broke the gun.

Doyle was at the house one day and we were on the porch with BB guns. One of us held a target for the other to shoot; then we switched places. While I was holding one for Doyle to shoot, he purposely shot my finger, then started laughing. I knew the only way I could get him back would be to pretend that he hadn't hit me, let him hold a target for me, and then shoot him.

So I acted like he hadn't hit me and I said, "What are you laughing about?"

He said, "I shot you."

"No, you didn't," I told him. "Now it's my turn to shoot."

He couldn't figure out how he had missed. But he picked up the target and held it for me to shoot. I shot him on the hand, and when he started crying, I didn't feel a bit sorry for him. In fact, I kind of enjoyed it.

At Uncle Ben's one night, John, Doyle, Donald, and I were alone. The others were gone somewhere. John inserted a 22 bullet in an old radio battery, and we shot at that bullet with a BB gun. We were trying to make it go off, just like it would in a 22 rifle. We shot and shot, until finally I hit it. Since the bullet couldn't go forward because of the battery, the shell came back toward us. It hit John on the cheek. If it had hit him in the eye, he would have been blinded in that eye. What unthinking boys won't do.

Chapter 48

UNCLE BOB JOHNSON

We had a cemetery on our land. It was about two hundred yards east of our house over in the pasture. There were seventy-two graves in it. No one had been buried there since Dad and Mom had bought the farm in 1935, but occasionally they had Decorations there. Rumor had it that a seven-foot Negro had been buried at the edge. Mom used to tell us kids that you could walk up to his grave and ask, "Whatcha doin', John?" and he would say, "Nothing." She really meant that he would say nothing.

Every year an old white-haired stooped-over man came from Clarksville and cleaned up the cemetery. When he finished, he always had it looking neat and pretty. He would paint the cedar trees around with whitewash. We called him Uncle Bob, though he was no kin to us. His last name was Johnson and his mother and father had been buried in the cemetery. He was related to some of the Johnsons at Oak Grove.

He rode from Clarksville to Russellville, then got a ride to the Barham Store. He walked to the cemetery and cleaned it until he was finished for another year. He had been doing this ever since Dad and Mom bought the farm.

One day when he got off from his ride, he went into the store for a few minutes, and he told the Barhams he was sick. Then he proceeded to the cemetery one-fourth mile away and began his work. Our family was sitting on the front porch of our house. It was too hot to be in the house on that summer day. We had no air conditioner or fan in 1947.

Suddenly we spied Uncle Bob walking toward our house from the cemetery. He was coming across the field in a big hurry. He came across the road and into our front yard and up to the house. Dad was sitting on the front of the porch with his legs dangling and I was sitting on the door steps. Uncle Bob hurried toward Dad. He said, "I'm sick, and I'm going to die."

"You'll be all right," Dad said. "You've just gotten too hot. We'll get you a cool drink of water, and you'll be okay."

Suddenly Uncle Bob collapsed into Dad's arms. Dad caught him and the old man died right there. We kids were very shocked. We had never seen anyone die before. We carried him into our house and placed him on the bed where Dad laid a sheet over his body. He put quarters on his eyes to keep them closed.

Mom sent Betty to the store to tell the Barhams. When Uncle Sewood came in from working at the sawmill, Dad had him drive to Clarksville and tell Uncle Bob's widow. When he arrived at the Johnson house, he told Mrs. Johnson, "I have some bad news about Uncle Bob."

"Is he sick?" she asked Uncle Sewood.

"I'm afraid it's worse than that," Uncle Sewood told her. "He passed away."

Mrs. Johnson gasped. She put her hand to her mouth. Then she began to cry. She said, "I tried to get him not to go to the cemetery today. He didn't feel well, but he was determined to go and clean it up."

Uncle Bob's body stayed overnight at our house before the funeral home people came and picked it up the next day. All of us were very sorry about Uncle Bob. He was a good old man.

Since Uncle Bob had died there, John and June thought our house was haunted. They were superstitious. We were in the house on the mountain one day where our Grandpa Gray had died, and suddenly John said, "Let's get out of here! This is where Old Mr. Gray died!" He was talking about his own grandpa.

THE GRAVE WORKER

He always came once a year
To clean the grass and weeds away,
To freshly spade and shape the dirt
And quietly kneel to pray.

How he treasured that hallowed ground
Where his own were laid to rest.
Neighbors would offer to come and help,
But he thought he could do it best.

He would ride the mail from town
And work til the job was done.
He labored hard and fought his task.
He cursed the scorching sun.

But when that man had finished
His work for another year,
Pride would show all over his face.
His eyes would fill with tears.

He really loved those old Oak trees
That gave shade round about,
and even the five-string barbed wire fence
That kept the cows and horses out.

I remember the last time Uncle Bob came.
I was a kid, but it's all so clear.
He was so excited as he began his work-

To do his duty for another year.

The day was hot, no rain in sight.
No clouds for the sun to hide.
I'm sure that I will not forget
The day Uncle Bob Johnson died.

I saw him hurrying across the field.
To the house he came in a run.
He grabbed my dad and held him tight.
He said, "This time I know I'm gone."

Dad said, "You've just gotten too hot.
Everything will be all right."
"No," he said, as Dad cooled his head.
"I won't make it to the night."

There on the steps of the front porch
Uncle Bob breathed his last breath.
In my daddy's arms he passed away,
He left for his eternal rest.

Now, as I look across the field
At the clump of tall Oak trees,
It seems as if I hear him still,
But I know it's just the breeze.

The Lilacs still grow, and so do the weeds,
But it's a peaceful place of rest.
No one tends to the graveyard anymore…
I guess God can do it best.

Donald Gray—1970

Chapter 49

THE BIG NOSE

One day we were sitting on the front porch when an old stooped-over man came walking into the yard from the road to the south. He had the biggest nose I had ever seen and he had black-rimmed glasses. He was using a cedar stick he had found in the yard for a walking stick. He kept walking toward the porch without saying a word. All of us stared at him so hard that he must have thought we were dummies. None of us said anything to him. As he neared the porch and still didn't say anything, I saw Dad stoop down and pick up a baseball bat one of us kids had left there.

When Dad did that, the old man started laughing and he straightened up. He decided it was time to reveal his identity before Dad conked him over the head. He took the glasses and big nose off and it was Uncle Ben! He had really pulled a good one on us. None of us had ever seen the big nose with the glasses before. We heard giggling from the corner of the yard, and when we looked, John, June, and Doyle came walking out from where they were hiding. They had been watching the whole thing.

Everyone had a good laugh about the prank Uncle Ben had played on us, but we felt a little foolish too, for being the butt of the joke. Uncle Ben was going to church at Buttermilk now and soon after the prank on us, he walked into the church house while wearing the nose and eyeglasses. Church was already started and he went to the front and sat on a seat. None of the people there had ever seen the big nose and the glasses before, so their attention was drawn to Uncle Ben instead of to the church service.

After a few minutes, Marshall Patterson sat down beside him and said, "I'm sorry, but I'm going to have to ask you to leave. You are distracting the church service."

So Uncle Ben left, and as far as I know, he never told Marshall or the others who he was.

Chapter 50

THE WILD HOG

Dad came from the mountain one day, where he had been to check his crops, and he said some animals had been eating his corn. From the looks of the tracks, he thought they were goats, but he wasn't sure. Whatever they were, they were making a mess of the corn.

He went back up there two or three times and by the damage done to the corn, he knew he had to do something about the animals. So he had John bring his big Redbone hound and we took our little dog, Tippie, a half Fiest, and walked up the path to the cornfield. Dad hoped the dogs could trail the animals to wherever they went after they finished their dinner in the field.

We hadn't yet reached the top of the mountain when the dogs ran on ahead of us; then we heard them barking and we heard animals running through the cornfield as fast as they could go. We ran fast after them, with the others going on ahead and leaving me behind, but I ran after them as fast as my short legs would carry me. They were headed south, in the direction of the Rockhouse. The dogs were very excited. In a few minutes we could hear them barking treed, and that was one of the most exciting sounds I had ever heard. "What in the world did the dogs have treed?" I thought.

When I reached where the others were, Dad was trying to put a rope on a wild hog, as Tippie jumped all around and barked as hard as he could. John's Redbone hound was nowhere to be seen. Later I found out he had gone after the old sow's pigs. So it was a sow and pigs that had been in our corn! The sow was a mountain hog if I ever saw one. She was black, long and slim. She had a snout on her a foot long. Her tusks were as sharp as razors. She got Dad down on his back! I was scared that she was going to hurt him badly. But we boys were helpless to do anything.

The sow was trying to get at Dad's throat! She would have made it if he hadn't got her by the ears, one in each hand. He was holding her off. "Put the rope on her!" he yelled at Jerry and John. "Get the rope on her!"

John finally had the rope on her after a few tries. It was all Dad could do to keep his hold on her ears. John and Jerry got the rope around a nearby tree. They pulled on it and soon had the sow off.

Dad wasn't hurt, but he was shaken up and he was dirty. "Let's go get the pigs!" he yelled. "Randall, you stay here with the sow!" He knew I wouldn't be able to keep up.

Tippie went with them, so I was all alone with the sow and I was afraid. She made a lunge at me! "What if that rope broke?" I asked myself. She would get me. I was sure that I couldn't hold her off like Dad had done. Then she made another lunge. I found the nearest tree and climbed as high as I could. It was large enough that I could just reach around it and the limbs were so high I didn't bother to try and reach them.

In the meantime, Dad and the other boys were trying to catch up with Old Red and the pigs but they had too big a start on them. They never got close enough to even hear Old Red bark. They finally turned back toward where I was.

As I hugged that Pine tree, some men drove by in a wagon pulled by a pair of mules. They must have thought I looked funny, clinging to the trunk of the tree. They stopped and asked what was going on and I told them. They headed up the road, which led off the mountain. I stayed up that tree until Dad and the boys returned.

Dad was my hero that day. He already was, but after the struggle with the sow he became even greater in my eyes.

He brought a wagon with a crate on it and put the sow in it. He fattened her up and sold her at the livestock auction. We never saw the pigs again. We heard that Alfred Brewer, who lived on the mountain, caught one or two of them and that Check Kinder, J.C.'s dad, had caught the others.

Chapter 51

TIPPIE AND LADDIE

Someone gave us a little dog to go with Tippie, the little dog of wild hog fame, and we now had a pair that couldn't be beat. The new dog was named Laddie. Jerry was eleven years old now and he hunted with Tippie and Laddie. He claimed the dogs as his, but the rest of us kids claimed them too. Those little dogs were all over the place. Every car that came by going thirty miles an hour had Tippie and Laddie to contend with for a little way down the road. Our growing family gave the two dogs plenty of attention, as we grew to love them just as much as they seemed to love us.

They went with us everywhere. When we walked to church, they would be right there. When we went to the mountain, ditto. They helped round up the cows and they kept the horses and mules in line. They went swimming with us and played in the water.

A mad dog scare had been out for some time. Everyone was scared to death just at the mention of mad dog. Stories went around about them being seen in the area. When we were at Grandpa and Grandma Maxwell's house, Donald and I were afraid to walk down to Uncle Doc and Aunt Opal's house to play with our cousin, Patsy, because we were scared we might run into a mad dog.

Early one morning, Mom woke us up. She said a mad dog had come to our house during the night and had fought with Tippie and Laddie. The mad dog had left our house and went on to the neighbors' houses. Roger Cagle had killed it. Dad had taken Tippie and Laddie over in the pasture and shot them. We were shocked! Losing them was just like losing members of our family. It was like losing a part of ourselves.

I wrote the following in memory many years after their deaths. They were gone but not forgotten.

*   *   *

How great is the value of a dog in a boy's life? It is so great that no value can be put on it. When a small boy makes a mistake, an older person will scold him or nag him to do better, sometimes over and over. But a dog only has to be petted, talked to and fed and it will show its love in a hundred different ways.

It will wag its tail, rear up and lick his face over and over to let him know that it loves him. And it will be the same every day, no change if it happens to be feeling a little bad.

Old Tippie and Laddie were two dogs we had,

And they seemed close as brothers to a growing lad.

They'd tree possums by dozens, it seemed to me,

And squirrels and raccoons up most every tree.

The groundhogs and rabbits could never come out,

Because Tippie and Laddie were always about.

The cars that ran past them were never quite safe,

For Tippie and Laddie would always give chase.

The time comes in life that every boy must know

When suddenly he loses something he loves so.

A mad dog bit Tippie and Laddie one night,

And a small boy had to learn a sad lesson in life.

Now dogs can be feisty and can dig up the yard,

And can tear up good clothes left carelessly athwart.

But the parents who deny a dog for with their boy to play

Have taken the best part of being a boy away.

Chapter 52

OLD SMOKY

Old Smoky came into our lives that year. Nobody knew where he came from, but he was one fine dog. He was a pretty, smoky-colored English Shepherd looking dog, of medium build, winning our hearts right from the start. We didn't know how old he was, but he was young, the way he could get around. Maybe God sent him to take Tippie and Laddie's place. His fur was almost as long as a Collie and it protected him when he was fighting. He needed it too, because the hound dogs in the area sometimes jumped him.

He never started a fight, but he would end it by catching hold of the other dog's tail near its base and hanging on. Of course the other dog couldn't do a thing as long as Smoky had its tail, and when Smoky finally let go, that hound wouldn't have any fight left. He would tuck his tail between his legs and hightail it.

When I had some food, like a biscuit, I would tell him to bark for it, and he would. I would toss the biscuit into the air and he would grab it as it came down.

At the Old Miller swimming hole we would toss a stick way out in the water. Smoky would jump in and get it. Then he would swim back to the bank, climb out of the water and drop the stick at our feet. He would shake himself off and water would fly everywhere. Until we learned to get out of his range, we would get water all over us.

Smoky loved to chase rabbits and when he jumped one he was so fast he could catch it. We didn't have to use much ammunition when we rabbit hunted with him, unless the area was brushy. When we squirrel hunted, he was just as good. When he treed a squirrel and we reached the tree, he would be grabbing a bush and shaking it, trying to get the squirrel to jump out. We didn't need for him to do that, because we had our twenty-two rifle. If he was by himself when he treed a squirrel, he might jump it out and catch it.

As the years passed, Old Smoky slowed down, just as every animal does when it gets older. The rabbits learned to dart to one side when he chased them, and he couldn't see where they had gone. He would jump high into the air as he tried to spot them. Hound dogs learned to gang up on Smokey, so we had to watch out for him when we went anywhere hound dogs were. At the store one day, Grady Barham was talking about the hunters running coyotes with their dogs.

Coyotes had just recently invaded our area. He said people should get rid of their cur-dogs because the hounds couldn't tell some of them from the coyotes. Since he was a grown man and I was only ten years old, I didn't say anything, but I thought to myself, "Get rid of Old Smoky? No way. He's crazy if he thinks we will get rid of him."

One day we were gathering corn for Uncle Sewood and Smoky was run over by the wagon. One of the iron tires went right over his body as the mules pulled the wagon forward. I was afraid our dog was badly hurt, but he didn't seem to have any broken bones. He did take it easy for awhile.

After that, he seemed to go down in body faster. He became very hard of hearing. Once we were walking down the road toward Uncle Ben's place when a car came along. Donald and I got over to one side of the road but Smoky kept walking in the middle.

The car slowed to a crawl and blew its horn. Smoky jumped like he had been shot. This happened quite often.

It was painful to see him go down so fast but that's the way life is, and we just have to learn to accept it. None of us remember when Old Smoky died. Maybe he just faded away.

Chapter 53

UNCLE JACK

We had a neighbor we called Uncle Jack Ford, who lived in an old house on the old Atkins-Appleton road. The road had been bypassed in 1928 or 1929, and the wilderness had about taken it over twenty years later. Uncle Jack's wife had died several years back, and he was all alone in the world. No one knew where he came from, but he talked with a New York accent.

Sometimes he would walk the mile to our house and ask Uncle Leonard to spend the night just to keep him company. He usually kept some alcohol to drink, so our uncle was happy to go with him. It became almost a weekly ritual for him to visit Uncle Jack.

One night a storm came up and Uncle Jack wanted to go to the storm cellar, which set on the edge of the yard in the road embankment. It was just a dugout which ran ten feet or so back from the old road and it had logs over it for cover. There were cracks in several places, and as the two men carried a light and opened its door, it looked very snaky to Uncle Leonard. This was summertime and the snakes were out. Uncle Leonard later said, "I was a lot more afraid of snakes than I was of the storm." They made it okay though, since they weren't bitten, struck by lightning, or blown away.

We often passed by Uncle Jack's on our way to the Old Miller swimming hole. Sometimes he would come out on the porch and talk to us. Once he showed us his pistol. If he wanted to impress us with it, he succeeded, because I had never seen a real pistol before.

A few years after I got to know him, he moved to a house on the new highway at the intersection of highways 124 and 105 where 124 turned off to go to Appleton. In the afternoons when we passed his house on the school bus, many times he would be playing cards, dominoes, or checkers with someone who had stopped by. Sometimes men who worked for the highway department would stop and visit.

One Saturday when my cousin, June, and I were walking to our house from hers, as we neared Uncle Jack's house, we saw several cars parked in his yard. As we got closer, we could see people going in and out. I asked someone what was going on and he told us that Uncle Jack had shot himself in the head, and he was dead.

June and I entered the house, to see his body lying face down in his bedroom by the bed. His pistol was on the floor beside him. It was the same one he had shown us a year or two before. Blood was all over the floor. When Uncle Leonard heard about Uncle Jack, he said, "He tried to shoot himself the last time I was down there, and I took the pistol away. He thought he had cancer and wanted to die suddenly and get it over with."

Apparently someone knew more about Uncle Jack than we did because his sister was at his funeral and she had to have been notified. Mrs. Barham told Mom that Jack Ford was not his real name—it was an alias. Anyone who wants to know his real name will have to look on his tombstone in the Crossroads cemetery. He was buried there beside his wife.

I have heard two versions of why Uncle Jack changed his name and came to this area. One was that he deserted the army during the Spanish-American War in 1899. The other is that he deserted the German army sometime in the past. I will take the first one because of his New York accent. You can take either one you want.

Chapter 54

SEWELL FORD

Louis Ford lived on the bench of the Iron Ore a mile or so north of Oak Grove. The bench ran all the way north for a mile and then turned east to butt up against the Big Mountain. The bench was called the Little Mountain.

The part of it abutting the Big Mountain was where Grandpa John Gray had lived when he died in nineteen thirty-five. His house was a half-mile west from where the road began on its climb up the Big Mountain. Uncle Leonard had inherited Grandpa John's eighty acres there, and Uncle Ben had bought them from him. Louis's house sat near the bench's southeast end, across the hollow between the Big and Little Mountains.

Louis owned 500 acres or so, part of which he had homesteaded, and part of which he had bought for a very small amount of money. His wife was related to Mr. Singleton, from whom Dad had bought his Big Mountain place. He and his wife lived about like most of the people in that area in the early nineteen hundreds.

He had a small apple orchard and a small peach orchard, from which he sold some fruit to make a little money, and he worked for other farmers. In the fall he descended from the mountain to go to the Atkins bottoms to pick cotton. It didn't take much for him and his family to get by, because they were very frugal. Sometimes he left his wife and little boy and traveled farther than the Atkins bottoms to earn more money.

They didn't have a family water well, their water being obtained from a spring about ten feet down from the top of the mountain. It was a very good spring, but it must have been hard to carry a bucket of water from there because the path was very steep.

Louis was a regular sort of guy. Lawrence Biffle told this story about him. "When I was a kid, my mother made me wear a dress until I was a great big youngster. One day while I was playing outside, I had the dress on and here came Mr. Ford. I climbed a nearby tree because I was afraid of him. When he saw me in the tree, he got down on his hands and knees and started barking like a dog, acting like he had me treed."

Louis had a lot of good pine timber; Dad and everyone else around sold their timber to be cut and made into lumber. Louis wouldn't sell so it kept on growing, getting taller and bigger. Timber buyers drooled at the mouth, wanting to buy it.

Mr. and Mrs. Ford had an only son named Sewell. He was a twin, but his brother had either died at birth or when he was very small. Sewell attended school at Oak Grove and Mom had him as a student when she taught there. He was intelligent in many ways, but he was very odd in many ways, too. Her younger sister, Norma, attended there and Sewell had a crush on her, but she didn't want anything to do with him. He would follow her around, but she avoided him as best as she could.

Sewell told Mom, "Miss Lois, I don't know why Miss Norma doesn't like me. Father and I have all that timber. I would think that she would love that about me."

Louis was off somewhere working in the early nineteen thirties, when he became sick with pneumonia. He wrote home that he was coming home to die. He made it home but was very sick. Doctor Linton climbed the mountain and did the best he could for him but his patient didn't get any better.

Sewell climbed the Big Mountain to where Dad lived and he asked him if he would come down and sit some with his father. Of course Dad told him that he would and he said that Uncle Leonard would be glad to go with him. The two brothers walked to the Ford home and they were shocked to see that their house didn't have heat. It was very cold during this winter time.

"Why don't you build a fire and warm this place up?" Dad asked Sewell.

"We're afraid to," Sewell replied. "The house might catch on fire."

Dad could see that the house was a tinderbox, so he didn't say any more, but he knew that Mr. Ford didn't have much of a chance to make it in that cold house. He and Uncle Leonard sat up with him a few more times. Doctor Linton came and checked on him often but without more modern medicine than they had back then, he succumbed to the dreadful disease.

Sewell had the job of caretaker now for the beautiful pine forest that he and his mother had inherited.

Sewell hired Charlie Foster, who lived at Oak Grove, to help do some work on his roof, so he and his mother could keep a fire going in the stove to heat their house. Charlie was a pretty comical fellow, and somehow he went a little too far with one of his practical jokes. He told Sewell that Lawrence Biffle was out to get him. Whatever he meant by that he didn't exactly make clear. Lawrence had now gotten married, and he lived off the mountain just across the road on the west from the Ford property.

A few days later they finished repairing the Ford house's roof, and before Mr. Foster told Sewell that he was only joking with him about Lawrence, Sewell spotted Lawrence coming across his property and he was holding a shotgun in the crook of his arm! Lawrence was only squirrel hunting, but Sewell didn't know that. Back then people didn't mind for others to hunt on their land.

When Lawrence neared where Sewell was, Sewell ran over to him, grabbed the shotgun, and tried to club Lawrence over the head with it! He would have hurt him, but Lawrence threw his arm up to ward off the blow. Sewell only hit him one time. Lawrence asked Sewell, "What on earth did you do that for? I didn't think you cared for me hunting on your land!"

Sewell didn't say anything. He broke open the single-barreled shotgun to discover it wasn't even loaded. He apologized to Lawrence and headed toward his house.

Sewell constantly walked over his property. After Donald and I were old enough, we played in our woods and in Sewell's. Often we were accompanied by our cousin, Doyle. He was Uncle Ben's youngest child, three years younger than I was. We often met Sewell as he surveyed his wooded kingdom. I guess he liked to shock little boys. He educated us about the birds and the bees. He was a strange one. He was an average size man, about five feet-ten inches in his almost knee-length rubber boots, or other heavy shoes, depending on the season. His face was ruddy, tanned by the wind and sun. He had a large mole on one cheek, with long hairs growing out of it, and he had a medium-length fairly straight nose. He had a huge tongue and would often stick it out below his lips. He had a deep baritone voice. He wasn't bad-looking, but the little girls were afraid of him. Once when Irene Hudson and her daughter, Jana, visited them, he asked Jana if she was going to school. When Jana told him she was, he asked her, "Do you know what $H2O$ is?" Jana told him she did, that it was water, and he said, "That's good."

Dad was somewhat of a friend to Sewell, as close as anyone could be to him. Everybody knew he was odd, but they tolerated him. A rumor went around the neighborhood that he was a "peeping tom". After Otto and Irene Hudson bought a farm that joined Sewell's land, he passed by their house often. He had a mule that sometimes got out of its pasture, and it would end up at Otto and Irene's. Their son, Sammy, would help him catch the mule and one day he told Sammy he was going to leave that mule to him in his will. Sammy laughed about that. He said, "That mule was almost 30 years old, and he died a long time before Sewell did."

Bobbye and Betty made a playhouse under some trees about fifty feet from Sewell's land. Dad and Mom's land joined his for a half-mile. Sometimes while they were playing, they could see Sewell watching them from the bushes. He didn't know they could see him. He was at least a mile from his house.

Before people started building stock ponds on their farms, the only place they could get water for their cattle during dry spells was from everlasting springs and waterholes in creeks. Most wells were too shallow to provide water. Until people put in bathrooms, it didn't take much water for a house. We didn't have a good drought-resistant spring on our land, but there was an excellent one just across the fence on Sewell's place, and the water ran down to us. We watered our cattle and horses there in the summer. There wasn't a lot of water that came from it, but it did keep a few shallow water holes filled on our land. After the fall and winter rains came, there was plenty of water from a little branch that flowed from the mountain, so we didn't need the spring then.

Sewell didn't get to use the water, because it was much too far from his house. It must have really bothered him for us to have use of his water, when he couldn't use it, and he would sneak down and stop up that spring so it wouldn't run. We had to keep a close eye on it. Dad sent some of us kids over many times to clean it out. As far as I know, there was never any communication between him and Sewell about the spring, but finally Sewell quit stopping it up.

He didn't have a car. He walked and caught rides everywhere he went. Most of his rides were with the mailman. One day he told the mailman, "I ought to pay you something for riding with you."

"Oh, you don't have to do that," the mailman said.

Sewell insisted that he pay something, so the mailman said, "Well, if you insist. I will let you pay me something just to keep you happy."

The mailman later said, "He reached into his pocket, pulled out some small change, and gave it to me."

Some man took a one and one-half ton truck to the Atkins bottom during cotton picking season and I rode with him once. With school and our own cotton to pick, I seldom got to go. Their cotton was much better than ours.

There was a truck load of people going that day. As we neared Sewell's road, we saw him waiting for us and the truck driver stopped to pick him up. We picked cotton all day and then headed home.

Two girls in my class at school were with us, and on the way back home, they smooched Sewell. They were only doing it for a joke, but his eyes got as big as small saucers. Very small saucers. I'll bet he had sweet dreams that night.

Sewell would have loved to have gotten married. We felt sorry for him. He started calling on a neighbor eight miles away. The woman he was calling on was not right in the head. They would sit in the porch swing and talk. One day Sewell told the woman's mother that they wanted to get married, and her mother said, "Sewell, she can't take care of herself, and she sure can't take care of you." That was the end of that.

Through the years his timber continued to grow, and the sawmill owners continued to drool. One day when Sewell looked out of his front door, he saw Elmer Virden and his son walking up the road toward the house.

He knew what the two were after—they had a sawmill. Sewell was selling Cloverine salve, and he had just received a new case of it in the mail. As soon as Elmer and his son were within hearing distance, he called out to them, "Do you want to buy some Cloverine salve?"

"Yeah, I'll take some," Elmer replied. "How much do you have?" Sewell told him he had a whole case. Elmer said, "I'll take it all." He was trying to get on the good side of Sewell. Then he was going to hit him up to buy his timber. Sewell told him how much he owed him and Elmer gave him his money.

He was just opening his mouth to start talking about the timber, when Sewell beat him to it. "If you run onto anyone who wants to buy my timber, tell them it's not for sale."

I was squirrel hunting on the Ford land one day, and as I neared their house, I got the wild idea to go by their house and visit. Both Sewell and his mother were there. They were very nice to me, inviting me inside and asking me to eat lunch. I hadn't realized it was lunch time, since it was cloudy. Their house was old, but I thought it was as neat and clean as ours was. I ate with them, and the food was good. They had several pretty Jersey milk cows tied to trees. I thought that was strange. We never tied ours to trees.

Jerry said he stopped by and ate with them once, and the food Mrs. Ford served had lots of dog hair in it. He didn't want to hurt their feelings, so he ate it, but he had a queasy stomach for a while. He said, "There's no telling how many dog hairs I ate." At the time he ate with them, they had a big dog, but when I ate, they didn't have one.

They milked their cows and sold the cream when they separated it from the milk. Many of the other farmers in the area did the same, including us. Sewell would carry a full cream can the half mile to Highway 105 and leave it for the mailman to pick up and take to the creamery.

Chapter 55

JERRY'S GOATS AND RABBITS

One of Dad's favorite pastimes when he wasn't working in the fields was to attend the livestock auctions around the area. He went to the Russellville, Atkins, Morrilton, and sometimes the Fort Smith auctions. There was no telling what he might bring home. One day it was a saddle, another time lespedeza seed.

Once at the Russellville auction, something was brought into the auction ring, and the auctioneer tried to get someone to bid on it. No one seemed interested. Dewey Kinder, who was sitting four rows up, said, "If Boyd Gray was here, he would bid on it." About that time, Dad did bid on the item. He was sitting a few rows behind Dewey, and Dewey hadn't known he was there.

Jerry was now old enough to go to the auctions with him. At eleven years of age, he was good company for his dad. Jerry had once had a goat, which he kept tied to a tree, but something had happened to it and he wanted another. He loved that goat. One day at the Russellville auction, as Dad and Jerry watched from up high in the stands, suddenly a whole group of goats was herded into the ring.

There were all kinds of colors, some white, some black, some brown and some spotted. There were billy goats, and nanny goats. One billy had long sweeping horns. Those were the prettiest goats Jerry had ever seen. He just had to have those goats, and he urged his daddy to buy them.

Dad said, "We don't need those goats. What would we feed them?"

"I'll bring in sassafras tree branches with leaves on them," Jerry said. "That's what I fed my other goat." After he begged and begged, Dad gave in. He knew that Dewey Kinder had some goats and they had cleaned up a brushy pasture.

Dad won the bid for the goats and hired a man with a truck to haul them to our farm. They unloaded them inside one of the mule stables. My, was Jerry proud of those goats! He hurried to the fence row where all the sassafras bushes were growing and he cut bush after bush and dragged them to the barn. Those goats loved the sassafras leaves and he felt like he was just about the happiest boy in the world that day.

The next day the goats were hungry again. My, were they hungry! They had eaten just before their previous owner had brought them to the auction but now they had been without feed all night. Jerry chopped down sassafras trees all morning before the goats finally had their fill. He wasn't as happy with them as he had been yesterday. With all the grass growing around the barn, he wondered why he was having to drag bush after bush of sassafras to them.

He also had to carry water from the house. It took two trips. Later in the day when he checked on the goats, he could tell they were hungry again, the way they crowded around. He dreaded to have to feed them. He was having second thoughts about being the owner of those goats. With all the grass that grew around the barn, he wondered why he couldn't just turn them out for a few minutes, let them fill up, and then put them back in the stable.

He went outside and looked around. He saw his dad's field of six-foot high corn across the cow lot, but it had a net wire fence around it. Surely the goats couldn't get into that field. Besides, goats were supposed to be mostly browsers, eating tree leaves, tin cans, and things like that.

Yeah, that's what he would do. Dad was over in the field working on the pasture fence and Jerry could have them back in the barn before he returned. He would never know the goats had been out. So Jerry opened the stable door and hurried them outside.

The goats looked around. They didn't seem to be as hungry as he had thought they were. They nibbled on the grass a little, but then got whiffs of that delicious corn across the way. Those goats were the best jumpers Jerry had ever seen. They sailed over the cornfield fence like it wasn't there. One hopped upon one of the fence posts, looked around for a minute or two, then hopped down and started nibbling on a half-grown ear of corn. My, was it delicious! The other goats were having their fill of the corn too. They would make short work of that cornfield and Jerry was going to be in one heck of a fix.

The only thing he knew to do was catch the goats one at a time and take them back to the barn. He ran back as fast as he could, found a rope, and rounded them up one at a time. There was no one around to help him, so he was on his own. It took hours to get all those goats back in the barn, at least that's the way it seemed to Jerry.

Dad didn't like it when he saw what the goats had done to his corn. He asked Jerry, "How did they get out?"

At that moment Jerry was afraid of his daddy, so he lied, "They just ran over me when I opened the door."

Dad said, "They must have been really hungry. Now, what do you say about selling those goats?"

This time it was Jerry who relented. "That suits me just fine," he said. "When is the next auction around here? I don't even want to wait until Friday to take them to Russellville."

So that is the saga of "Jerry Gray and his goats". Experience is the best teacher and that boy sure got an education those few days he had them.

The saga of "Jerry Gray and his White Rabbits" didn't turn out quite so badly but it would have if the rabbits had been as big as the goats. At the auction, he talked Dad into buying two white rabbits with their cages and bringing them home. They were females. My favorite one was Old Jeannie. She was solid white and had beautiful pink eyes. I think she was an Albino. Jerry thought the rabbits were his but everyone of us kids claimed them. Soon afterwards, he put a buck with them. That's when the trouble began. Before long baby rabbits were running around everywhere. Soon they were tunneling all under the barn.

Years later, I asked Jerry why we didn't eat the rabbits. He said we didn't like their taste. The varmints did though, because they moved in on them. One day when I was on the way to the barn, Old Smoky, our Shepherd dog, began barking as hard as he could from out in the weeds near the barn.

Then he quit barking and I saw him going around and around. I ran toward him. He had a big black snake by the tail and was slinging it. An egg came out of that snake's mouth, then a baby white rabbit. What an experience for an eight-year old boy.

Chapter 56

THE LONG WALK HOME

Dad was willing to try anything to make a little extra money. When the pickle plant opened in Atkins, we started growing cucumbers. The only vehicle we had was an old run-down 1937 Chevrolet car he had traded a pair of mules for and it would quit on us at the worst of times. He didn't know anything about mechanics.

The two acres of cucumbers that year added to the work we already had with the cotton and corn. We almost lost the cotton on the mountain because of so much rain, but we finally got it hoed. Aunt Molly, Dad's ex-step-mother and Mom's aunt, had moved into the little house we lived in the year after our house burned.

Her two grown boys, Chalmer and Hubert, visited her for a few weeks and she made them help us with the cotton. The two men were single, so they didn't have families of their own. They grumbled about all the grass in the cotton but they were a big help to us and we were glad to have them.

The ground Dad chose to grow the cucumbers on was in a Johnson grass field and we'd have to hoe them every few days.

Sometimes we thought he just wanted us to have to work all the time. It was a rich spot of land and we had made a killing when we grew snap-beans there before the cannery in Russellville shut down, when the government inspectors had found something wrong with their products.

By the time the cucumbers were ready to pick, the fifteenth of June, we had just finished hoeing the grassy cotton, and we didn't get the usual rest we had been getting the years before. To pick the cucumbers, we had to stoop over all the way to the ground and hunt the little rascals. It wasn't long before we thought we had died and gone to hell. Our backs started aching and didn't quit.

I learned to get on my knees some, and that helped, but as soon as I had to get in another position, it was back to the bending once again. We had to be careful and not damage the vines any more than we could help.

We also had to watch out for honeybees. They were all over the vines, and they stung, and it hurt! When one stung us, it would lose its stinger and die, because its guts would be pulled out of its body with the stinger.

So the bees had it worse than we did. Many times the stinger would be left sticking in our skin, and we would have to pull it out. I was somewhat allergic to their poison, and whenever I was stung the area would swell up to twice normal size.

A neighbor from California, who had bought the old Russell farm, put in some cucumbers and he didn't make his teenage daughter pick. She said her head started hurting when she began picking them.

That excuse from one of our family wouldn't have cut it with Dad for one minute. He would have said, "You'll be as well off in the cucumber patch as you will be at home," or "You'll get to feeling better after a while if you continue working." You know, he was usually right about the last one.

Dad had put enough cucumbers in that it took us two days to get over the patch.

Talk about being happy to get finished that second day, I was. Now I thought we could have a good rest. But not so. Dad told us we would start picking the cucumbers again the next day. What?? I asked. "Why do we have to pick them again. I thought we were finished with them."

"Not quite," Dad told us. "Those cucumbers are not like cotton. They have to be picked every other day."

"Then why didn't you just grow enough that we could pick one day to get over them and then rest one day before we picked them again?"

"It doesn't work quite that way either," he explained. "The pickle plant operates every day, so they have to have cucumbers always coming in. Another thing is that we can make more money by picking them every day."

"How long will we be working in the cucumber patch?"

"Six weeks."

"Six weeks?"

Yes, and then we'll start bailing hay for a month. By then the corn will be ready to gather. After that it will be cotton picking time. We'd have to stay out of school two days a week until the cotton was finished.

That summer seemed much longer than the previous ones. Dad had mercy on us and he started paying us 25 cents a bushel for every one we picked. At the pickle plant he received $2.00 a bushel.

He said the extra money would help pay for all the expenses of growing them and for our living expenses. That sounded reasonable enough but we would be expected to pay for our school clothes and for our lunches at school as long as our money lasted. By working hard, I could pick eight bushels a day, so that was $2.00.

Jerry and I had a few cucumber fights when Dad wasn't around. There were always culls laying in the row middles. They were too big to sell and we often pelted each other with them.

All the work we had to do on the farm helped us children decide to further our education after high school.

All of us except Jerry got further schooling. He left for Michigan and stayed gone for twelve years, until he could buy some of the cheap land in Pope County. Then he returned and worked at Purina Feed Mill and raised hogs.

To haul cucumbers to market Dad would take out the back seat and place full sacks there. He would also load the trunk.

In order for us to stay busy with the milk cows and other work, he would take the pickles to Atkins after dark. There was room in the front seat for two of us boys to go and after the day's crop was sold, we could stop at a café and get some ice cream.

As we drove onto the grounds of the pickle plant that first night, the aroma of brine was in the air. I'll never forget that smell. I had never smelled anything like it in my short life and I actually liked it.

Dad backed the car up to the cucumber grader and one sack at a time the cukes were emptied into it. The grader separated the cucumbers by size with the smallest ones being midgets, which brought the most money per pound.

Next were the number ones, the number twos, the number threes, and finally the culls, which the plant wouldn't buy. We had to haul them back home. The culls were the largest and the pigs and hogs thought they were delicious.

After Dad picked up the check for the cucumbers and we were in the car ready to go get that ice cream and then head home, he turned the ignition to start the car.

Nothing happened. No sound at all. No hum from the motor. Nothing. He got out and raised the car's hood and looked at the engine but he knew nothing about mechanics.

We pushed the car off to one side where it wouldn't be in anyone's way and started walking home. As we passed the café in the middle of town, there was no mention of ice cream.

The night was pitch dark, no moon, and we had no light except for the stars. It was okay while we were in town, but after we turned north toward home, we soon reached the outskirts and then we were on our own. We soon reached the open country where every house had one or more dogs and they let us know they were there with their barking, growling and snarling. I was scared to death we were going to get attacked and ripped to pieces, but Dad didn't pay any attention to them.

A mile or so north of Atkins we came to a house that belonged to a man Dad knew and he took us into the yard. There were no lights, but he knocked on the door and yelled until the man came to see what was happening. Dad told him our car had broken down and asked if he would take us home. The man said he would but he grumbled about being so tired after having worked all day. He said he was going to have to get up really early the next morning and go to work again. Boy, was I ever glad to get that ride. I was still tired from picking cucumbers all day and I wasn't looking forward to the long walk home.

The next day Dad asked Floyd Byrum, a neighbor and shade-tree mechanic, to take him to get his car. Floyd had the car going in a jiffy.

A few days later it again was Donald's and my turn to go to deliver the cukes. This time we would get the ice cream we had missed out on the first trip—or so we thought.

After the drive to the pickle plant and after the cukes were once again unloaded and graded, once again the car wouldn't start. And once again we started for home with no ice cream, with no light and again with barking, growling, snarling dogs to contend with.

The only thing different this time was when we reached the house of the good Samaritan from the last trip, we kept going.

I kept waiting for Dad to turn off and go into his yard, but he kept walking. He wasn't going to ask him to take us home again. We also had the dogs to contend with for eleven miles more than we had before.

The highway was gravel-not paved. During the weeknights in 1948 very few cars traveled that road and there wasn't one car that night for the next four hours or so.

That happened a long time ago and I still remember the walk as if it was yesterday. I remember Dad saying if one walked at a fast pace, he could cover a mile in fifteen minutes. That would be four miles an hour and twelve miles in three hours.

Since then I have read about men walking 50 miles a day back in the days of yore, so our twelve-mile trek paled in comparison to what they did. But I still didn't like it. Remember, we had worked hard all day and we didn't keep eight-hour days back then. We didn't know what those were on the farm.

When it came time for Donald and me to go with Dad a few days later and he asked if I wanted to go, I said, "No thanks."

"I'll get you some ice cream on the way back," he promised.

After thinking it over for about two seconds, I replied again, "No thanks. I don't care all that much for ice cream anyway."

Chapter 57

CONCLUSION

The view on the Iron Ore Mountain is just as magnificent today as it was on that day eighty-four years ago when Mom first set foot on it.

The Petit Jean Mountain can still be seen to the south as it surveys all that goes on along the Arkansas River. The Crow, Buck, Nebo and White Oak Mountains continue to keep watch over the valleys below.

The wind still whistles softly through the pines, while the Mockingbirds keep singing out their melodies to all who will listen.

But the houses are gone. Only the spirits of those who once lived there remain. If you stand quietly on the brink of the mountain, you may be able to hear the faint yelling and laughing of children, or the patter of little feet running through a house.

Sometimes the faint sounds of "I was seeing Nellie Home" may come floating through the hills and hollows high on the mountain, as of long ago, or perhaps it is only the wind as it whistles through the pines.

The house at the foot of the mountain where Dad and Mom lived when Jyles was killed is gone. The cedar tree where he buried his marbles died and was cut down. The chimney rocks were hauled away and used in the foundation of our new home. All that remain are the well, hickory tree, and the daffodils. Each spring there are thousands of daffodils.

Dad, Mom, Uncle Ben, and Aunt Nora lived within sight of their beloved Iron Ore Mountain until their deaths. Dad died at eighty-four in 1985, Mom in 1995 at age ninety, Uncle Ben in 1989 at age 89, and Aunt Nora age 95 in 1999. I can imagine not a day went by that they didn't wistfully gaze upon the mountain and relive all their memories so dear to them of long ago.

They have children, grandchildren and great grandchildren scattered from Arkansas to the west coast. This book was written for them, that they may not forget this small chapter of their heritage.

Ricky and Jerry now live on the home place. The family and a cousin own all the land that Dad and Mom owned.

I own Grandpa and Grandma Maxwell's old place on Pea Ridge. I live four miles away in the country around Moreland.

Bobbye lives in Little Rock, Betty in Oregon and Donald in Washington state.

The house built in 1942 still stands proudly facing the Iron Ore Mountain.

*   *   *

TAKE ME BACK

Take me back to the place that I love so,
To the land that I'll always call home.
Take me back to the mountains of Arkansas,
To the pathways where I used to roam.

Take me back to the fields long forgotten,
Where the cotton and the corn used to grow,
Where we worked from daybreak until the setting sun,
And the hoot owls and the whippoorwills would call.

Take me back with my mother and my dad,
And my brothers and my sisters on the farm;
With Old Smoky, Tippie, and Laddie, and
The horses, cows, and mules 'round the barn.

Take me back, take me back, oh take me back.
Take me back to the land from which I sprung.
Take me back, take me back, oh take me back.
Take me back to the hills where I belong.

Randall Gray - 1970

Made in the USA
Charleston, SC
31 March 2013